CASH ON DELIVERY

CIA SPECIAL OPERATIONS
DURING THE SECRET WAR IN LAOS

THOMAS LEO BRIGGS

ROSEBANK PRESS
ROCKVILLE, MARYLAND

Rosebank Press
Rockville, Maryland 20850-2819

Orders: www.rosebankpress.com

Printed in the United States of America

Briggs, Thomas Leo.
    Cash on delivery : CIA special operations during the secret war in Laos / Thomas Leo Briggs.
    p. cm.
    Includes index.
    LCCN 2009907322
    ISBN-13: 978-0-9841059-4-6
    ISBN-10: 0-9841059-4-6

    1. Vietnam War, 1961-1975~Campaigns~Laos.
2. Vietnam War, 1961-1975~Secret service~United States.
3. United States. Central Intelligence Agency. 4. Laos ~Politics and government.   I. Title.

DS557.8.L3B75 2009   959.704'342'09594
                            QBI09-600122

Dedicated to Mom and Dad

And to Hom, Somneuk and Thong who survived and to the memory of Viroj, Niphon, Somsit and Boonsong aka "Pete" – who did not

DISCLAIMER

All statements of fact, opinion, or analysis expressed are those of the author and do not reflect the official positions or views of the Central Intelligence Agency (CIA) or any other U.S. Government agency. Nothing in the contents should be construed as asserting or implying U.S. Government authentication of information or CIA endorsement of the author's views. This material has been reviewed by the CIA to prevent the disclosure of classified information.

ACKNOWLEDGMENTS

This book is a personal memoir and I alone take responsibility for its content and accuracy, nevertheless, it could not have been completed without the generous assistance of many people. I thank all who helped me along the way and especially John Cusimano, Lloyd Duncan, Larry Ratts, Jim Hix, Frank Kricker, "Ratana", Roger Warner, Merle Pribbenow, Robert Destatte, Lee Gossett, Sarisporn Bhibakul, Southchay Vongsavanh, Mac Alan Thompson, Allen Cates, Jerome DeBruin, Ray Roddy, Rick Atchison, Albert "Durf" McJoynt, Ian G. Baird and Bill Howard.

"And ye shall know the truth, and the truth shall make you free."

–John 8:32

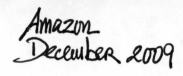
Amazon
December 2009

CONTENTS

PREFACE

"Let every nation know, whether it wishes us well or ill, that we shall pay any price, bear any burden, meet any hardship, support any friend, oppose any foe to assure the survival and success of liberty."

–John F. Kennedy Inaugural Address
Washington, D.C. January 20, 1961

Three issues have often hampered the success of our 21st century volunteer armed forces when they have deployed overseas in the post 9/11 world: limited numbers of deployable troops for the job, protracted deployment overseas, and foreign population objections to the presence of large military forces.

The number of active duty, reserve and National Guard troops available for commitment to countering terrorism, conventional wars (whether large or small), and other missions, is not large enough to handle more than one or two such missions. Since 9/11, the commitment of troops to Iraq and Afghanistan has stretched U.S. military forces to the limit.

The American public is not tolerant of long troop deployments. When we become involved in foreign wars over any extended amount of time and casualties mount, political pressure on the home front builds to end our presence overseas and bring the troops back home, thus risking ending our counter terrorist or counter insurgent effort before it is complete.

The presence of large numbers of Americans on foreign soil often causes anger against the United States rather than gratitude for our effort and sacrifice.

One solution to these problems is to use very small numbers of American military specialists and Central Intelligence Agency (CIA) officers to recruit, train, advise and direct indigenous surrogates. Such surrogates would conduct unconventional intelligence collection and combat operations to find and neutralize terrorists or insurgents operating in foreign countries or training to attack the American homeland. While the American military preferred model for operations against any enemy is the use of all-American units or, at the least, units led by Americans down to the lowest levels, it is possible to conduct successful intelligence collection and unconventional combat operations without having Americans "on the ground." This would satisfy the need to respect other cultures and traditions and keep the American profile as low as possible while still being successful and achieving American goals.

Policy makers can learn important lessons from the CIA's conduct of large unit combat operations and small unit special operations in Laos during the Vietnam War. The CIA suffered very few casualties and did not cause any cultural clashes with the population of Laos while using battalion and regiment sized indigenous combat forces, as well as small special operations teams of two to ten men to gather intelligence and conduct combat operations. Lao irregular battalion and regiment sized combat units advised by American CIA officers succeeded in winning some of their battles against regular North Vietnamese Army units. Overall, the CIA succeeded in causing the North Vietnamese Army to commit significant numbers of troops in Laos that could not be sent on to the Republic of Vietnam to fight against U.S. forces and their allies. Lao irregular special operations units, in small teams of two to ten men, collected intelligence and inflicted casualties on the North Vietnamese Army in many successful operations.

The following pages describe how approximately three hundred Lao irregulars, with the support of about ten Thai and Lao interpreters/operations assistants, were successfully directed by one CIA officer in unconventional special operations deep in enemy held territory. This force of irregular small teams obtained important intelligence by capturing North Vietnamese Army soldiers, by recruiting local villagers to obtain enemy locations that were successfully bombed by U.S. and Lao aircraft and by intercepting important enemy coded messages.

These teams operated in enemy held territory without the presence of American or third-country advisors on the missions in the field with the teams. The teams in the field were entirely Laotian. These teams brought in seventeen captured or defected North Vietnamese Army soldiers. The debriefings of these enemy soldiers produced important intelligence information. The teams also conducted other successful intelligence collection and combat operations. One team collected information for over three months on enemy troop locations and passed that information to American forward air control- lers who guided many successful air strikes against those enemy positions. There is no telling what the effect would have been in Laos if the CIA had duplicated these operations ten-fold or a hundred-fold.

With an absolute minimum loss of American lives, CIA helped to defend Laos from communist takeover and helped to inflict significant damage on the North Vietnamese Army's infiltration and supply line, although it never actually cut that line. Moreover, rather than sending all their troops to fight U.S. and allied forces in the Republic of Vietnam, the North Vietnamese Army had to keep large numbers of troops in Laos to defend its supply line, the Ho Chi Minh Trail. Given that the American military preferred model is that indigenous forces cannot achieve American preferred objectives without Americans on the ground shoulder to shoulder with them, the CIA's results using indigenous troops were remarkable.

If it was possible for Lao irregulars to achieve these successes against the North Vietnamese Army, why would it not be possible to train and direct other indigenous peoples to collect important intelligence or conduct combat operations against urban or rural terrorists, insurgents or even the military units of other nations?

There is already a model for the use of American special operations forces[1] in foreign countries. Robert D. Kaplan describes this model in two recent books[2].

Roger Warner, author of *Shooting at the Moon: The Story of America's Clan- destine War in Laos*, has described another model in the documentary film,

---

[1] Special operations forces consist of U.S. Army Special Forces (Green Berets). Delta Force and Rangers, U.S. Navy Seals and Special Warfare Combatant-craft Crewmen (SWCC), U.S. Air Force special operations units and Marine Force Recon.

[2] Robert D. Kaplan, *Imperial Grunts: On the Ground with the American Military, from Mongolia to the Philippines to Iraq and Beyond* , Vintage Books, New York, 2006; and *Hog Pilots, Blue Water Grunts: The American Military in the Air, at Sea, and on the Ground*, Random House, New York, 2007.

Once Upon a Time in the CIA.[3] In this model, a CIA case officer, Bill Lair, directs foreign special operations trainers who blend into a country and who provide the same training American military special operations forces provide.

The following chapters describe how a CIA case officer directed special operations by surrogates when CIA policy did not allow American participation in the actual operations. This is not a recipe for use in today's world. It would be a recipe for failure to follow it item by item. Rather, it should provide inspiration for the development of new recipes for use in the 21st century's counter terrorism and counter insurgency environment.

Please note that employees and retirees of the CIA are required to submit their manuscripts for review by the CIA because they signed a secrecy agreement which requires submission of manuscripts so that the CIA can insure that classified information is not released to the public. In a few minor cases, the CIA found references in this manuscript that it asked me to change or remove. I complied with their request and either obscured the reference or took it out so that the CIA was satisfied that no classified information is released in the manuscript. This should not be construed as hiding anything from the public only that information that should be classified continues to remain classified.

Finally, there are many instances where I have quoted dialogue. In the chapter, "Raven 42 Is Down", for example, the three Raven pilots, CIA officer Ratana and I corresponded voluminously about the events surrounding the rescue or Raven 42. The dialogue was recreated based on the memories of all the participants. In other instances I used literary license to transform what would have been straight prose into dialogue to make the narrative a little more lively and colorful for the reader. Whether prose or dialogue the text describes the way things were to the best of my ability and recollection.

---

[3] *Once Upon a Time in the CIA,* documentary film by Roger Warner, Northern Light Productions, 2007.

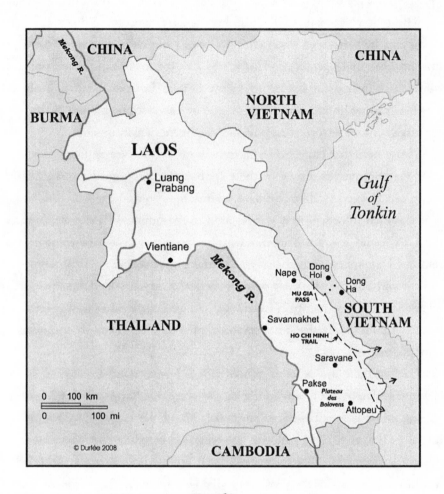

Map of Laos

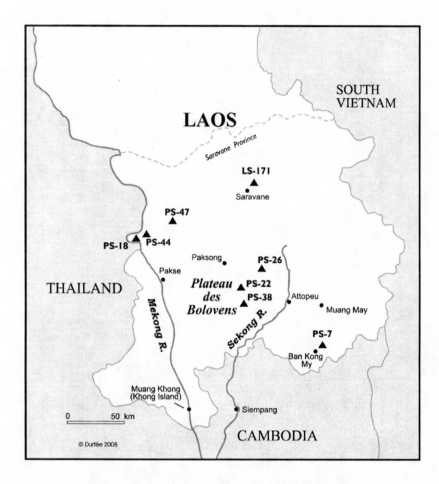

Map of southern Laos showing Pakse area of operations

INTRODUCTION

———◆———

"And so, my fellow Americans: ask not what your country
can do for you – ask what you can do for your country. My fellow
citizens of the world: ask not what America will do for you, but what
together we can do for the freedom of man."

–John F. Kennedy (1917–1963), Inaugural address, January 20, 1961

R ichard H. Schulz, Jr.[4] asserts that the Central Intelligence Agency (CIA) had responsibility for special operations and unconventional warfare in North Vietnam at the beginning of President John F. Kennedy's administration. According to Schulz, President Kennedy was not satisfied with the CIA's performance and decided to transfer responsibility for these operations to the U.S. Armed Forces. The objectives for the U.S. military program were: agent operations and deception in North Vietnam, interdiction and commando operations against the North Vietnam coast, psychological warfare operations in North Vietnam, and cross-border commando operations against the Ho Chi Minh Trail. This transfer of responsibility resulted in the formation of Military Assistance Command Vietnam, Studies and Observation Group (MACVSOG or sometimes MACSOG). MACVSOG conducted its operations in North and South Vietnam, Laos and Cambodia using U.S. Army officers and enlisted men and indigenous Vietnamese and mountain tribal soldiers. Every one of these operations was subject to high-level review in an effort to limit the possibility of the capture of an American soldier in North Vietnam, Laos or Cambodia. The policy makers did not want to face the political consequences that would result from evidence of American troops in these countries.

MACVSOG was able to conduct its cross-border operations reasonably well until the North Vietnamese Army built its security apparatus to the point where they were intercepting MACVSOG teams as they landed in Laos or within hours of landing. By 1970, the North Vietnamese Army was thwarting

---

[4] Richard H. Schulz, Jr, *The Secret War Against Hanoi: The Untold Story of Spies, Saboteurs, and Covert Warriors in North Vietnam*, Harper Collins Publishers, New York, 1999.

most if not all of MACVSOG's cross-border infiltrations. For anyone interested in the details of MACVSOG's efforts, Mr. Schulz's book is a good starting point. Nevertheless, CIA was responsible for all special operations in Laos even as MACVSOG was responsible for special operations in Vietnam, as well as operating in the border areas of Laos and Cambodia adjacent to Vietnam.[5]

CIA had full responsibility for all special operations and unconventional warfare in Laos subject to review by the American ambassador to Laos. The United States Air Force and the United States Navy provided close support from bases in Thailand and the Republic of Vietnam and ships off the coast of the Republic Of Vietnam. They supported CIA with propeller-driven and jet strike aircraft, various types of fixed wing gun ships, and helicopter infiltration and exfiltration. The U.S. Army had attaches in Laos to advise Royal Lao Government military units and to coordinate issue of weapons, ammunition and other supplies to those units. The CIA's goals in Laos were to bolster the Royal Lao Government and help it remain a buffer between North Vietnam and Thailand, to prevent its military takeover by the North Vietnamese communists, and to interdict or harass the North Vietnamese Army's infiltration route and supply line into the Republic of Vietnam. To pursue those goals the CIA organized indigenous irregular military forces whose mission was to prevent the North Vietnamese Army from using an ancient infiltration route into northern Laos to attack and seize the royal capital of Luang Prabang and the administrative capital of Vientiane, and in southern Laos to harass and possibly interdict the Ho Chi Minh Trail. Additionally, every North Vietnamese Army soldier remaining in Laos to defend the Ho Chi Minh Trail was one less combatant able to go to the Republic of Vietnam and fight against American and allied forces.

Initially, the CIA formed irregular battalions in northern Laos, consisting primarily of Hmong (at that time known as Meo) hill tribesmen, and in south-

---

[5] John L. Plaster, SOG: *The Secret Wars of America's Commandos in Vietnam*, Onyx, New York, 1997, for a detailed look at MACVSOG operations:.

ern Laos, consisting of lowland Lao and southern hill tribesmen (among which were Ta'oi (Brou) and Lave (Brao) among others). Most books about the CIA effort in Laos concentrate on the Hmong units in northern Laos, but CIA undertook an equally important effort in southern Laos involving lowland Lao and southern hill tribesmen. CIA formed irregular units because the Royal Lao Government was not supportive of allowing the CIA to dilute regular Royal Lao units with large numbers of men it would have to deal with when the Americans were gone. The Royal Lao Government allowed CIA to build up irregular units and then the CIA was going to be responsible for disbanding them. The Royal Lao Government would have no responsibility to keep them on when the war was over. Prior to 1970, CIA used the southern Laos irregular battalions for reconnaissance, surveillance and interdiction of the Ho Chi Minh Trail. The concept was that the battalions would send teams (10-15 men) or large patrols (50-100 men) out to collect intelligence on North Vietnamese Army activities on the Ho Chi Minh Trail, or to conduct ambushes of trucks or troops. Special Guerrilla Units (SGU) of about 500 men might even conduct these reconnaissance or combat operations. Additionally, CIA established a roadwatch and riverwatch program to place small teams at strategic positions on the Ho Chi Minh Trail to observe enemy movements and report them to their CIA case officers for further transmission to CIA headquarters and dissemination to the intelligence community. Presumably, MACV and MACVSOG were potential consumers of this intelligence.

The secret war in southern Laos began heating up in early 1970. Prior to that, the North Vietnamese Army had confined itself to protecting its Ho Chi Minh Trail supply line. When they did venture into areas west of the Ho Chi Minh Trail, it was usually to coerce Lao citizens into labor gangs, to forage for food to buy or seize from the Lao, or to conduct reconnaissance or intelligence collection operations.

The North Vietnamese viewed the CIA bases in northern Laos on and near the Plain of Jars, and similar bases on the Bolovens Plateau in southern Laos, as serious threats to their activities in the north and to their Ho Chi Minh Trail supply line in the south. They also feared a U.S.-South Vietnamese joint operation to cut the Ho Chi Minh Trail.[6] In addition to the Ho Chi Minh Trail, they also maintained a supplemental supply line via ship to Sihanoukville on the western side of Cambodia for transporting it overland eastward through Cambodia into South Vietnam on Route 110 also known as the Sihanouk Trail. The Cambodian route was lost after March 1970 when the Cambodian government, led by Lon Nol, closed Sihanoukville to the North Vietnamese.

As a result, in 1970 the North Vietnamese Army began a series of opera-tions throughout Laos designed to protect its only remaining supply route into South Vietnam. It expanded its control of Lao territory further to the west of the Trail, it seized CIA bases and it attacked and tried to wipe out irregular Lao and Thai CIA units wherever it could find them. The North Vietnamese Army attacked CIA forces and bases on the Plain of Jars, Royal Lao Govern-ment forces at Attopeu in the valley between the Ho Chi Minh Trail and the Bolovens Plateau, CIA bases on the Bolovens Plateau, and CIA irregular forces in Saravane.

Then, in the beginning of 1971, North Vietnamese anxiety over any U.S. effort to cut the Ho Chi Minh Trail from South Vietnam across Laos, was justified as Operation Lam Son 719, a U.S. supported South Vietnamese Army operation, was launched from bases on the Khe Sanh Plain in South Vietnam. The goal was to reach Tchepone, a village in Laos, thus cutting the Ho Chi Minh Trail in half. The North Vietnamese thwarted Operation Lam Son 719 and then immediately sent the same forces that had won the battle of Lam Son 719 to attack Dong Hene in central Laos and Paksong in southern Laos.

Southern Laos had been the scene of significant combat and serious Lao losses beginning in early 1970. By mid–May 1971, the beginning of the rainy

---

[6] "*Military Region 4: History of the Resistance Against the American to Save the Nation, 1954-1975*" (Quan Khu 4: Lich Su Khang Chien Chong My Cuu Nuoc (1954-1975)). Editorial Direction: Military Region 4 Headquarters and the Current Affairs Commit-tee of the MR-4 Party Committee (with the personal assistance of Major General Tran Van An); Senior Writer: Senior Colonel Vo Van Minh; People's Army Publishing House, Hanoi, 1994. Translated by Merle L. Pribbenow.

season, there was even more peril. This was when the North Vietnamese Army usually chose to begin heavy combat operations, because the weather included heavy cloud cover making it difficult to provide U.S. air support to Lao and Thai irregular units.

To prepare for the campaigns that began in 1970, the North Vietnamese Army's Truong Son (Ho Chi Minh Trail) Command had amassed 62,000 personnel organized into four divisions or division-equivalent units: Group 470, the 968th Infantry Division, Group 565 (Vietnamese advisors to Pathet Lao forces in the area), Group 571, and thirty way stations (binh trams] and regiments. These units were directly subordinate to the Command's headquarters and 144 battalions and battalion-equivalent units were directly subordinate to the way stations.[7]

North Vietnamese Army planners believed they needed to protect their strategic transportation line (the Ho Chi Minh Trail), consolidate and expand their liberated zone adjacent to the Trail, and crush the military efforts of the American imperialists and their lackeys in Laos. The North Vietnamese decided to expand their southern liberated zone to include the Bolovens Plateau, Paksong and Saravane.[8]

As a CIA special operations case officer, I arrived in Laos in February 1970 and was assigned to handle roadwatch programs being run out of CIA's Pakse Unit. I spent the next two years shutting down roadwatch operations and converting them to any special operation that could produce valuable intelligence or verifiable action operations. This is the story of my evolution from green young first tour officer to veteran CIA special operations officer.

---

[7] *"The Road Through The Annamite Mountains: A Memoir"*, (Duong Xuyen Truong Son: Hoi Ky), Colonel General Dong Si Nguyen, with Duy Tuong and Ky Van, People's Army Publishing House, Hanoi, 2001 (Second printing, with corrections and additions). Translated by Merle L. Pribbenow.

[8] *"Second Division, Volume 1"* (Su Doan 2, Tap 1), Da Nang Publishing House, Da Nang, 1989; Editorial Direction: - 2nd Division Party Committee and Division Headquarters- Lieutenant General Nguyen Huy Chuong. Translated by Merle L. Pribbenow.

BACKGROUND

---◆◆◆---

"I offer neither pay, nor quarters, nor food; I offer only hunger, thirst, forced marches, battles and death. Let him who loves his country with his heart, and not merely his lips, follow me."

–Giuseppe Garibaldi (1849), Italian Patriot and soldier

Recruitment

In 1962, at the beginning of my junior year at the University of Delaware and after completing two years of the basic Reserve Officer's Training Corps (ROTC) program, I voluntarily joined advanced ROTC because I expected to be drafted and I wanted to serve my time in the military as an officer. I believed that if drafted I should serve. I served on active duty in the United States Army from August 1965 to May 1968. After Military Police Officer's Basic (MPOB) training at Ft. Gordon, Georgia and airborne training at Ft. Benning, Georgia I remained at Ft. Benning until May 1967 serving in the 552nd Military Police Company and the 139th Military Police Company where I served under Captain Karl L. Sannicks, one of the three best officers I ever met in the army. I volunteered for a third year in the army and for assignment to the Republic of Vietnam. I served as a platoon leader in "C" Company, 504th Military Police Battalion and in the Provost Marshal's Office in Cam Ranh Bay. My commanding officer in C Company was Captain Gerald L. Kelly, the second of the three best officers with whom I served. The third officer in this category is Colonel Thomas Guidera, who was Commanding Officer, 18th Military Police Brigade and Provost Marshal, Vietnam. As a relatively young officer, I made the mistake of not fully informing my superiors of an incident that happened in An Khe involving the military policemen in my platoon and a non-commissioned officer (NCO) from the 1st Cavalry Division. The NCO had been apprehended for a curfew violation and then physically attacked several MP's while in custody. He was subdued and placed in the conex container we used as a detention cell.[9] After being released to his unit, the NCO made allegations of police brutality, specifically against Sgt. Buford Cox, Jr. one of my squad leaders and me. Neither Sgt. Cox nor I had actually been present in the platoon area when the incident had occurred. I was called in by the 1st Cavalry Division Inspector General (IG) for an interview. I was not told I was being investigated or that allegations had been made against me. The two field grade officers interviewing me asked me to write a statement about the incident but did not advise me of my Miranda rights at any time during the interview. By that time, I had realized they were trying to sandbag me and readily agreed. I said, "It really makes no difference if I write a statement, you haven't read me my Miranda rights." That caused them to huddle their heads together for a few minutes and then ask me to go ahead and write the statement, which I did.

I did not think any more about it until Captain Kelly summoned me to company headquarters. He told me that the 1st Cavalry Division IG's office had forwarded a complaint to Headquarters, Military Assistance Command Vietnam (MACV) and then it had gone to Colonel Guidera, whose staff had sent a query up the chain of command to the 504th MP Battalion commander and then to Captain Kelly. That, of course, had caught all the military police chain of command at a loss and he asked me what had happened and why I had not reported it. I described all the events from the NCO's apprehension to my interview with the 1st Cavalry Division IG officers. I said that they never mentioned they were investigating anything, never told me what they were going to do, and had not read me my rights. I had assumed it was not a big deal. Captain Kelly told me he would let me know what was going to happen next.

A few weeks later I was informed that Colonel Guidera would visit the 504th MP Battalion and specifically, outlying units like mine, which was a separate platoon assigned to work with the 1st Cavalry Division. Flying in by

---

[9] Conex containers were large steel cubes 8 feet on all sides. Long vertical rectangular slots were cut into them at eye level for light and air. They were in use all around Vietnam up until 1967.

helicopter, Colonel Guidera and his entourage arrived at my platoon head-quarters and I gave him a briefing on the platoon's mission and activities. At the end of my briefing, he asked me about the incident with the NCO. I described the whole thing and made sure to describe how my fellow officers had tried to sandbag me. At the end of my recitation, Colonel Guidera said something like this, "Son, you made a mistake not informing your chain of command of this incident. Don't do it again." I replied, "Yes, sir." He then said, "Now I'm going over to the 1ˢᵗ Cavalry Division and chew some ass. No one treats my officers like that." With that, he earned my undying admiration. He had listened to me, made a decision that I had made a mistake he should admonish me for, and then declared that the 1ˢᵗ Cav officers made a bigger error and he was going to take care of it. The final note to this incident is that a few weeks later an order went out that conex containers would no longer be used as detention cells by military police in the Republic of Vietnam.

I left the Republic of Vietnam in May 1968, returned home to Newark, Delaware and spent the summer trying to decide what I wanted to do next. The one thing I knew was that I did not want to spend my life selling "wid-gets" in the business world. I was interested in public service. I had tried the army but realized I might have difficulty in such a regimented environment. Even though I was attracted to public service, I did not want to test water or read gas meters. After the military, it was a paramilitary type of organization, such as the Federal Bureau of Investigation (FBI) or the Central Intelligence Agency (CIA), that interested me. I had enjoyed the extra bit of glamour attached to being in the military police so the FBI seemed appealing. I thought I understood what the FBI did, but I had no idea what the CIA was all about. At this time, I was 25 years old, had just finished my military service and was temporarily living at home with my parents in Newark, Delaware. I obtained an FBI application and began filling it out. In the meantime, I had been interviewing for various jobs and had an interview at a company north of Philadelphia. I looked up the CIA in the Philadelphia telephone book and found an address in the center of the city. On my way back from the job interview, I stopped at the CIA office. I told a man there that I wanted to apply and he gave me a very long, multi-paged form and told me to go home, fill it out and mail it to Washington, D.C.

My FBI application eventually wound up only half completed. A story appeared in the newspapers about how J. Edgar Hoover, the FBI Director, had fired one of his employees. The young man was engaged to be married but Hoover had learned that he was living with his fiancé prior to the wedding. I was not engaged or even in a serious relationship. I thought that if I ever were it would not be my supervisor's business whether I decided to live with a woman or not. I decided I could not work for an organization run that way.

I took the CIA application form home and began to work on completing it. It was extensive and asked for information that I did not have on the tip of my tongue. After two weeks or so, I was still working on it when I received a letter in the mail telling me that the CIA was aware that I had military experience that was of interest to them and asked me to go to their office in Philadelphia if I was interested in employment with them. I went to Philadelphia and was directed to talk to the same man who had given me the long application form. I asked him if he remembered me. He hesitated long enough for me to understand he did not, but he said he did. I showed him the letter I had received from the CIA in Washington, D.C. and asked him if my previous visit to Philadelphia had resulted in this letter. He said he did not think there was any connection and asked me if I was interested in pursuing this employment opportunity. I said I was and we began the application process. To this day, I have no idea how or why the CIA decided to send me that letter. CIA recruited me to become a special operations officer. During my entire career in the CIA, I met only one other former military police officer who had also been recruited for duty in Southeast Asia as a special operations case officer. All the rest of my colleagues in the special operations program were ex-Special Forces, ex-Seals, ex-Army or Marine Corps infantry officers, ex-military intelligence officers, ex-long range reconnaissance patrol, or ex-some other combat or intelligence or special operations specialty.

Filling out the application form caused me a small problem. Right near the top of the first page, there was a question along the lines of, "Have you ever been known by any other name or names or aliases?" I was born Thomas Briguglio in Staten Island, New York. My paternal grandparents, Gaetano Briguglio and Rosina Perniciaro, had emigrated from Sicily, my maternal great grandparents Giovanni Cucco and Maria Spadola had emigrated from Potenza, Italy and my maternal grandfather, Christos Daras, had emigrated from Skiros, Greece. When I was five years old, my father legally changed our family name to Briggs. I had been known by another name until I was five years old and I was worried that this was going to cause me problems. As it turned out, my career in CIA resulted in using aliases from time to time. All my life I never hid the fact that my ancestry is Italian but it caused problems trying to explain how I could have three quarters Italian and one-quarter Greek ancestry with a name like Briggs. For a long time, well into my forties, I deflected all questions about my name. My stock response was something like, "It was one of those Italian names you can't pronounce. I really don't remember what it was." However, I decided to change my response and since then, I tell people my birth name was Briguglio. My dissembling about my original Sicilian surname was not bad practice for developing the ability to use an alias while protecting an actual true name. In the end, I entered all the data about the legal name change and stopped worrying about it.

During the summer of 1968, the CIA invited me to visit its headquarters and take a series of personality and intelligence tests as well as a polygraph test. Since that summer ended without hearing anything further from the CIA, I began teaching the 4th grade at the Elkton Elementary School in Elkton, Maryland only about five miles from Newark, Delaware. I wanted to try teaching high school but I was told there were no openings for history or social studies teachers, which I thought would be natural because my college major was history with minors in English and political science. However, the school informed me that if I wanted to try elementary school there was a need for male teachers. Since I had not found anything else that interested me and I had not heard from the CIA, I accepted the position. It was a big mistake. The principal liked me and thought I would make a fine teacher, but I knew I would not be able to remain in elementary education. I knew there was a new

teacher they wanted to hire who was going to graduate from college in December. He was older with a wife and children. He would not be able to start work
until the following fall unless my job opened up. I went to the principal,
explained my problem and asked for release from my one-year contract. She
was very nice about it but I think it was easier for her to do knowing she could
replace me right away with some one who needed the work sooner rather than
later.

While I knew I had to leave teaching, there was some regret. I would never
be able to commit myself to it in the way that a good teacher must. However,
there were rewards in it. I never thought I had much talent for math, but
perhaps my problems with it made it easier for me to teach others. I read once
that people who are talented at something find it hard to teach it to others
because the talented sometimes cannot understand why others cannot learn.
However, those who have had problems and have figured out how to overcome those problems can also understand how to help others learn. Perhaps
that was why I could teach math better than I myself could learn. The math I
was teaching was not difficult and was material I understood. I was leaving at
Christmas time and the students brought in Christmas cards for me. One of
them, a quiet, reserved young girl wrote in her card that I was the best math
teacher she ever had. I was quite touched. On the other hand, the day before
my last day the local police came for one of my young boys. He was more than
quiet - he was silent. He was well behaved, he just did not participate in class.
My students and I had been quite surprised when he brought in a Christmas
tree we could decorate. The police were there because they said he had taken
money from a gas station cash register, which he had used to buy the tree.
How could you be angry with a nine year-old boy who thought enough of the
class and his classmates to go out and get a Christmas tree to bring in to
school? However, what do you do when that boy, who in no way seemed to be
a bad boy or troublemaker, decided to steal the money to buy the Christmas
tree? Both of these children needed more than I could give. I had to move on.

As it was just before Christmas, I decided not to worry about a new job
until after the holidays. I was at home about one week when I received a letter

from the CIA saying they wanted to offer me employment and telling me to telephone them if I wanted to accept. I made the telephone call and the CIA asked me to report to its headquarters on the first workday of January 1969. I agreed and so my CIA career began as a contract special operations case officer. I went through one year of training courses.

Training

CIA hired contract special operations case officers as qualified candidates became available. There was no formal training program. We were put into the courses they thought we should have as those courses became available. One other new guy was hired at the same time that I was, so we went through our year of training together. Other new guys were hired in groups of two, three or four and each group went through training together. We all received essentially the same training, just not in the same order. From time to time, we all came together in one particular course if we were all available for it at the same time.

I reported to work at the CIA in the second week of January 1969 and my training partner, Ken, reported the week before me. We were the only two new Special Operations Division (SOD) case officers reporting in at that time so we were teamed up to go through training together. When the Agency first began recruiting new people for its special operations programs in Vietnam and Laos, they recruited older military people who had been field grade officers or senior enlisted men. We were in a new program designed to recruit junior officers and enlisted men. As far as we could tell upon looking back a few years later, the primary goal of our training was to have us go through the Operations Course Phase II, which was the special operations phase, and the Escape and Evasion course. The Operations Course was divided into two phases, OC Phase I and OC Phase II. Phase I was the traditional tradecraft course. It was a mystery to us why they limited us to the special operations course. All of us came from at least two or three years of military training and for most, extensive special operations experience. As it turned out, an assignment in Laos involved standard military and special operations skills for most case officers assigned there, but an assignment to Vietnam was much more oriented toward traditional tradecraft than special operations skills. It would have made much more sense to put us through both phases, but they did not. While we were waiting for the regularly scheduled OC Phase II and Escape & Evasion courses to come around, we took a variety of courses designed for traditional operations personnel. They included the 4-week operations familiarization course (that provided a minimal exposure to traditional tradecraft), reports writing, counter intelligence, the records system and name tracing, counterterrorist driving, clandestine photography, and locks and picks. There were courses aimed specifically at Vietnam assignments, such as, Vietnam Familiarization and Police Administration. From time to time there were specialty courses set up for us like demolitions, vehicle armoring, or weapons training on the Swedish K, Israeli UZI, and Italian Beretta sub machine guns, M-16, M-1 Garand rifle, M-1 carbine, M-14 rifle, AK-47, .45 caliber pistol and the Browning 9mm pistol. The trainers assigned to provide weapons instruction had done a study and decided that the best all around handgun was the Browning 9mm and so it was the preferred pistol used in training, even to the point where the weapons instructors tried to brainwash us about it. It was the only handgun officially issued to CIA personnel. I was experienced with the Colt .45 caliber pistol, having been a U.S. Army military policeman, and preferred it. No brainwashing could change my mind. We not only learned to fire the weapons but also learned to field strip and clean each of them. Through all these courses, except some mundane administrative courses, I was in pig heaven. We took photos and then developed and printed them in a dark room, or went out on firing or demolitions ranges, or learned defensive driving where we did 180-degree turns or broke through roadblocks. All of this was entirely enjoyable and I often thought, "All this and they pay me, too!"

CIA conducted demolitions training at a special clandestine training site run by what was then called Technical Services Division (TSD). TSD officers were our SOD "cousins." They were often former military personnel with specialties useful in special operations and unconventional warfare. They had a belief system and attitude that fit in with special operations. They were involved in many different technical specialties, both traditional and special operations, such as, locks and picks, clandestine photography, forged documents, demolitions, special weapons, and much more. As in all things in the world of intelligence, there were secret compartments and if you did not have a need to know, you were not given access to a compartment. I am sure there are many exotic and useful things that TSD officers did for which I did not have a need to know.

For me, demolitions training was extremely enjoyable. We sat in the classroom and listened to lectures and then went out on the demolitions range and blew things up. TSD prided itself on providing "hands on" training and, indeed, in the case of demolitions it was a very practical approach. The instructors were very strict about following the teaching and procedures. The penalty for screwing around was a lost limb, other mutilation or possibly death. There was a TSD preferred way to do things and they wanted us to follow it. At the beginning of the course, they gave us notebooks and suggested we make good use of them. The instructor said we would submit our notebooks and they would grade them. When we were on the demolitions range, they wanted us to follow procedures to the letter and instructors came around to look at our creations to see that we did. I was suitably impressed with their warnings and kept meticulous notes with every "i" dotted, and every "t" crossed. On the demolitions range my work was as close to theirs as I could make it. I guess I bought in to their teaching because I wanted to be sure I did not cause any harm to my buddies or myself. We built and detonated a wide variety of demolitions most often using C-3 or C-4, "det–cord" and time pencils of various types. [10] They kept a variety of old vehicles, mostly automo-

---

[10] C3 and C4 are malleable forms of explosive, sometimes called plastic explosive, evolved from Gelignite, invented by Alfred Nobel in 1875. Detonating cord (det cord) is a high-speed fuze which explodes and thus detonates plastic explosives such as C4. Time pencils are chemically activated time fuzes used with detonating cord to explode plastic explosives.

biles and trucks, on the range for us to practice on. At the end of the course, the instructors assigned each one of us a vehicle and the final demolition was to blow up the vehicle. We had a limited amount of C-4 so it was more important to place the charge well as there was not enough C-4 to blow away the entire vehicle. I managed to place my charge so that I produced a satisfying fireball by detonating some residual fuel. I had a bit of a special operations inferiority complex because I did not have the background my classmates had so I was especially gratified at the end of the course when the instructors announced that I was the top graduate. I have always felt that my meticulous notebook won the day since I noticed that my more seasoned classmates, who had seen and done it before, were not as keen on note taking as I was.

The escape and evasion (E&E) course was usually three weeks long, two weeks in the desert and mountains and one week in a hot/wet climate. However, for some reason they had an extra week available and several of us were brought together for four weeks of E&E, two weeks in the desert and mountains and two weeks in the swamps. We went south first. We flew down and then drove to where all the equipment was kept at a site that had been associated with the Bay of Pigs operation. The instructors told us which equipment to take and we loaded it into the transportation vehicles. We loaded canoes, paddles, jungle hammocks, and other field gear. The jungle hammocks, nicknamed the "Jungle Hilton" were especially interesting. In addition to the normal hammock, there was a special double roof and mosquito netting all around. First, the instructors showed us how to rig the hammocks from trees in the normal way. Then, they showed us a way to support the hammock on the ground. We were shown how to cut support branches – four branches cut with a Y at one end and two branches cut straight. If you put two Y branches at the head standing vertically touching the ground and connected them with a straight branch horizontal to the ground and did the same at the foot, you could support each corner of the hammock so that it made quite a comfortable bed. At first, I did not think I wanted to go to the effort of cutting the six supports, even when the instructors told us they would not be any extra weight as we could stow them in the canoes. The first night in the hammock, I had a terrible nightmare in which I dreamed that I was hanging over a cliff only keeping myself from falling by clinging to the edge of the cliff. I was dreaming that I was struggling to pull myself back to safety when I awoke and found myself in the hammock, tilted perpendicular to the ground, holding on to the side of the hammock and trying to scramble to bring it back to parallel with the ground. That morning I cut six branches and thereafter slept well in a very comfortably supported hammock-bed.

With all the equipment in the trucks, we drove to the embarkation point. After visiting a local food store to buy supplies we drove to a location where we put the canoes into the water in canals that led to the coast. We were assigned two to a canoe. Ken and I did not have much experience in canoes so the first few hours we cut zig-zag lines in the water as we tried to master driving the canoe in a straight line. The narrow canals led to more open water where there were islands consisting of mangrove trees. There was not any land or earth, as such, just the mangrove roots above the water. We noted the high water mark on the roots and set up our jungle hammocks above the water line. The first night I realized I should have taken the sag of the hammock with my weight in it into account. During the night, it became apparent I was only an inch or two above the water at high tide.

As we paddled through the waterways, we saw a variety of wildlife to include several sightings of the dorsal fins of what we took to be sharks. We wound up at an island on the coast where we gathered oysters, clams and other flora and fauna to cook over a campfire on the beach. We took the canoe, paddled around the island and saw oyster beds visible at the bottom. It was easy to lean over the gunwale of the canoe and uproot oysters and bring them into the canoe to take back to the campfire. We learned a lot of wood-craft during those two weeks. We also conducted a training exercise where we had to travel around among the "islands" while the instructors played the part of an enemy patrolling in speedboats. It was an uneven game of hide and seek.

The second two weeks we traveled out west to spend one week in the desert and one week in the mountains. We spent several days traveling into a national park for weapons training, map and compass exercises and land navigation. Part of the training was in mountains near an Indian reservation. The training was oriented toward learning how to survive in these environments in addition to the jungle or swamp environments. We learned such things as how to take water from a cactus, which snakes and plants are poisonous, how to catch and cook lizards and snakes, which insects can be eaten, how to remove the skin from a chicken without removing the feathers, and how to cook fish without beheading, scaling or gutting them. Jerry and Red were two of the instructors for both the jungle and desert training. Jerry was an older, long time outdoorsman, hunter and fisherman. He reminded me of a 20th century reincarnation of Jeremiah Johnson. He was a good old boy who had probably forgotten more than we would ever know about the woods. One of my army instructors would have said that Jerry had more time on the crapper than I would ever have in the woods. Red was a former U.S. Air Force survival instructor. He countered Jerry's homegrown knowledge of survival and woodcraft with solid, military knowledge and experience. They were both excellent instructors and taught us a lot. We learned about setting traps to catch animals to eat, including how to use Jerry's famous three-pin trigger. We learned what equipment you needed in various climates and which brands and models performed best. One day at the beginning of a field lecture Jerry, who was a big but quick and agile man, came bursting out from behind a tree carrying a tomahawk and whooping like an Indian. He ran past us and then threw the tomahawk in perfect looping revolutions right into a target placed on a tree.

In addition to the tomahawk, they taught us to throw knives. Red believed the only knife you really needed was a bowie knife. Much like the character in the movie "Crocodile Dundee", Red had a large bowie knife that he called "a real workin' knife." He went into detail about how to make the knife out of the best steel you could find anywhere, which he said was in a USMC bolo machete. He even gave us an outline of his bowie knife so if anyone wanted to buy a USMC bolo machete and make one he could. After the course, I ordered a machete from a company I found in an outdoor magazine. While on leave before departing for Laos, I had a machinist in Delaware cut the machete into a bowie knife. I took my bowie knife with me to Laos and carried it in my survival kit for two years.

The photography course was given in a building near the main State Department headquarters at 23rd Street and Constitution Avenue. They taught us how to use a 35mm single lens reflex camera including how the camera operated as well as how to use shutter speed and aperture to affect depth of field or to take into account the lighting conditions. They sent us out into the streets of Washington, D.C. to take photographs and taught us how to load the film into development tanks and develop it, followed by lessons in using an enlarger and developing prints. By the second week of the course, we were shown special equipment and given exercises (*that the CIA does not want me to describe.*) We then had to develop the film and prints from the negatives. If you had never photographed documents yourself you would have had training that let you understand what an agent was going through or which could help you if you had to train an agent. We also went through other practical exercises where we took photographs and developed them. It was a very interesting and useful training course.

In the locks and picks course we were shown the insides of a number of different types, sizes and models of locks, padlocks and the locking mechanisms of safes and vault doors. The instructor said that if you could visualize the inside of a lock and you knew how the locking mechanism worked, you could pick or crack the lock. They showed us how vault doors had safety features to allow a person trapped accidentally inside to easily open the vault door from the inside. The first vault doors with this safety feature consisted of a round knob that you could pull and turn and the door would just open, even though on the outside the vault door lever could not be pulled down to open the door unless the proper combination had been dialed in. The instructor pointed out that on such doors you merely had to apply torque to the lever and then whack it a good shot with a rubber mallet. The whack caused the mechanism to jump back as if it had been pulled from the inside, and the torque on the lever let the lever go all the way down once the equivalent of the inside pull was simulated. He told us that the company that made these vault doors had solved the problem by putting a little door with a latch pin in it so that the door blocked the rod from being pulled back until the person on the inside removed the latch pin and moved the door out of the way so the handle could be pulled back. Problem was, the company did not notify any of its customers of the problem and would only put the little door in place if called to service such a vault. He said it was unknown how many vault doors in the metropolitan area opened with some torque and a whack.

From January to December Ken and I sat in classrooms to learn report writing or how to write cables and do name traces, went to jungles, mountains and swamps, walked the streets of Washington, D.C. practicing clandestine tradecraft, fired weapons, learned to armor cars, exploded C-4, crashed cars through roadblocks or spun them through 180 degree turns. We slowly learned many skills or gained knowledge that might or might not be useful to us on our first field assignments. Toward the end of my thirty-two years of government service, I often wondered what sort of employment I would find, after retirement, where I could use the skills, knowledge and experience I had built up as a CIA case officer.

Eeney, Meeney, Miney, Moe – Assignment to Laos

The CIA hired me specifically for assignment to Vietnam, but as the year of training proceeded, one thing led to another. I decided to get married. The wedding was in August 1969. I had completed about two-thirds of my training and I had learned that there was another possible assignment for a special operations case officer - Laos. I had no idea, which assignment would be more desirable, but I knew that Vietnam assignments were unaccompanied[11] and Laos was an accompanied assignment. My new wife was willing to go to Laos for two years so I had to find a way to get an assignment there.

---

[11] Most CIA assignments allowed a spouse to accompany the employee overseas, but when an assignment was unaccompanied, the spouse had to stay at home or live in a nearby "safe" country.

A case officer whose assignment was really quasi-personnel work handled all the new hires in the special operations program. We did not know much about Jerry Sohl, but he seemed a decent sort. We heard that he had worked in Cuban operations out of Miami, but no one knew any details. He was actually the one who had interviewed me during the hiring process. They invited me to Langley, Virginia to the CIA headquarters building. When you entered the building and walked over the CIA seal, that so many have now seen in a variety of television shows and movies, you were taken into an waiting area just to one side before going through the turnstiles that badged employees used to enter the building. The large room had two desks manned by receptionists and a variety of couches and easy chairs. Against one wall was a row of doors leading into small windowless interview rooms. After reporting to the receptionist, you waited on a couch or in an easy chair until they called you. When they called me, I went into the interview room and sat down opposite Jerry who was on the other side of a desk. His first question was, "What's a Blue Hen"? I was actually familiar with the origin of the nickname from fighting roosters that members of American revolutionary war units from Delaware brought along with them. I quickly recited the story and Jerry was impressed. He knew the origin because he had graduated from Washington College in Chestertown, Maryland back when Washington College was a sports adversary of the University of Delaware. From there he conducted a comfortable session and I left thinking I had at least not messed up the interview.

In September 1969, with about three-quarters of my training completed, I went to talk to Jerry and explained that now that I was married I wanted to take my wife with me on my assignment. I said that if there were no such assignments and I had to go to Vietnam I would give serious consideration to resigning from the Agency. I did my best not to be demanding or confrontational and maybe he believed I was worth keeping in the program. He made no promises and just said he would see what he could do. As it turned out, two positions in Laos came up just about the time I was ready to go into the field.

My training partner, Ken, was a graduate of the University of San Francisco and a former U.S. Army infantry officer who had served in Korea. The openings in Laos were at Udorn Base and Savannakhet Unit. We did not learn this until much later, but when they sent a cable to Vientiane to nominate us for assignment to Laos, they put my name on Ken's background and his name on my background. Bill Dodds, the officer in Vientiane who had the responsibility to monitor such things was a retired U.S. Army infantry colonel who had graduated from West Point. His attitude was that the infantry officer should go to Savannakhet and the military police officer should go to Udorn. The Udorn assignment was a staff job while the Savannakhet assignment was a field assignment. There was no way the former regular army colonel could see an MP officer doing special operations fieldwork better than an infantry officer. The only problem was that my name was on the infantry officer's background so I was accepted for the assignment to Savannakhet and Ken's name was on the military police officer's background so Ken was accepted for Udorn. In one of those strange twists of fate, one day while we were still in Washington making final preparations for our departures, the chief in Pakse so enraged one of his case officers that the case officer went after the chief and punched him in the face. The chief was sitting behind his desk and the angry case officer lunged across the desk grabbed the chief by the shirtfront with one hand and popped him in the nose with the other. This caused quite some turmoil until Vientiane and Udorn decided to transfer the pugnacious Pakse case officer to the empty Savannakhet position. They sent a cable to CIA headquarters telling them that I should report to Pakse. As a result of bureaucratic confusion and a chief's deficient interpersonal skills Ken wound up in the one job in all of the Vientiane Station best suited to his skills and temperament and I wound up in the best job I ever had in my life.

My wife and I departed Washington, D.C.'s Dulles Airport in February 1970 and flew to Los Angeles, where we had a few hours layover. An aunt and uncle live in Los Angeles and my aunt met us at the airport and we had a nice visit. From Los Angeles, we flew to Hawaii where we spent ten days vacationing on Maui, Kauai, and Hawaii, the Big Island. When we married on a Saturday near the end of August 1969 my new bride had to go to work on the following Monday so we had not had a honeymoon. Our ten days in Hawaii was our delayed honeymoon. We departed Hawaii and flew to Guam for a fueling stop and then to Taipei, where we stayed a few days. From Taipei, we flew to Bangkok, arriving about 9 p.m. A CIA representative assigned to Air America met us. He drove us from the airport to a hotel. Along the way, he told us his idea of a hilarious story. It seems a Thai couple had died on their wedding night because their hotel room was stuffed with flowers from well-wishers suffocating them from lack of oxygen because the flowers used it all up. We thought it would not be a good idea to stay out here too long if this was what you came to think was funny. I spent the next day processing paperwork at the Air America office and then we flew on to Vientiane. On the plane to Vientiane, we met several of the wives of authentic Air America employees. They were all chatting, laughing and having a good time. We became alarmed, however, when talk turned to whether the crane at the end of the airport runway had been removed yet, and if not, whether an arrival after dark would be a problem for the pilots. They all thought it was so funny that the Royal Lao Airlines pilots had such a hard time maneuvering around the crane to avoid crashing into it. Perhaps they were having fun with the obvious green horns, but we were apprehensive until we landed without incident.

We were met at the Vientiane airport and taken to the Lang Xiang Hotel. While it had the reputation as the best hotel in the capital, it was somewhat of a dump even by modest standards. A bellhop showed us into a barren room that was very depressing. We were even more depressed when the bellhop took out a large bug sprayer and began to spray the whole room with DDT while swarms of mosquitoes flew out of the curtains. After the bellhop left we looked in the bathroom to find an old French style commode with the water tank on the wall above our heads. The walls were stained in rust and green. We have a photograph of my wife sitting on the edge of the bed looking as forlorn and depressed as a newlywed 25-year-old bride could look. Now, that photograph seems funny to us.

We decided the best thing to do was go down to the lobby and find a good strong drink. In those days, I liked bourbon and she liked scotch, but the only thing we could find in the hotel bar was White Horse scotch. We each ordered a scotch and water and when two very large water glasses arrived filled half with scotch and half with water we not only drank the whole thing but ordered seconds. After that, we returned to our rooms and, anesthetized by the alcohol, fell asleep and forgot how down we were.

We did some more processing in Vientiane, this time in the CIA Station. We both had an interview with the deputy chief of station, Clyde "I Am the Whip" McNeely (not his true name). We did not know his nickname at the time but when we heard it later, we thought it quite appropriate based on our short interview with him. He had a rather small office with a window air conditioner on the wall behind him in a windowless office. The air condition-er was high on the wall almost touching the ceiling. He spoke in a soft low voice which the noise from the air conditioner almost drowned out. My wife and I both leaned forward trying to hear what he was saying but we missed parts of it. Neither one of us felt we could ask him to speak up so when we left his office we asked each other what he had said, only to find there were parts neither of us heard. We never did figure it out and promptly forgot about it without any known detriment to us.

From Vientiane, we flew to Udorn, Thailand in a converted C-47[12] called 50 Kip. The last letters and numbers on the airplane's tail were 50K. It was common practice for the pilots to use only the last two or three letters and numbers on the tail of the aircraft as their radio call sign using the military system of A is alpha, B is bravo, C is charlie, etcetera. In the military system, K equals kilo but the local currency in Laos was the kip, artificially kept at 500 to the U.S. dollar by the U.S. government. Somewhere along the line, the airplane had become 50 Kip instead of 50 Kilo. The aircraft call sign 50 Kip was operated by Continental Air Services, Incorporated and flew a regular

---

[12] The C-47 is the U.S. Air Force military version of a modified Douglas Aircraft civilian DC-3 airliner.

schedule from Bangkok to Udorn to Vientiane to Savannakhet to Pakse and return. We were catching a Vientiane to Udorn leg. We flew to Udorn and my friend and training colleague, Ken, met us. He had gone out to his assignment a few weeks before me.

Udorn was a base and the chief was designated Chief of Base (COB), Udorn. When I arrived in Udorn I visited the base office, met the COB, Pat, the DCOB, Jim and all the other people I had to know who would be my support element when I was up-country. Vientiane Station, in the capital, directed all CIA operations in Laos. Udorn Base, in Thailand, directed all special operations in Laos and had five operational up-country units, Nam Yu, Luang Prabang, Long Tieng, Savannakhet and Pakse. The first three units were in north Laos, while Savannakhet Unit in Lao Military Region III and Pakse Unit in Lao Military Region IV were in southern Laos.

After a couple of days of meetings and orientations, we were ready to fly to Pakse and report for duty. Since 50 Kip was not scheduled to fly to Pakse, we were manifested on a C-123[13] cargo plane that was flying cargo down to Pakse. They told us to wait in the Air America waiting room until called to board the aircraft. Finally, after what seemed like hours, they called us out and directed us to enter the aircraft by the ramp at the rear. The cargo area was empty and the red canvas sling seats on each side of the bulkhead were down so we took seats as far forward as we could. We sat there for a while and then they asked us to disembark. They then began to load all manner of large boxes and wooden crates. When we looked inside the entire cargo area was full of boxes and crates. Along the bulkheads, the aluminum and red canvas drop down seats could only be reached by crawling over and around the cargo. We scrambled to seats, belted ourselves in and waited uneasily. I had done this sort of thing in the army in Vietnam, but here I was with my wife taking my employer's transportation to report in for work. It did not seem to bode well. When we went over the rear ramp into the aircraft the engines were running,

---

[13] The C-123, built by Fairchild Aircraft, was a U.S. Air Force military transport aircraft.

propellers were turning, and the pilot was revving the engines. Before the aircraft moved, however, they asked us to get off again. We got down on the tarmac and stood back watching the aircraft sit there while the pilot revved the engines, shut them off, then revved and shut them off several times. Finally, one of the engines flared a large cone of fire. When the flames died away, they said we could board again and the flight would begin. We looked at each other, shrugged our shoulders and boarded. Thankfully, the flight from Udorn to Pakse was uneventful and we arrived in the early evening.

Unknown to us, our colleagues in Pakse Unit were eagerly anticipating our arrival. They had initially been told we would arrive at noon so as many as possible had driven to the airfield to form a welcome committee for us. When our arrival was delayed to 3 p.m., the group gathered again, just fewer of them. By the time we arrived, about 9 p.m., only Mark and Joanie, our sponsors, were there to greet us. We were unaware of the larger welcoming group until they told us the story a few days later. We were happy to see Mark and Joanie, and they drove us to our house. It was late and we were very tired from a long day of traveling. Mark and Joanie did not stay long and said they would spend more time with us the next day. We noticed that our refrigerator was stocked with some basic foods, some soft drinks and there was ice in the ice trays. We both decided to have a big cold drink with lots of ice before going to bed. We spent the next three days flat on our backs with severe cases of "Ho Chi Minh's Revenge." Thinking about it after we had been in country a while, we decided Joanie's maid had probably filled the ice trays with water from the tap. The entire time we lived in Laos, we always boiled all our drinking water and then ran it through a filter, except obviously, for the water in those ice trays.

The U.S. government provided the housing for CIA employees in Pakse. A housing compound had been built so that all the houses would be adjacent to each other to make it easier to provide security. There were a few individually leased houses around the city and State Department or U.S. Agency for International Development employees usually occupied these. The houses in the compound had been built to U.S. government specification but out of locally available materials and designed for a tropical climate. The houses were built on concrete pads with thick concrete support columns at each corner. The ground floor had three rooms on the rear half, one for a kitchen, one for a storeroom and one for a laundry room. These rooms took up about half of the floor space. The rest of the ground floor was open and enclosed with screening. This allowed the occupants to have a patio protected from rain by the ceiling supporting the second floor and from bugs by the floor to ceiling screening. At the center of the ground floor was a staircase leading up to the second floor.

The second floor consisted of a large living room, two bedrooms and a bathroom. The wood to build the house was local teak. The furniture was made of bamboo and there were rugs made of thatching material. The kitchen was furnished with a propane gas stove, a sink, refrigerator, table and chairs and a water filter. We boiled water and then put it into the filter. It held several gallons of water. We used boiled and filtered water for cooking, drinking and ice cubes. The electricity for lights, refrigerators, and other electrical appliances came from the housing compound generator. Nevertheless, we had an ample supply of candles for when the generator failed and we had to wait for repairs. We ate breakfast at the table in the kitchen, and we had a dining room table out in the patio area for dinner and entertaining guests. One corner of the patio area had a coffee table and chairs. We used this area in the evenings and for entertaining guests. As the security situation deteriorated over our time there, we converted the storeroom into a bedroom. It was the middle room so it had concrete walls on sides and the back, buffered by the kitchen and laundry room spaces on either side. The back wall was covered on the outside with a wall of sand bags and the front wall had sand bags from floor to ceiling except for the doorway. The doorway had sand bags piled floor to ceiling in a way that allowed one to come out of the room turn right then left and out into the patio area while still protected by sand bags.

The laundry room had an old style washing machine with a ringer, the kind little kids sometimes get their arms stuck in while helping their mothers feed bed sheets into them. I know this because as a child, we had a washing machine just like it and I caught my arm in it while feeding a sheet into it for my Mom. Wet clothes were hung outside on a clothesline in the dry season and inside in the patio area on a clothesline in the rainy season. The house had a fence around it and a lawn inside the fence. We planted various bushes and flowers around the house for decoration. After we first moved in we planted a vegetable garden but one day my wife came home to find that the maid or gardener had left the gate open and water buffalo had wandered in and eaten the vegetable stalks. Another morning my wife was sitting on the patio having coffee when she heard a strange sound outside the screening. She looked out and not more than a foot or two away she saw a cobra, in strike pose, swaying back and forth looking in at her. She was able to get up and get out of the house through the front door. She went down the street looking for help and found Eli Chavez at home, because he was sick with a fever. Eli got up, even though he was as sick as a dog, came down to our house, found the cobra and beat it to death with a rake. My wife felt a lot better until someone mentioned that many people believe that cobras mate for life and are usually found in pairs. We could only hope the dead cobra was a young single. We lived in that house for one year until the chief of unit decided we would be safer in a separate house across the river. We did not want to move to the new house because we felt it was much less secure than living with our colleagues in the housing compound. This difference of opinion caused a lot of hard feelings.

Up until the house dispute, I had been a bit of a fair-haired boy with the chief of unit. He seemed to like me and I was getting more and more responsibilities. The Pathet Lao had tried to rocket the airfield once before we had arrived and during our first year, they had rocketed it again. They would set up their rocket launchers aimed at the airfield. Unfortunately, the housing compound was between their rocket launch site and the airfield and they were poor marksmen. During the first rocket attack, some rounds had landed quite close to the housing compound. One of the intelligence collection case officers had had a few drinks, went up on the roof of his house and was using the security radio net to describe where each round landed and proclaim that it had not hit anything. One of the special operations case officers radioed to him to cut it out because he was functioning as a forward observer for the enemy if they were listening to our radio net. One night while we were sleeping in our bunkered bedroom an unusual sound awakened us. My wife sat up in bed, "Tom, what's that?" she asked. I replied, "It sounds like incoming rockets." There were heavy thudding, explosion sounds and the ground was shaking. She asked, "What should we do?" I said, "We stay right here until the explosions stop." We put on our clothes and waited. When it stopped, we waited for ten minutes or so and then I went outside to see what was going on. I took a radio, my handgun and an M-16. The assumption was that the Pathet Lao, the military arm of the Lao Communist Party, would shoot their rockets and disappear but there was always the chance that the rockets were preliminary to a ground attack. I met my neighbor, another case officer known as Khamsing, at the fence between the two houses and we chatted over the fence not much differently than two suburban neighbors except we both had assault rifles and carried tactical radios. Khamsing had been in country longer than I had and was more experienced. He had been on the radio net and said that all reports indicated it was only a rocket attack and there did not seem to be a ground attack. We talked a while and then decided we could go back into our houses and try to sleep until morning.

The new chief of unit knew all about the rocket attacks. While he was still in Washington, he had decided he was going to reduce the risks by moving us all out of the housing compound. We all preferred to remain in the compound where we could mutually assist and defend each other. Moreover, if Pakse came under ground attack we could all move to the airfield and meet helicopters that would be sent in to evacuate us. If all of us were together in the compound we could quickly locate everyone and the case officers could provide security while moving the wives and children to the airport. If we were dispersed around Pakse, we could not support each other and it would be much more difficult for us to travel securely to the airfield. The house they chose for us was across the Sedone River. Pakse was on the banks of the Mekong River. The airfield was on the northwest side of the city. National

Highway 13, which ran all the way from Vientiane through Pakse to Phnom
Penh and then on to Saigon, went past the airfield, past the housing compound, across the Sedone River through Pakse and out the eastern side. The
Sedone River ran perpendicular from the Mekong River first north northeast
and then east and had a one and a half lane bridge crossing it. The house was
also adjacent to a Lao army ordnance camp. The Mekong River was south of
the house and the ordnance camp was north of it. The only way to get to
Highway 13 from the house was through the ordnance camp. The most likely
enemy approach to Pakse was from the east and the ordnance camp was a
lucrative target. If we were in the house when a ground attack commenced, we
would have to make our way through the ordnance camp where attacking
enemy or defending friendly forces would be equally dangerous to us. If we
made it to the highway, we would still have to make it through the city and
across the Sedone River bridge, if it were still there. Our choices would be
immediate flight to the airfield in the hopes of helicopter evacuation, defense
at our house alone, or flight and hiding in the city or countryside where we
would stick out like a very sore thumb. The chief of unit might be protecting
himself from criticism if a rocket hit the housing compound, but we were not
being protected from the dangers of ground assault. In our bunkers and our
proximity to the airfield and our mutual protection, we felt safe against both
dangers.

At first, we tried common sense and persuasion and when that failed, we
just dragged our feet. The chief of unit took it as a serious threat to his ability
to manage and he took my resistance to be very harmful to his ability to
supervise the unit. He did not realize that he permanently damaged his ability
to manage us with a variety of illogical decisions and would never be able to
command our respect for the rest of his tour. He called me into his office and
told me to move across the river or pack up and go home. He won and we
moved, but not happily at all.

The Pakse Unit had a chief of unit, deputy chief of unit, chief of operations, chief of support, special operations case officers, humint case officers
and a variety of support officers for communications, logistics, finance,

etcetera. After I recovered from the bad-water sickness, I was able to go in to the Pakse Unit offices that were in a large white windowless building next to the United States Agency for International Development building. I once heard a local missionary call it "The Great Whitened Sepulcher." I was introduced to the chief of operations. Ray was a retired senior army NCO recruited into CIA special operations during the time when such recruitment had concentrated on former senior NCO and field grade officers. He was the best supervisor I worked for in Laos. He was a natural leader and one who expected his subordinates to get their job done with a minimal amount of supervision. He told me I was going to be the roadwatch and guerrilla battalion (GB) case officer at PS-38[14]. Ordinarily, the PS-38 garrison consisted of one special guerrilla unit (SGU) battalion, two GB battalions and the roadwatch teams. The senior case officer on the site was Dunc, a retired U.S. Marine Corps lieutenant colonel. He was the SGU advisor and the junior case officer was supposed to run the roadwatch teams and be the GB advisor. The SGU battalions were recruited to fight anywhere in Laos while the GB battalions were local defense force units recruited to fight only in their home province. Dunc's SGU had been sent to Long Tieng under the supervision of another case officer and Dunc had remained behind at PS-38. I never knew why nor did I ever ask. What it meant to me was that Dunc had taken over advising the GB battalion leaving me only the roadwatch teams with which to work.

Dunc was a very taciturn person. He rarely said much to anyone he did not know well or did not like, which did not leave many people. He and Ray had been together in Laos for several years. During their first years in Pakse, they had been roommates. By the time I arrived, Ray's wife was living with him in Pakse and Dunc was rooming with the finance officer. I would guess that Dunc was about five-foot nine or ten inches tall and about 150 or 160 pounds. He was trim and seemed fit. His hair was all white and cut in a Marine brush cut. He always wore the same style square bottom shirt and wash

---

[14] PS stood for Pakse Site.

pants with Vietnam jungle boots. I do not ever remember him carrying any weapons, but he probably carried at least a handgun in a survival kit. Again, I never asked and he never volunteered. I didn't think he liked me much. He was not friendly or welcoming. If I wanted to ask questions to find out how things worked I asked my contemporaries like "Khamsing" or "Heng", former Army Special Forces enlisted men, or Bill ("Uncle Billy"), also known as Mr. Noy, a former Marine Corps lieutenant. The Lao found Uncle Billy's Lao name, Noy, amusing since it means "little" or "small" and Uncle Billy was a large guy. Finding Dunc to be so unfriendly, I spent my time with my Thai operations assistants. In the long run, this was better for me as I tried to learn to speak Lao, to understand the Lao and the tribal Lao Theung cultures, the personalities and capabilities of the men on the roadwatch teams, and the enemy order of battle. Dunc's unfriendliness and lack of communication, however, almost cost me a lot of money.

Not too long after I began working at PS-38, the enemy attacked it during the night while we were in Pakse. At this time, we rotated the duty officer assignment of remaining over night (RON) at PS-22, but no case officers RON'd at PS-38. The enemy overran PS-38 but withdrew before dawn. Usually, when Dunc and I arrived each day on a Pilatus Porter[15], we would circle the site and establish contact with one of the English speaking Lao officers before landing. On this morning, our ground contact informed us of what had happened. The Continental Air Services Porter pilot did not want to land at first, but Dunc convinced him. We landed and went to the office building we had on the site. I was still in the main building with Dunc when rockets began to fall on PS-38. We could not tell exactly where they were landing but you had to assume they were targeting our buildings. Dunc was very experienced and knew we had to get to the aircraft and take off. Dunc immediately snatched up the gear he had brought with him and running out the door told me to follow him. I did not understand we had to get to the

---

[15] The Pilatus Porter (PC-6) is a short take and landing (STOL) aircraft capable of operating in areas that are inaccessible to many other aircraft.

aircraft as fast as we could and I was trotting along behind him. He turned while still running, told me, "Mister, you better move a lot faster." and then turned and resumed running, all without much break in stride. He would have made any football team's defensive backfield coach proud. The pilot was still with the aircraft when the rockets began to fall so he had the engine running ready for takeoff and the doors open. There was no thought whatsoever that a Porter pilot would take off alone and save his own skin, so we arrived, jumped in and he took off. We climbed to a safe altitude above the arc of the rockets the enemy was using and radioed a report to the Pakse air operations officer. We then made contact by radio with one of the English speaking Lao officers on PS-38 and he assured us the enemy had not begun a ground attack. If they had, we would have served the site best by calling for and coordinating air support from the U.S. Air Force via the daytime Airborne Battlefield Command and Control Center (ABCCC) C-130 aircraft, call sign, Hillsboro, or from Pakse via the Ravens[16] and the Royal Lao Air Force T-28's. Once it became apparent all was quiet, we landed once again on PS-38.

Dunc and I both had combination safes in which we kept sensitive documents, money and other valuable property. I kept money and a supply of about twenty .45 cal. automatic pistols. Demolitions of some kind, probably C-4, had been used on the safes to blast them open. They were rugged and difficult to break open manually but the C-4 had opened them enough for the money to be removed. We suspected, but could not prove, that our own troops had stolen the money. That evening after we returned to Pakse I was told to write a cable to Vientiane and Udorn telling them how I had lost the money and how much. No one told me there would be any repercussions. It seemed to me that you just described what had happened, it was recorded and life went on. I was obviously naïve about how things worked in the CIA. This was not like the army where I would have been more wary of bureaucratic traps. I had been a military police officer and I had seen how the unsuspecting

---

[16] Ravens were U.S. Air Force forward air controllers assigned to live and work in Laos.

might be ensnared. However, all I had been exposed to in Laos was a loose, can do, let's just get it done attitude. I did not even think about it, but if I had, I would not have expected any trouble. I reported the full amount of money that had been lost.

I had no idea what Dunc had written in his cable. The cables were handled separately. Dunc and the finance officer were roommates, but I did not focus on that at all. A few weeks after I sent my cabled report, Pakse received a visit from the Vientiane Station chief of support and the chief of finance. It seemed like it was a normal visit to see how things were going in the Pakse Unit. I was told they wanted to talk to me and I went to see them. I thought they wanted to interview me about support or finance issues. They were friendly and spent some time establishing rapport with me. They eventually sidled their way up to questions about the lost money. The more we talked about it the more apprehensive I became. I began to detect that a bit of an adversarial process was underway. They were trying to see if I could be held accountable for the loss of the money without the courtesy of telling me what they were doing. It turned out that keeping money on the site, even in a locked safe, was against regulations if no CIA employee remained on the site. The only thing that saved me was that I insisted that I was just following procedures that all the case officers working on up-country sites followed. I said that everyone kept money in safes on the sites and everyone left them unguarded over night. I found out later that to pursue punishing me for violating regulations meant exposing higher authorities to rebuke. Leaving money unguarded had gone on for so long there was no way unit, base and station supervisors could claim they had not had enough time to discover and correct it. I was let off without punishment, otherwise management would be exposed for not doing their jobs.

Once the two investigators returned to Vientiane and it became apparent they were out to get me, if possible, I became aware that there was no investigation directed at Dunc. I knew however, that Dunc had lost more money than I had. I asked questions and was finally quietly told that the Pakse finance officer had advised Dunc that if you lost $300.00 dollars or less it could be written off without investigation, but if you lost more than that it had to be investigated. Dunc was advised to report less than $300.00 and to make the rest up out of his pocket and thereby avoid being punished for ignoring the regulations. No one told me I was being investigated for reporting the full amount, which was over $300.00. One of my father's favorite sayings was, "schemers always out scheme themselves," and this was certainly proof. They wrote off my entire loss but they only wrote off $299.00 for Dunc. I wondered where the rest of the money came from, but as with other things, I did not know and I did not ask.

ROADWATCH

---

*"Now, the reason a brilliant sovereign and a wise general conquer
the enemy whenever they move and their achievements surpass those
of ordinary men is their foreknowledge of the enemy situation.
This 'foreknowledge' cannot be elicited from spirits, nor from gods,
nor by analogy with past events, nor by astrologic calculations. It must be obtained from
men who know the enemy situation."*

*"Now, there are five sorts of spies. These are: native,
internal, double, doomed and surviving spies."*

*"When all these five types of spies are at work and their
operations are clandestine, it is called the 'divine manipulation
of threads' and is the treasure of a sovereign."*

–Sun Tzu, "The Art of War"

The typical CIA Special Operations Division case officer wanted to be Lawrence of Laos, leading the indigent resistance forces against evil invaders. T.E. Lawrence led Arabs against the Turks and they wanted to lead the Lao against the North Vietnamese. Having been infantry or special operations they wanted to lead troops and do battle. I called them, not in a demeaning way, "ammo-humpers." because in reality they could not go out into combat with their troops. Their job, at least until the operation to retake Saravane in March 1971, was to organize and train irregular units, plan and coordinate their activities, and provide logistical support from rear areas. They also coordinated resupply during combat and air strike support from U.S. Air Force and Royal Lao Air Force resources.[17] A large part of their responsibility was logistical, to get food, weapons and ammunition to their troops in the actual combat areas, thus, my use of "ammo-humpers." They were users of intelligence but I didn't know many who were really interested in running irregular operations solely for the purpose of collecting intelligence. On the other hand, I had no interest whatsoever in being a Lawrence of Laos. If anything, my heroes were the men of the World War II's Office of Strategic Services (OSS). I had read books about the OSS and British Special Operations Executive (SOE) who had run intelligence and action teams into Thailand during that war. The goal of collecting and disseminating intelligence fascinated me, not just the activities of running the teams. Because all my ammo-humper colleagues were so interested in being

---

[17] In March 1971, the operation to re-take Saravane was launched from CIA's up-country site, PS-47. When the U.S. Air Force helicopters loaded the troops the GM case officers got right on the helicopters and rode with the troops right into the helicopter landing zones in Saravane. The chief of station (COS) was there, observing. No objection was raised to prevent them and the previous ban on case officers going into combat with the troops was over.

Lawrence of Laos it left the field wide open for me to take on the operational responsibility for all the special operations intelligence operations in the Pakse Unit. To paraphrase bluesman Mississippi Fred McDowell, I didn't play no rock and roll, and in the world of special operations, I didn't hump no ammo.

The roadwatch program was one of the oldest continuous programs in Laos. It had a long, honorable history going back to World War II in the OSS. It was descended from the island coastal watchers in the Pacific who sat and watched for Japanese naval activity and then reported it. OSS had done well assigning small teams of observers, in both Europe and the Pacific, to watch for enemy activity and report it. It must have been easy to get approval, once again, to set up an enemy activity observation project. OSS' use of names for the teams had also been resurrected for the Lao program with all the teams having names like Team Cranberry, Team Onion and Team Gin. It seems to me that it was quite common for intelligence officers to retool successful concepts and adapt them to new programs and requirements. In this case, no one had ever reviewed the concept as it was being applied in Laos and it was a failure that, just like the Energizer bunny, kept on and on. To a certain extent, military thinkers tend to do such things a lot, and a large percentage of case officers were former career military or at least military experienced. To the military mind, it was usually better to be doing something rather than nothing at all. Intelligence collection in Laos by human assets was almost nonexistent and the lack of a disseminable intelligence product was no reason to end the roadwatch program since it was one of the Vientiane Station's few special operations intelligence collection programs.

A roadwatch team consisted of a team leader, deputy team leader, radio operator and team members. The number of team members varied according to the mission, but generally, there were three to five men. Roadwatch teams were supposed to sneak into positions from which they could observe the enemy moving along the Ho Chi Minh Trail. They were to count the soldiers, vehicles or pack animals and report the date, time, numbers and travel direction of each. We accumulated these reports and sent them to CIA headquarters in Washington every ten days as field intelligence reports. Obviously, the biggest problem with this was that no one had any idea what was in the vehicles or on the pack animals or where the soldiers were going.

During my year of training before departure for Laos, my training partner Ken and I had a two-week period where we had no training classes scheduled. The chief called us in and asked us to take on a special assignment. The Lao Desk of the Far East Division had told Wayne, a branch chief in SOD, that the Directorate of Intelligence (DI) analyst receiving the roadwatch field intelligence reports had them piled up under his desk and could find no useful way to interpret them. Wayne told us to work with Dave so we looked him up and told him we were at his disposal. Dave was quite a character. He had been around the Southeast Asia programs a long time. He had even once ridden a motorcycle from the DMZ to the Mekong Delta not too long after the initial establishment of the DMZ line of demarcation. The DI analyst had told Dave that he could not come up with any way to analyze the data and so he just piled up the reports under his desk and was not using them.[18] Dave brought us a monstrous stack of roadwatch intelligence cables and set us up at two desks in a cubicle in the middle of all the other Special Operations Division cubicles. He told us, "See what you can do to make some sense out of all this."

Ken and I took over the small cubicle in the center of the area and began to try to figure out how to analyze the information. We quickly learned that the sightings of enemy trucks, troops, pack animals, riverboats and such, reported to roadwatch case officers in both Savannakhet and Pakse, were accumulated for a period of time, usually ten days, and then summarized into intelligence reports and sent to CIA headquarters. Traditionally, an intelligence report was sent out when intelligence information had been collected by a human asset, a recruited agent or spy, or from a technical operation, perhaps a wiretap or an audio device, and the information was in the hands of a case officer. Disseminable information usually meant the information was deemed valid and responded to a known requirement. In Laos, CIA headquarters had decided that roadwatch teams were human assets and their reported sightings should be reported in

---

[18] DI analysts were responsible for analyzing information from all sources to write and publish finished intelligence products.

intelligence reports. The problem was that a team could not say what was inside a truck or on a boat, nor could it tell its destination. The team could not identify the unit designations of the troops it saw nor discern where they were going or why. The DI analyst was not receiving anything he could use. After looking over a sampling of the intelligence reports, we decided to get a map of the area. Since most of the road watching activity observing the Ho Chi Minh Trail was conducted in MR III from Savannahkhet and MR–IV from Pakse, we went to the map library and requisitioned maps of the area and set up a big map board of 1:50,000 scale maps. We then tried to plot each team's observation posts. We wanted to tie the reported sightings over one year into one or more specific places along the Ho Chi Minh Trail. The problem we ran into was that no one point on the map was covered continuously. One team might cover it for a month or two, but then when the team withdrew the next team did not always move into the same area, not even close. There were also gaps in the times of coverage, so that we could not find one place or one lengthy time period when a specific position was covered.

We devised a code for the types of sightings, i.e. troops, trucks, boats (some of the reporting locations were along rivers that the North Vietnamese Army used in the rainy season because they were easier to travel), pack animals, etcetera. After tinkering with many different sets of reporting data, we decided to take the best one and total up all the data. We went through all the reports for the sample we wanted and noted the information on graph paper. We had columns for trucks, troops and such and we wrote down the numbers under each column from all the reports that we had set aside. Finishing that, we discovered that we had an unwieldy long column of numbers that we needed to add up. Ken went off and found an old adding machine, one of those with a crank. You tapped in the numbers and then cranked the handle. We took turns either reading out the numbers or tapping them in and cranking the handle. It was monotonous work and we took to droning the numbers. In a cubicle in the middle of a lot of others, everyone could hear someone's voice announcing incomprehensible numbers followed by tap, tap, tap and then crank – over and over again. It sounded like this:

Me: "2, 1"
Ken: tap, tap, crank

Me: "3, 2, 2"
Ken: tap, tap, tap, crank

Me: "7"
Ken: tap, crank

We did this for hours on end. We counted, totaled and sub-totaled for two weeks. We had become quite anal about it. We were intent on producing some kind of report at the end of the two weeks. We were driving our neighbors in the surrounding cubicles crazy.

They finally could not take it any longer and went to Dave. "Dave, if you don't stop those guys we're going to strangle them."

Dave asked us, "Hey, it's almost the end of two weeks. Have you two gotten anywhere?"

We told him that as far as we could see there was no way an analyst could make any thing useful out of the data and we sympathized with the analyst and wondered why he had been so patient and not just destroyed the pile of useless paper a long time ago.

When it was all over, we had to go to Wayne and tell him there was no way to make sense of the data. There was no continuity of coverage of the same locations. If you did not know what was being transported and you did not know where the troops were going or why, you might be able to interpret something if you could analyze the flow between the same two points. However, over the approximate five-year period covered by the intelligence reports there was never any reasonable length of time when any one point had been consistently observed. The entire output of the roadwatch project in Pakse and Savannakhet was useless. While this revelation should have been enough to cause the termination of the program that would never happen in a government bureaucracy. A lot of time and money had been spent and egos and reputations were on the line.

At the end, I said to Ken, "How is anyone going to admit that something so useless was allowed to run for so long without ever reviewing it or questioning it?"

Thus, I went to Laos knowing the Directorate of Intelligence was ignoring the intelligence output of the roadwatch project. I did not know I would wind up involved with roadwatch teams for my entire two year tour in Laos. I had no idea I would need to adapt and improvise their activities so that Lao team soldiers would be more effective and would come to be feared and therefore pursued by the North Vietnamese Army whenever they thought our teams were behind North Vietnamese Army lines.

In early 1970, Pakse Unit's area of operations was divided into three guerrilla zones. Each zone had one case officer for its special guerrilla unit (SGU) battalion and one case officer for the roadwatch program plus the two local-force guerrilla battalions (GB). Guerrilla Zone I was headquartered at PS-22 and was in the central part of MR-IV. Two special operations case officers, Dutch and Jack, were in charge of PS-22. Guerrilla Zone III was headquartered at LS-171[19] and covered the northern part of MR-IV. CIA special operations case officers "Heng" and "Noy" were in charge of LS-171. Heng was a former U.S. Army Special Forces non-commissioned officer and Noy was a former U.S. Marine Corps company grade officer who had already completed a CIA tour in Vietnam before arriving in Laos.

Guerrilla Zone II was headquartered at PS-38 and was responsible for the southern part of MR-IV. I was assigned as the roadwatch and GB case officer operating out of PS-38. The senior case officer on PS-38 was Dunc, a retired Marine Corps field grade officer. Dunc was responsible for SGU-2, which was on assignment to Long Tieng, but Dunc had remained at PS-38 and had taken over directing the two GBs. CIA special operations case officer "Khamsing", a

---

[19] LS stood for Lao Site, or Lima Site (because "lima" is the military phonetic pronunciation for the letter L).

former junior Army NCO, was the commando/raider case officer and split his time between PS-38 and LS-165.

My Lao code name was "Chanh." The idea of the Lao code names was that we were supposed to use those names with the Thai and Lao, and whenever we talked on the radio. It was supposed to be better than using American names or nicknames, but it seemed silly. We all looked like Americans and we spoke English over the radio. Nevertheless, the Lao and Thai all called us Mr. Chanh or Mr. Noy, as appropriate. The lowland Lao and the Lao hill tribesmen called the Thai operations assistants and the American case officers "Nai Kou." a Thai term used for someone in a position of respect. I asked my Thai operations assistant, Somneuk, about it once and he told me it was how a Thai would address a teacher or instructor in school. Our call sign procedures were different from the ones used in other units such as Long Tieng or Savannakhet where they used call signs such as "Kayak", "Mule", "Sword", and "Boston." These were really radio call signs not chosen to disguise that the user was an American. Actually, everyone in Pakse, even the secretaries and other support personnel were assigned Lao names but the case officers were the only ones who made use of them.

Pakse Unit was still using the SGUs for what they called interdiction operations while the GBs were supposed to be security forces for the villages still under Lao government control. The GBs sometimes conducted "offensive" operations near the villages but it seldom amounted to any actual combat. An SGU might form 20-50 man teams to go out to the area of the Ho Chi Minh Trail to conduct ambushes, trying to kill enemy soldiers or destroy cargo carrying trucks or boats. Sometimes they were effective and sometimes they tried their best to avoid any contact with the enemy. As is usually the case this was a function of whether the unit had good Lao leadership or not. About this time, a change was going on and SGUs were just beginning to be asked to leave MR-IV and go to Long Tieng to help the Lao MR-II commander, Vang Pao, in a more conventional role. This change in mission eventually led to a reorganization of the SGUs from single battalions to three-battalion regiments, called Groupements Mobile (GM) using a French military term.

There were a few teams out on these missions on the day I arrived and for a while, I continued to send replacement teams as needed. Roadwatch was a year round activity conducted during both dry and wet seasons, but when the rainy season came, we added riverwatch teams because we knew the North Vietnamese Army used rivers for transportation when they were full from rain runoff and roads were hard to use because of the mud and water.

Roadwatch teams infiltrated by helicopter to areas near the Ho Chi Minh Trail and could then reach it in two to three days walking. That provided a bit of security because the helicopter landing zones were not in areas heavily patrolled by the North Vietnamese Army. Their patrols were much more numerous closer to the trail network. Once on the ground the roadwatch team walked several days to reach an area where they could establish a command post (CP). The observation post (OP) then had to be set up so the team could observe enemy movements on the Ho Chi Minh Trail.

For comparison, consider that infiltrating and operating against the Ho Chi Minh Trail was the equivalent of trying to do the same within the boundaries of Nazi Germany before the invasion of Normandy. Operating in the rice growing areas surrounding the Bolovens Plateau and on the Plateau was equivalent to operating behind enemy lines in France. In Germany, an unconventional unit would not expect to get any assistance from local German citizens and would have to operate very covertly. In France, an unconventional unit could expect to find help from resistance fighters or friendly French citizens who would provide intelligence and logistical support as well as possibly fighting along side the special operations units.

Another type of team operation was the truck ambush. Since the teams had experience traveling out to the Ho Chi Minh Trail, management thought they could infiltrate close enough to one of the roads used by North Vietnamese Army trucks to destroy them. My predecessors had been sending out teams to try for troop or truck ambushes as targets of opportunity. Once on the ground the team would reconnoiter until they found a place where they believed they could ambush a truck or North Vietnamese Army troops. They would execute their ambush and then hightail it out of there. We tried

American shoulder fired rockets, captured Soviet rifle propelled grenades (RPGs) and a variety of exotic Technical Services Division (TSD) designed truck destroyers. One of the more interesting weapons was a triple rocket tube designed and built by TSD officer Greg M. The tube had a long wire and a pressure sensitive trigger. I had to train the teams to get literally within a stone's throw of the center of the road. They were supposed to wrap one end of the wire around a rock and throw it into the center of the road and then extend the wire back to where the triple rocket tube would be setup. They then had to go to the center of the road and dig the pressure sensitive trigger into the earth in the road. After concealing the triple rocket tube where it had a clear line to the road, they could withdraw to a safe place back from the road and wait for a truck to drive over the trigger. The weight of the truck would close the loop allowing electricity from a battery to ignite the rockets and send them screaming toward the cab of the truck. When done properly the triple rockets could demolish a truck cab and part of the rest of the truck. The problem was – could I believe the team had really done it when they said they did? I issued cameras to truck ambush teams but I do not remember ever getting photographs of demolished trucks after a mission. The teams felt it was too dangerous to hang around an ambush site taking photographs for the Nai Kou since three 3.5-inch rockets exploding into a truck would draw a lot of attention. Even if the truck were the only one, and more often it was the lead truck of several, the North Vietnamese Army soldiers would immediately be off on both sides of the road looking for the ambushers. The normal result of an ambush was to stir the North Vietnamese Army up and cause them to begin searching for the perpetrators. The teams knew that and were not likely to remain in the area after an ambush, if they remained for any length of time at all before. There was not much a case officer could do to verify a team had actually done what it claimed. Generally, previous case officers relied heavily on the polygraph to try to determine if the team was telling the truth about their missions, but I did not like or trust the polygraph and especially the polygraphers. Not that I thought the polygraphers were dishonest or incompetent, there were just too many cultural ambiguities involved in Americans administering polygraphs to lowland Lao or Lao Theung mountain tribesmen on American terms. Moreover, some polygraphers had come to believe all roadwatch personnel were fabricators and they were there to uncover that fabrication, not to determine if there were fabrication or not. As my tour wore on, I was able to find other ways to test my teams or to produce results that would not need polygraphs for verification.

An example of the negative impact of the polygraph because of cultural disparities happened to one of my best team leaders. After spending some time up-country in Laos, a good case officer was capable of telling which team leaders were honest and which ones needed careful watching. Khampeng, the leader of Team 704, had established a sterling reputation over several years with a number of different case officers. He had returned from an intelligence collection mission and it was time for another polygraph. John, the polygraph operator, was newly arrived in Laos. He was assigned to assist Bob, who had been in country for several years but could not keep up with the large number of cases. Polygraphs had to be administered to all assets, special operations as well as foreign intelligence agents. John was a rather normal looking man, except for one noticeable habit. His body was always suffused with the aroma of the man's cologne, Canoe, which I've heard pronounced ka-new and some-times ka-no-way. The aroma of Canoe was pleasant enough but intense and unusual in up-country Laos. John arrived at PS-47 for the polygraph sessions and we had a straw hut set aside for him. He had been adamant that the venue for the polygraph session be in a place that was private and out of view. On a site like PS-47 that was almost impossible except inside a straw hut. It was 100 plus degrees and humid when John arrived in a Porter and even hotter and airless inside the straw hut. John could not speak Lao, so he could not interro-gate his subjects or question them with the polygraph machine. Therefore, we had to assign one of our operations assistants to work with him. I assigned Somsit, one of my Thai assistants, who spoke Lao with a heavy Thai accent, to work with John. Away they went into the straw hut and I went about my business. After a while, John came out of the session and told me he was sure the team leader was fabricating and would have to be terminated. I was shocked

and asked John to wait a few minutes while I conferred with my senior operations assistant, Hom, as well as with Somsit. I explained to them that John
wanted to fail the team leader. Hom and Somsit conferred in Thai. Then Hom
asked if he could substitute for Somsit. Would John try the test again with
Hom? I asked John and he agreed. Back they went to the straw hut and after an
hour or so John came back and said the team leader had passed. I asked John
to continue the other examinations with Somsit and I went to find Hom.
Ordinarily, Hom might not want to be too forthcoming, since the explanation
involved several cultural differences and only embarrassment would ensue if
they became public. Hom and I had built a reasonably good rapport in our
time together since PS-22 and he explained what had happened. First, the
team leader was an ethnic hill tribesman and Lao was not his native language.
Since Somsit had a heavy Thai accent, the team leader was having great
difficulty understanding Somsit. When asked a question he generally did not
understand it, but he could not cause Somsit to lose face by telling him he
could not understand Somsit's Lao. Therefore, he would guess no or yes
without being able to understand the question. Whatever stress John's polygraph machine was registering it was most likely the team leader registering the
stress of not being able to understand and not being able to tell Somsit why.
Further, the team leader told Hom that John's perfume made him very uncomfortable and within the confines of the sweltering straw hut, it was overwhelming. The only place the team leader had ever been in the presence of such
overpowering perfume was in a brothel. It was a strong association and he was
very uncomfortable smelling such perfume on a man. When Hom took over he
spoke excellent unaccented Lao despite being Thai, and he helped the team
leader ignore the perfume problem. With the questions now clear and the
perfume problem addressed, he was able to answer the questions without stress
and he passed the polygraph test.

One has to wonder how many team leaders may have not passed the polygraph because of cultural differences rather than whether they were fabricating
information. In my opinion, the polygraph is merely a piece of technology,
which in the hands of a skilled interrogator can help the interrogator determine

if the subject might be fabricating. If you go into an interrogation or interview as an interrogator/interviewer using a piece of technology as an aid, that is one thing, but, if you go into the interrogation or interview as a polygraph operator whose polygraph test must be passed or it means you are fabricating, that is very much something else. At one point, I wanted to know why they could not train me to use the polygraph so I could use it on my teams myself. It was the first time I ran into the "breaking someone's rice bowl" explanation. I was told there was no way the Office of Security would let someone from the outside, that is the Directorate of Operations, be trained in how to use the polygraph. Providing polygraph operators was Security's "rice bowl" and letting in outsiders might result in that rice bowl being broken.

After my first five years in the CIA I decided to transfer to the Drug Enforcement Administration (DEA) where I became a Special Agent (1811-Criminal Investigator). During my three years in DEA before I transferred back to CIA, I became friendly with a long-time Special Agent who had been a Houston homicide detective. As part of his training for interrogating murder suspects, he was trained in graphology also known as hand writing analysis. He could analyze a suspect's handwriting and then use the insights he gained into the suspect's personality and character to guide his interrogation. It was an aid. A suspect did not fail the handwriting test. The CIA polygraph people did not seem to me to think of the polygraph as this sort of aid. On one hand, you can think of yourself as an interrogator who uses an aid called a polygraph, or on the other hand, you can be a polygraph operator who uses the polygraph to trap and uncover fabricators or liars. One invests himself in his skills as an interrogator and the other invests himself in his machine. The latter is a formula that can lead to failure. Once you lose sight of the human dimensions of interrogation and trust only the machine invalid results are possible. The polygraph can be beaten, it can be fooled, but more than that, the polygraph operator can be fooled. However, if the polygraph operators have come to see their machine as infallible they will not recognize when they are being beaten. If they do not see their machine as infallible then they must see themselves as interrogators first and polygraph operators second, and I never met one who felt that way. One other facet of using the polygraph is its use on CIA employees. The holy grail of the polygraph operator examining an employee or employment candidate is an "admission." That is, if the polygraph operator believes the machine is indicating the subject is practicing deception he must get the subject to admit that she or he is being deceptive. A person cannot be declared deceptive because of the polygraph, the person must admit deception. However, in Laos and in many other agent polygraph examinations, it is not necessary to get an admission, an agent might be terminated just because the polygraph operator declares the agent is fabricating. From a case officer point of view, this places the validity of the operation totally on the skills and ability of the polygraph operator, something that is not acceptable to a case officer and can be the source of a lot of friction between case officers and polygraph examiners. This subject will come up again during a discussion of the teams we sent into Cambodia in early 1970.

In addition to truck ambush, the roadwatch teams supplied the manpower for wiretapping and radio intercept operations, in coordination with the Pakse Unit signals intelligence officer. The North Vietnamese Army used military field telephones connected by stringing wire on wooden poles with porcelain insulators. They also communicated using Soviet made World War II era radios, NATO code-named "Mercury Grass", operating in the 66.0 to 69.97 MHz range. When they wanted to pass sensitive information, they used code sheets. A message would be put into four or five-number groups. Using the radio, the sender called in the clear, that is not using code, and when he established contact said that he had coded message. When the recipient was ready, the sender would read the coded groups of numbers. At the end, he would sign off in the clear. We did not have much experience with wiretapping but we did not think they used code for conversations over the wired field telephones. The North Vietnamese Army patrolled their wired telephone poles extensively and my teams were never successful in finding North Vietnamese Army wires and tapping them. Whenever we had a wiretapping target, I would get the equipment from the Office of SIGINT Operations (OSO) officer assigned to Pakse

Unit. He supplied a tape recorder, a clamp for tapping into the wire and enough wire to reach from the tapped wire to the tape recorder. This was not a popular mission as the team soldiers felt very exposed and vulnerable sitting close to a telephone pole with a clamp on the wire. In my two years, we never had a successful wiretap operation. From time to time a team would come in with what they alleged were Pathet Lao wiretaps but they never had anything interesting on them and I never had to try to authenticate them. We did conduct one very successful radio intercept operation described in a later chapter titled, "This Is the Monthly Report for Binh Tram 35."

We also sent the teams out on intelligence collection missions, which involved sending a team into an area, which was under enemy control, and in which one or more of the team members had friends or relatives. The team traveled from Lao government controlled territory to a safe place near their target location and then set up a clandestine camp from which they could secretly try to contact their friends or relatives. They would try to enlist their contacts to report enemy activities that they then reported back to me. In the beginning of my tour, I sent the teams out by helicopter to be delivered to landing zones in the vicinity of their targets. After disembarking from the helicopter, they would walk the rest of the way to their intended campsite. I inherited this methodology from previous case officers because most missions were out to the Ho Chi Minh Trail and it was deemed the most efficient and timely method. That is the way they had done it for years.

However, I quickly became disenchanted with helicopter infiltrations because the enemy often attacked my teams within a few days after disembarkation. It was not hard to understand. As the helicopters flew out into enemy territory, the enemy discerned the general area where the helicopters landed and then worked to encircle the area to find and engage my teams. My teams were rather adept at fleeing from such attacks and in two or three weeks they would eventually straggle in to our operations base without weapons or equipment, having chucked it all as soon as gunfire broke out. They bolted out of the kill zone firing their weapons in all directions and throwing hand grenades, if they had them. They made their way through the underbrush until they were safe from enemy bullets and then simply walked home. I decided that if they could walk out they could walk in. I made it my policy to give them money to pay for local transportation as far as they could go into enemy territory. From that drop off point, they would then walk the rest of the way.

In southern Laos, Military Region IV, there was territory controlled by the Lao government (mostly in a wide swath along the Mekong River), territory controlled by the North Vietnamese Army (mostly in a very wide swath along the Ho Chi Minh Trail), and a neutral buffer zone between the two. The North Vietnamese Army allowed the neutral buffer zone to exist with its villages and farming as it gave them an area where they could buy or confiscate agricultural products and animals for food. Lao regular and irregular military forces did not like to venture into the neutral buffer zone because they feared running into the North Vietnamese Army who might be foraging through the area. The Ho Chi Minh Trail was heavily bombed but the neutral buffer zone was not. My teams moved through the neutral buffer zone villages either by going around the ones they did not know or through the ones in which they expected a friendly reception. Their passage through enemy territory was made easier because they dressed like the local villagers. The local villagers went about their business and rarely reported team activity to the North Vietnamese Army.

These intelligence collection missions were not satisfying to me as they resulted in the teams reporting hearsay information from the villagers who were unsophisticated observers. Generally, the information consisted of an estimate of the number of enemy soldiers, a description of the weapons they carried and perhaps an idea of the activity the enemy unit was conducting. I wanted better than that but it took me some time to figure out ways to use the teams to better effect. Eventually I came up with operational ideas that had much more impact than I could have imagined.

The roadwatch program included the emplacement of sensors (described in detail in the chapter titled "Remote Sensors and Beacons") and action operations included troop, truck and boat ambushes. In true guerrilla fashion, my teams never went after the enemy unless they were sure they outnumbered them and had a clear path to escape if things went wrong. In reality, I did not want them to do otherwise. Early in my tour in Laos, intelligence collection consisted of talking to villagers about enemy activity and reporting that back to me. There was no intention to use the information to attack the enemy positions. As my tour progressed, I added collecting intelligence to find and capture North Vietnamese Army soldiers and bring them in. I also added sending teams to contact villagers behind North Vietnamese Army lines and then using the intelligence collected from the villagers to visually locate the enemy and guide Raven forward air controllers (FAC) to them so they could be bombed. I describe these activities in further detail in the chapters titled "Cash on Delivery" and "Find, Fix and Destroy."

Throughout my tour and in all my activities I had rules of engagement to follow. The rules included that we were to do everything we could to avoid allowing Americans into direct combat with the North Vietnamese Army. You could do that by staying in Pakse all day never going to a forward site and never flying out over the combat zones and the Ho Chi Minh Trail but then you would reduce your effectiveness significantly. Instead, you had to choose when and where you would run risks. Khamsing, another CIA special operations officer assigned to Pakse, and I had very different views about what you had to do to be an effective special operations case officer. We often had animated discussions about it. My position was that we were intelligence officers first and ammo–humpers second. There was a lot of money invested in making us intelligence officers and our job was collecting intelligence. Khamsing, on the other hand, believed he could make a difference with his Lao irregulars and could make a fight of it against the North Vietnamese Army. He could not ask his men to do things he would not do and so he felt he had to be as far out in front of the action as possible. I believed in letting the men do the fighting while I "manipulated threads"

Khamsing may have been right about needing to lead by example when the assignment was directing irregular military units, but it was not necessary to lead by example when directing special operations intelligence collection.

After a few months working in Laos, I decided to debrief a roadwatch team after its return from a mission. I carefully gathered all the details I

could, including information about the width of the road, the soil composi-
tion, the vegetation and anything else the team could tell me about the road
and the area around it. I meticulously wrote all of this mundane detail into a
Field Intelligence Report (FIR) and cabled it to Vientiane and CIA headquarters. CIA headquarters accepted the report for dissemination to the
intelligence community and I received credit for one "intelligence dissem" in
the monthly intelligence summary cable. In those days, Vientiane Station
was still keeping score on intelligence disseminations, a practice that had
begun when Theodore G. (Ted) Shackley was the chief of station. Shackley
distributed a monthly message listing all the case officers in Laos and how
many intelligence dissems for which each had been responsible. A lot of
special operations case officers did not care about the monthly intelligence
report summary cable but the traditional intelligence collection case officers,
mostly in Vientiane, and the few spotted around Laos did not want to be
placed far from the top of the list. It was not common for special operations
case officers to be above the halfway mark on the list because their jobs were
not intelligence collection. The practice did not last to the end of my first
year but during the time it was in use, traditional intelligence collection case
officers eagerly or fearfully awaited the monthly report to see who was at the
top and who was at the bottom. Usually a Vientiane based case officer was at
the top of the list because they were conducting traditional intelligence
collection operations and writing many intelligence reports. In a quirk of the
system, roadwatch officers might receive credit for as many as three reports a
month based on having all the roadwatch statistics accumulated for ten days
and then reported in a summary intelligence report. For some reason these
reports were always disseminated to the intelligence community. During
months when I added a few intelligence reports on top of my three automatic roadwatch dissems I gained the distinction of being one of the few special
operations case officers to top the list. Given the sad tragedy of the non-
dissemination of one truly important report, described in the chapter titled
"Our North Vietnamese Army Spy" this is a curious footnote to the history
of intelligence dissemination in Laos.

While the primary mission of the roadwatch program was intelligence collection on the Ho Chi Minh Trail, it also had other operational targets, such as radio intercept, wiretapping, and truck ambushing. Prior to 1970, most Pakse roadwatch case officers were content to run pure roadwatch missions and truck ambushes. In addition, some time near the beginning of 1970, CIA decided to organize a commando/raider program. The commando/raiders were to conduct special operations deep in North Vietnamese Army controlled territory or even in North Vietnam. The full details of the commando/raider program are unknown to me and will have to be the subject of another book written by someone knowledgeable of its details. I did not have a need to know about the program and so I was unaware of the details of its operations. I was not allowed access to that compartment. I believe the commando/raiders were involved in some intriguing operations.

In southern Laos, irregular battalions and roadwatch operations were directed from both Savannakhet and Pakse Units. In the Savannakhet Unit area of operations there was flat terrain all the way to the mountains containing the Ho Chi Minh Trail. In the Pakse area of operations, there was extensive jungle from Pakse to the Bolovens Plateau, rich rice growing areas around Saravane north of the Bolovens and around Attopeu east of the Bolovens, the Bolovens Plateau itself and then the mountains containing the Ho Chi Minh Trail. In 1970, Savannakhet Unit and the Royal Lao Government's military forces were already limited to operating from Savannakhet, a Mekong River city. Pakse Unit's irregular units were operating against the North Vietnamese Army from forward sites on the Bolovens Plateau, about 95 kilometers east of Pakse. Royal Lao Government Forces Armée du Royaume (FAR) units had military installations in the strategic towns of Saravane, Paksong and Attopeu.

By 1970, subsequent to the fall of the Sihanouk government in Cambodia in March, the North Vietnamese Army lost its alternate route of infiltration into the Republic of Vietnam and had to rely only on the Ho Chi Minh Trail. The North Vietnamese Army high command must have realized that they needed to widen and harden the Trail's security. The North Vietnamese Army began actions that were interpreted as intending to secure the Bolovens

Plateau to eliminate it as a launch base for irregular operations and to seize the rice growing areas and the villages to guarantee access to the rice and to be able to make use of the villagers in support of the North Vietnamese Army. Taking the Bolovens Plateau and the cities of Saravane, Attopeu and Paksong would push the irregulars and the FAR back to Pakse, also a Mekong River city.

The North Vietnamese Army began its westward advance toward the Mekong River in February 1970. As the North Vietnamese Army began to conduct operations further and further west from the Ho Chi Minh Trail toward the Bolovens and Pakse the CIA changed its method of operations from running single Special Guerrilla Unit (SGU) battalions (550 men each) to running Groupements Mobile (GM). GMs consisted of four 300-man battalions and a heavy weapons company. French designations were used because the FAR used them and CIA wanted the irregular units to appear compatible with FAR units. Unit numbering also followed the FAR pattern for the same reason.[20] Both Savannakhet and Pakse organized and trained GMs and began to use them as conventional units to combat the North Vietnamese Army advance westward rather than for Ho Chi Minh Trail interdiction. Nevertheless, the roadwatch and commando/raider programs remained the same. SGUs and later GMs had one case officer for each SGU or GM and the roadwatch and commando/raider programs each had one case officer. The difference was that SGU/GM case officers often had to work with a Lao officer assigned to command the unit and the unit's operations were subject to oversight by many levels of CIA management. In my case, I was left alone to run daily operations as I saw fit, something I earned from the chief of operations once he realized I could handle it and needed no close supervision. Sometimes he told me to try to run operations into a certain area, but that only happened once or twice. Generally, as the war became more conventional in nature, management lost interest in small team special operations and

---

[20] CIA numbered its irregular units according to the military region, e.g., MR IV units were numbered GM 41 and GM 42, while MR III units were numbered GM 31 and GM 32. This followed the Lao army practice of numbering units with the first number equal to the MR from which it originated.

focused mostly on the conventional large unit operations. As the enemy increased its activities off the Ho Chi Minh Trail, in the Attopeu and Saravane valleys and on the Bolovens Plateau, the roadwatch teams were no longer operating in a hostile, enemy controlled denied area, but rather in their own backyard. Rather than being strangers in enemy controlled territory, they were fish swimming in the sea of their own people. On the Ho Chi Minh Trail, they were under heavy pressure and had to hide from the enemy at all times. In their own backyard, they could move openly, if in disguise. Moreover, the North Vietnamese Army became more vulnerable as they had to move among the villages and villagers. On the Ho Chi Minh Trail, they had extensive security but in this new area, they did not have the same iron-fisted control. This change in the operating environment devalued roadwatching as a function of the roadwatch program, if indeed it ever had any real value. More viable operational options were intelligence collection, wiretapping, radio intercept, capturing North Vietnamese Army soldiers, ambush, target acquisition and forward air guidance of United States Air Force, United States Navy and Royal Lao Air Force bombing.

I started out running the roadwatch teams operating out of PS-38. The men who served on these teams were Lao hill tribesman from the village, Kong My, originally known as LS-407 but later changed to PS-7. PS-38 was on the Bolovens Plateau and Kong My was in the jungles south of the plateau about 15 kilometers from the Cambodian border. These teams were all numbered in the 500s and had names associated with alcoholic beverages, such as Team Gin, Team Whiskey, Team Rum, etcetera. While its headquarters was on PS-38, the 500 numbered teams lived in Kong My and were transported to PS-38 for missions by helicopter or fixed wing STOL (short take off and landing) aircraft. Kong My was located at about 500 feet of elevation approximately 40 kilometers on a straight line to the southeast from the edge of the Bolovens Plateau. This was an area of jungles and mountains above 4,000 feet extending west to east from Cambodia to Vietnam and north to south from Laos to Cambodia. The eastern end of this area included the well-known Parrot's

Beak and the communist sanctuaries just across the Vietnam border in Laos and Cambodia.

I worked at PS-38 until November 1970 when Pakse Unit management, decided to abandon it and move the PS-38 case officers and our Lao assets to PS-22, ceding control of the southern end of the Bolovens Plateau to the North Vietnamese Army. The North Vietnamese Army first attacked our positions on the Bolovens Plateau in September 1970 by climbing up 3,000 feet to PS-26 from the Attopeu Valley on the east side of the plateau. I describe our reaction to the North Vietnamese Army attack on PS-26 in the chapter titled "The Battle for PS-26." We temporarily retook PS-26 but it became apparent that the attack on PS-26 was just the opening move in the North Vietnamese Army's plan to kick us off the plateau so we could not mount our operations against the Ho Chi Minh Trail nor interfere with their western movement toward the Mekong River. It seemed that the North Vietnamese Army wanted to gain control of more of the neutral zone between the Ho Chi Minh Trail corridor they controlled, and the Mekong River corridor that we controlled.

Gaining more complete secure control of the buffer zone would provide greater security for them by reducing our ability to send out SGU units, commando/raider teams, and roadwatch teams. This would also give them access to more rice, because they would control the villages and rice paddies in the buffer zone, and have more access to the villagers, whom they could use as workers and porters, and who could sell them goods obtained from the Mekong River towns.

Pakse Unit roadwatch teams were composed of indigenous mountain tribesmen and lowland Lao. In the early days teams were usually homogenous, that is, an entire team was from one tribe or made up of all lowland Lao. By the time I arrived, some teams were going out with mixed lowland Lao and hill tribesmen as members. One particular tribe or certain tribes dominated each MR-IV Guerrilla Zone. The PS-7 teams were usually Lave (Brao) tribesmen, while the LS-171 teams were usually from the Ta'oi (Brou) tribe. At PS-22, the teams were a mix of hill tribesman and lowland Lao. The longer the war lasted the more the members of different tribes served together on the same teams.

The people referred to as lowland Lao made up approximately one-half to two-thirds of the population. They are racially related to the people of Thailand and during the Vietnam War period were called Lao Loum. Today it might be more appropriate to refer to them as lowland Lao. Some academics theorize that the Lao Loum immigrated into the Mekong River valley from northwest Laos or China. They tend to be wet-rice farmers and usually stay in areas that are no higher in elevation than 600 to 1,200 feet. Their religion is Theravada Buddhism, they eat glutinous rice and, to a lesser extent, steamed white rice and use their hands and a fork and spoon rather than chopsticks when eating. They often build their houses on stilts and men wear "pha salong" clothes around their waists, which resemble skirts rather than pants. Their language is in the T'ai family.

The languages spoken by the various hill tribes are used to differentiate them. The Lao Theung are thought to be the original inhabitants of what is now Laos and are Mon-Khmer speakers, a branch of the Austro-Asiatic family of languages. They are mostly animists who provide offerings to a variety of spirits, including ones who inhabit the forests, rivers, houses, etcetera. Their villages are usually in the uplands of Laos where they practice swidden agriculture, sometimes called the slash and burn method of cultivation. In southern Laos, some of these tribes were Ta'oi (Brou), Laven (Jrou), Nya Heun (Heugn), Kasseng (now known as Taliang), and Lave (Brao).

The Lao Soung migrated into Laos, Vietnam and Thailand from China. They are either Hmong-leu Mien or Tibeto-Burman speakers. Their villages are usually above 3,000 feet of elevation with houses built on the ground rather than on stilts. The Hmong (known during the war as Meo, a name they detest) made up the largest group of Lao Soung. They are further sub-divided into clans. They also practice swidden agriculture and often grow poppies for use in opium production. They practice animism as well as Taoism, Buddhism and Christianity. In fact, there are Christians among many Lao groups, however, generally in small numbers.

The tribal T'ai in northern Laos, known as Black T'ai, Red T'ai and White T'ai, plant sticky rice and live in stilt houses, much like the lowland Lao. Their religion is animist and their language is in the T'ai family.[21]

The PS-7 teams from Kong My were part of a Lao Theung sub-group known as Lave (Brao). The village of Kong My had multi-family long houses and they did some slash and burn, but not as much as in the past since a lot of rice was delivered to the village by the U.S. government via Air America. I saw many people in Kong My who filed their front teeth and inserted ivory plugs in their ears. The plugs were as big as one and a half to two inches in diameter and one-half to three quarters of an inch in thickness. When the plugs were not inserted in their ears, it left the ear lobe hanging in a big looping hole. The many wild orchids that could be found while walking around in the village are one other lasting memory of Kong My.

The teams headquartered at PS-22 were numbered in the 700s and had names like Flax, Garlic and Tomato. Eventually, while working at PS-22, I assumed responsibility for the teams that used to work from LS-171, near Saravane, and were numbered in the 300s and had names like Pomelo, Cantaloupe, and Durian. When we wrote our reports to Udorn, Vientiane or CIA headquarters we referred to the teams by their names, e.g. Team Rum, or Team Pomelo. When we dealt with the teams themselves, in person, over the radio or via Morse code messages, we referred to them as Team 305, Team 501 or Team 704. The English word "team" is pronounced "teem" in Lao. The Thai operations assistants had found it easier over the years to work with the teams by using numbers as their designations rather than trying to find Lao words for some of the names the teams were given. Thus, within the roadwatch program, that is, between the case officer and the Thai operations assistants, a team was known as Papaya/305 or Garlic/704. The team names were associated with the team leader in the minds of the CIA headquarters desk officers

---

[21] The term Lao Loum is used in Laos while Lao Lum is used in Thailand. The Lao hill tribes were sometimes called Kha, a derogatory term usually translated as 'slave.' Names of tribes are given by the name used by the Lao followed by the name the tribe used for itself in parentheses, e.g., Lave (Brao).

so whenever a team leader was lost, quit or terminated we had to come up with a new name and number for the next team leader.

As mentioned above, while I was running Team 500 and 700 roadwatch operations at PS-22, I inherited the Team 300[22] roadwatch from LS-171, the Guerrilla Force Zone III headquarters site at Ban Khok Mai (XC 5839). The two LS-171 case officers, "Heng," who had departed Laos and "Noy," who wanted to work with the Cambodian irregular units that were being trained at PS-18, needed to be replaced. The North Vietnamese Army was also attacking the Saravane area and management decided to move the LS-171 roadwatch operation to PS-22. Rather than assign Team 300 to another case officer it was easier to combine it all under me. Eventually, as the North Vietnamese Army advance on Paksong threatened PS-22, we moved all the roadwatch operations to PS-47, which was farther west of PS-22 and north of Pakse not too far from PS-18. PS-47 was previously known as LS-447 or Ban Koutlamphong. It was 500 feet above sea level and had a sod runway about 1,705 feet long and 114 feet wide.[23] The sites on the Bolovens, PS-22 and PS-38, were above 3,000 feet altitude, while PS-47 at 500 feet above sea level was much more humid and hot. Eventually, it became obvious that it might be better to locate all the roadwatch teams at PS-18. This site, previously known as Phou Lat Seua (LS-418) was located 575 feet above sea level. It had always been the primary MR-IV training site but, because of enemy advances on Paksong, was also being used for operations. It was on high ground near the river and my men could come and go by taking a taxi to a place on the river where they could then take a water taxi upriver to a landing near PS-18.

Roadwatch team operations had a small corner of PS-18 all to itself. The total number of men assigned to all roadwatch teams was about 300, but not all of them were on PS-18 at the same time. The general breakdown was about

---

[22] "Team 300" became the overall name, among my Thai operations assistants and me, for all roadwatch operations after the three separate roadwatch programs were consolidated under my supervision.

[23] Airstrip data comes from "*Air Facilities Data Laos*" (1974), a pamphlet compiled by Air America and distributed to its pilots.

one-third in the field on missions, one-third on leave in their villages, and one-third at PS-18 undergoing debriefing or training. We had several barracks buildings for the men, a small office building for Sergeant Vouk the roadwatch teams' camp commander, a building where the operations assistants lived, a supply building, and the roadwatch teams' headquarters building. I worked in this building and had a small office in it. I had a desk, a file cabinet and a small two-drawer safe. I kept unclassified files in the file cabinet and money, weapons and anything sensitive in the safe. Sensitive items would be anything worth taking and selling or anything that was operationally sensitive such as communications gear. The weapons were my collection of about twenty .45 caliber pistols that I issued only in special circumstances. We kept other weapons, such as M-1 carbines, M-16s, and AK-47s, ammunition and hand grenades in the supply building in a specially secured area.

There was also a main room where we had maps on the walls and which functioned like an orderly room in the U.S. Army. In addition, there was a communications room where we had three Morse code continuous wave (CW) base station radios for communicating with the teams. Our primary mode of communication was via Morse code. The teams carried the Delco 5300, a portable, high frequency (HF), solid-state transceiver weighing 7.5 pounds with its battery. The Delco 5300 looked like and was about the size of a lunchbox, colored olive drab. The batteries were about 6 inches square and about two inches thick. We always issued a team two batteries. One battery would last about one month when used for once a day sending and receiving of Morse code messages. Once the first battery was dead the team had one more month of battery life and we then airdropped two more batteries in the next scheduled air drop.

Our secondary mode of communications was the HT-2 very high frequency (VHF) hand-held radio, similar to radios known as "walkie-talkies." A Technical Services Division (TSD) officer told me that the HT-2 was specially developed by TSD for use in special operations/counter-insurgency operations. It had a limited range overland but was best for communicating with aircraft. Its crystals were in the same frequency range as the VHF radios in all the fixed-wing and rotary aircraft in use in Vietnam and Laos, that is, 118.1 to about 129.9. Standard D-cell batteries powered it. We used the HT-2s to talk to the teams from over-flying aircraft. We over-flew the teams anywhere from once or twice a week to almost every day if the situation was critical and we needed daily contact. The HT-2s were also used during helicopter exfiltrations and re-supply airdrops to talk to the teams and finalize details during the exfiltrations or airdrops.

When there were three separate roadwatch operations (PS-38, PS-22 and LS-171), each had its own Morse code frequency and its own base radio. Now that we had them all combined in one place, we had all three base radios in the communications room and used all three frequencies. Morse code for English is simply a matter of one Morse code sequence of dots and dashes for each of the 26 consonants and vowels. However, Lao has 21 main consonant sounds written with one of the 27 consonant symbols, and 38 vowel symbols, therefore, a system was developed to use numbers for each consonant and vowel. Thus, it was possible to transmit a message in Lao in Morse code. We did not want our messages sent "in the clear" so the radio operators used a one-time pad codebook. Each page of the codebook was filled with a series of four-number groups. The radio operator wrote out the message one letter at a time with the letter's number equivalent written into the codebook over each number in each group on the codebook page. The radio operator then used "false" subtraction to get the coded equivalent of the letter. If the numbers were 9 over 3 then the coded number was 6, but if the numbers were 3 over 9 then the coded number was 4 (the 3 was treated as a 13). The encoded numbers were written below the printed numbers in the codebook. The radio operator sent a message in the clear making contact with the base station and sending the one-time pad codebook number and page number on which the message began followed by the encoded numbers in groups of four.

One sending and one receiving codebook went with the team into the field and one sending and one receiving codebook stayed in the communications center. There were only two copies of each sending and receiving codebook and no other codebooks were identical to these two. The team had one codebook and one was in the base radio station. Since all coded messages were translated from letters of the alphabet into a series of numbers for each letter, a radio operator only had to know the Morse code for the numbers 0 to 9. The actual Morse code for numbers is a longer set of dots and dashes than the ones used for the alphabet. However, since we did not use the alphabet at all, but just single-digit coded numbers, we used a shortened set of dots and dashes for the numbers, which were called "cut numbers." Since all the radio operators knew the numbers for the Lao alphabet by heart, they could communicate without code by just sending the numbers for the Lao characters spelling out the words they wanted to send. They would establish contact in the clear, and then send the operational messages encoded. After a few months, I became aware that a lazy radio operator might begin sending messages in the clear rather than going through the encoding process with the one-time pad and I had to remind my Thai operations assistants to continue to monitor whether the code books were being used, otherwise our messages might be readable to North Vietnamese Army radio intercept operators.

Two soldiers operated each of the three base radios. One was a radio operator who sent and received the Morse code and would copy the messages down into the appropriate codebook. The codebook pages were then given to an assistant radio operator who decoded the message and wrote it out in Lao. The message, now in Lao, was given to a Thai operations assistant who translated it into English. All the translated messages were given to me and I read them over. I read them to extract anything of intelligence value or anything that needed to be tended to from an operational point of view, such as, requests for re-supply or requests for special items to be in the drop bundles. The Thai operations assistants from PS-38, PS-22 and LS-171 each operated with their original roadwatch teams, so I held meetings with the appropriate operations assistants for the teams in question.

In addition to the Delco 5300 and HT-2 radios, we used the Collins KWM-2A single sideband (SSB) high frequency (HF) radio for communicating from up-country sites to Pakse Unit headquarters, Udorn Base and Vientiane Station. The Collins KWM-2A came in two types, a fixed frequency radio and one that had a tunable dial. Each morning each up–country unit tuned its SSB radio to the SSB in Udorn. This was done by trading long counts. The Udorn Base SSB radio would keep its radio tuned to where it thought the correct frequency was and the up–country units would listen to the Udorn long count (counting slowly from one to ten and then back to one) and tune the unit radio until the Udorn long count was five by five (the first five being for loud and the other five for clear). We used a fixed frequency SSB at PS-7 so Pakse had to tune to it, as the PS-7 radio had no tunable dial.

Any single side band radio conversation that was not sensitive could be carried on in the clear, that is, not encoded, but if the conversation were sensitive then we used a substitution code. Each day all locations, except places like PS-7 which did not have a 24-hour 7-day a week American presence, were issued a code sheet. I had to remember to carry the day's code sheets with me whenever I visited PS-7. The code sheet consisted of a series of two-letter combinations with each combination representing a fixed word or phrase, for example, tank, rice, North Vietnamese Army, rifle, located, U.S. Air Force, bomb, etcetera. If you wanted to report "two NVA tanks are located at XC 546582 send USAF to bomb" the message would be something like this, "We have delta echo, uniform yankee, whiskey quebec at foxtrot delta, charlie victor, yankee tango, papa oscar, zulu sierra, yankee tango, lima kilo, delta echo send november bravo to echo mike." Each two-letter combination substituting for listed words on the code sheet. Separate letters, numbers or words not on the code sheet could be spelled as there was a two-letter combination for each letter of the alphabet and each number from 0 to 9. Code sheets were distributed in 30-day sets and kept in a combination safe, with yesterday's sheet destroyed at the beginning of each day and that day's code sheet taken out of the safe.

I took two walls in the main room of the operations building and put up all the 1:50,000 scale maps, necessary to show the entire MR–IV operational area. We carefully cut the borders off the maps and pieced them together so it looked like one big map and then covered them with clear plastic. The northern half of MR–IV covered one wall and the southern half covered another wall. We also had numerous copies of 1:50,000 scale maps of the operational area so we could issue them to the teams or take them when we went to contact the teams via air to ground radio, for infiltrations or exfiltrations, or for re-supply drops. At one point in time I had asked my Thai operations assistants to mark the wall maps with the team locations but it soon became too much of a chore to keep up. We were so familiar with the area that we would just plot the latest team location grid coordinates on the map whenever needed.

There were a variety of aircraft in use in southern Laos in support of CIA operations operated by Continental Air Services, Incorporated (CASI) and Air America. Fixed wing aircraft such as the Pilatus Porter PC-6, Curtis C-46, Douglas C-47, Beechcraft Baron, Beech Volpar, De Havilland DHC-4 Caribou, Fairchild C-123, De Havilland DHC-6 Twin Otter, Piper Super Cub, Helio Courier and a variety of Cessnas were used for transporting cargo and personnel and for special missions, such as, aerial photo surveillance, aerial radio intercept, communicating with ground units, or coordinating air cover for ground operations. Rotary aircraft such as the Sikorski UH-34 and Sikorski S-58T were used for transporting personnel and cargo and for operational infiltrations and exfiltrations. The most common United States Air Force aircraft supporting CIA activity in Laos were the fixed wing C-130 and C-123 for transporting personnel and cargo and for aerial command and control, the OV-10 Bronco (call sign 'Covey') for forward air control, and F-4 and A-7 fighter-bombers for close support of troops on the ground in contact with the enemy. The U.S. Air Force rotary aircraft were CH-3 and CH-53 helicopters for operational infiltrations and exfiltrations. U.S. Air Force Raven pilots, who lived in Laos and coordinated the air strikes of the Royal Lao Air Force T-28 pilots and also the U.S. Air Force and U.S. Navy pilots flying from Vietnam and Thailand, flew the O-1E. This was a U.S. Air Force version of the Army's two-seater L-19 spotter aircraft. It was a Cessna type aircraft with a slightly oversized engine that allowed it to perform well at slow speeds. It had a tail-wheel that made it quite versatile on rough, short fields, which describes most of the airfields in Laos. They were armed with smoke rockets for marking targets and sometimes with explosive rockets that could be fired at enemy targets on the ground.

For roadwatch operations, the workhorse aircraft was the Pilatus Porter PC-6 that was used for parachute drops of re-supply bundles, air to ground radio communication with teams on missions, transportation for personnel and materiel from Pakse to the up-country sites, and command and control of fixed and rotary wing aircraft during infiltrations and exfiltrations. Its ability to take off and land within incredibly short distances was remarkable and due in part to its propeller that could be reversed to blow air forward rather than backward. The pilot had a control that swiveled the blades to make this change. The Pratt-Whitney engine burned a form of jet fuel, JP4, which was highly inflammable and was carried in tanks in the wings over the top of the fuselage rather than slung under it. It had standard foot pedals and a stick for controlling the aircraft in flight and a wheel in the roof between the seats for adjusting the trim. None of the other aircraft in which I flew while in Laos had this control and the sight of the pilot reaching up and rotating the control from time to time while in flight or when getting ready to land is burned into my memory. In addition to the seat for the pilot, there was a seat and a control stick next to him for a co-pilot or a passenger. Behind the two front seats was an area that could have two, four or six removable seats or an empty cargo bay, depending on the mission to be flown. In the middle of the cargo bay were drop doors that could be opened to drop cargo rigged with a parachute.

The Sikorski H-34 was the rotary wing workhorse for roadwatch operations as it was used for transporting personnel and cargo from Pakse to the sites and for infiltrations and exfiltrations of the teams. From time to time, the Piper Super Cub was used in place of the Porters and U.S. Air Force helicopters were used in place of Air America H-34's when the landing zones were out on the Ho Chi Minh Trail.

We kept an exotic assortment of weapons for use in roadwatch operations. The M-1 carbine, M-16 rifle and AK-47 rifle were the primary shoulder fired weapons issued to the teams. As time went by, I tended to issue only M-1 carbines because they were light and very inexpensive or AK-47s because they made the men look like enemy soldiers from a distance. The other primary weapon I issued to the teams was the anti-personnel hand grenade. Finally, I issued them smoke grenades. The smoke was for signaling while the fragmentation grenades were the cheapest and most effective defensive weapon for the Lao irregulars. They tended to prefer to quickly toss as many hand grenades as they could when they were fired upon and use the noise and concussive effects as a screen as they immediately took off running away. A number of hand grenades were more effective for them for covering retreat than firing their shoulder weapons because they were so inaccurate with the shoulder weapons. In addition to the weapons issued to the teams we kept .45 caliber automatic pistols, Swedish K and Uzi 9mm sub-machine guns, M-79 40mm grenade launchers, and automatic shotguns for issue to case officers as their personal weapons. I tried carrying a Swedish K, Uzi and then an M-16 for a while but eventually only carried a .45 caliber pistol. If I was up-country on a site, I always kept shoulder weapons nearby, usually an M-16, but did not carry them around all the time. If I was flying between up-country sites and Pakse, I only had the .45 pistol and a small .22 caliber pistol in my escape and evasion kit. Some case officers liked to think they would be able to defend themselves with the shoulder weapons but I decided that if the aircraft went down I would not survive, or if I did, I would be picked up right away or I would need to take off into the jungle where stealth rather than firepower would be necessary. The Beretta .22 caliber pistol, with a six inch barrel and long rifle cartridges, was in my kit for survival hunting if I had to escape and evade for several days. CIA escape and evasion training instructors who taught the course I had taken had recommended such a pistol and I had bought one and taken it with me to Laos.

I inherited a dormant 5 x 7 index card system for keeping records on the men who worked on the roadwatch teams. Generally, Lao men have a given name and a surname, but the men working on the roadwatch teams preferred to be known by only their given names, or perhaps, among the tribal soldiers, they never had a Lao surname. That was just one of those things there was no need to insist that the American preferred model of given name, middle name, and surname had to be followed. I decided to revive the index card system and add a photograph to each card for identification. For about a month my Thai operations assistants used a 35mm camera with black and white film and took a head shot of each soldier in camp and then each one who returned from mission or leave. I had the photos developed in our photo lab and then affixed to each soldier's 5 x 7 index card. When I took over the PS-22 and LS-171 roadwatch programs my Thai operations assistants photographed the soldiers being added under my supervision. We kept some basic information for each soldier on the index cards and whenever a soldier went missing in action, we entered the date. If he came back from the missing, we removed the date, or if we became convinced he had been killed in action we entered that date. This was important information since we paid a death benefit to his survivor if he was killed in action (KIA). I would not pay a death benefit if a soldier was missing in action (MIA) and I had no acceptable proof he was actually KIA. In the years that the roadwatch program had been in existence, going back to the early '60s at least, there had been no such strict record keeping and soldiers were known to have gone MIA, had a friend report them KIA and collected the death benefit. They then went and joined another roadwatch program or another irregular unit, perhaps an SGU battalion, and continued to work under another name. My index card and photograph system put an end to that practice in the Pakse roadwatch program.

We did a lot of helicopter infiltrations and exfiltrations in my two years. Every one of them was a clean operation except one. During one of the North Vietnamese Army prisoner exfiltrations the team was attacked on the helicopter-landing zone as our aircraft were heading to their location. The team leader reported the enemy activity and I told him to go to the alternate helicopter-landing zone. We aborted the run in to the helicopter landing zone and the helicopters returned to Pakse airfield, known as L-11 (Lima One-One). The Raven, flying low, spotted the enemy and directed the covering strike aircraft to bomb them, helping the team escape. I stayed flying above the Raven and strike aircraft monitoring the team as it moved to the alternate helicopter landing zone. Once the team had escaped and felt safe, we agreed on a new pick up time. The Air America helicopters were already re-fueling at L-11. The Raven and Porter also returned to L-11 to re-fuel. As soon as the Porter was re-fueled, I went back out to monitor the team. I was worried that the helicopters would be diverted to something else or the Raven would not be able to get more strike aircraft but at the appointed time everyone was ready and the helicopters went in and picked up the team and the North Vietnamese Army prisoner. While the initial pickup was not quick and clean, as all my others had been, the team had reported enemy activity and then moved on to the alternate helicopter-landing zone. That sort of honesty was reassuring to the Air America helicopter pilots as they had been lured into hot helicopter landing zone's by scared troops that just wanted out as quickly as possible. Thus, I can say that no helicopter crew ever took ground fire on any of my infiltrations or exfiltrations, just that that one operation was not a quiet in and out.

One of the veteran Air America helicopter senior pilots once told me, "You are the only customer I feel comfortable working with. You give the most complete briefings and they rarely sound like bullshit. Some customers are so disorganized it makes me worry the whole operation will be a mess."

We ran all of my North Vietnamese Army prisoner retrievals with Air America helicopters but Air America was not authorized to go when an infiltration or exfiltration was all the way out on the Ho Chi Minh Trail. In those cases, the U.S. Air Force from Vietnam or Thailand would provide the helicopters, sometimes CH-3 and sometimes CH-53. The sight of my small, scraggly, randomly uniformed, AK-47 wielding teams boarding the warlike and well kept U.S. Air Force helicopters under the gaze of a nicely uniformed U.S. Air Force crew chief was ironic at best. Once one of my Kong My PS-7 team leaders decided he did not want to get off the helicopter as it approached the helicopter-landing zone. He later told my Thai operations assistant that the spirit ceremony before the mission had not gone well and he was sure the spirits would not be supportive. He was feeling spooked and had not really wanted to get on the helicopter. He probably boarded because he did not want to lose face. Nevertheless, on the ride out his uneasiness must have overcome his worry over losing face so he took out a ballpoint pen, wrote "PS-38" in large letters on his hand and showed it to the U.S. Air Force crew chief, followed by vigorously pointing in the direction of PS-38. The crew chief told the helicopter pilot and the pilot told me, flying overhead in a Porter. I told the pilot to continue the mission and put the team out on the helicopter-landing zone, which they did. It did not do me any good as a week later the team straggled in to PS-38 telling me they had been set upon after leaving the helicopter-landing zone and had to escape and evade to make it back. I had no reason not to believe them since one of them was obviously wounded by gunshot. You had to be a terrible cynic to believe one of them would volunteer to be wounded just to convince me they had been attacked.

The use of the helicopter for infiltrating and exfiltrating intelligence teams provided both advantages and disadvantages. Putting a team on a helicopter and taking them out into the area saved a lot of time, and wear and tear on the team members. On the other hand, the North Vietnamese Army could easily spot the helicopters as they flew into an area. Neither the U.S. Air Force nor Air America was allowed to fly infiltrations or exfiltrations at night. The best that could be done was to schedule the infiltration for just before dusk. As long as the enemy was not close enough to find the team before dark, the team had the night hours to try to move to a safe location. This only worked when infiltrating the teams into an area they knew. If they were going into an unfamiliar area, dusk infiltration only delayed their discovery by a few hours. Saving time was an American bureaucratic consideration that I dismissed early in my tour. I was more interested in getting the team covertly into place so they could survive for the duration of the mission. Saving wear and tear on the team members was also an American consideration. I found that these hardy mountain tribal people could walk over rough terrain for weeks without complaint and could stay on mission for two to three months. An American soldier was making extreme sacrifices when trekking through Lao terrain. If he was on mission, a Lao mountain tribesman was living as he usually did. There was not a lot of difference between living in a mountain village and living in the mountains. Moreover, we dropped supplies to them, something that never happened in their pre-war lives in the mountains. It became obvious to me that the only way to infiltrate my teams was by sending them in walking overland. When a mission was over and they were eligible to return to base I also had them walk out. This was usually agreeable to them because they were being paid for each day on mission and the mission was not over until they arrived at base camp. Of course, if they had been attacked and had wounded or just needed to be pulled out of a hot environment, or had an North Vietnamese Army prisoner, I would run a helicopter exfiltration to get them out as quickly and safely as possible.

In the early days of the roadwatch program, when CIA managers in Laos must have thought they were actually obtaining useful intelligence from teams supposedly perched somewhere overlooking the Ho Chi Minh Trail, case officers were under pressure to insure that teams in a target area overlapped each other, that is, that it could not be said that the target area had gone unobserved for any length of time. Since I had learned that the CIA intelligence analysts were piling roadwatch reports under desks, I knew there was not going to be any uproar if we left a target area uncovered. In fact, I surmised there would be no analytic outcry if roadwatch reporting just faded away. To be sure I would have to be able to point to some new more valuable use of the roadwatch teams if I expected to get away with ending the missions of just going out and trying to observe a section of the Ho Chi Minh Trail. At any rate, it was my decision to send most teams by foot and it eventually became the primary mode of infiltration for Pakse roadwatch and intelligence teams.

A team could carry a certain amount of supplies, usually about seven to ten days worth. As they walked toward their mission area of operation they passed through territory controlled by the Royal Lao Government, then contested territory, and finally, they passed into enemy territory. I usually did not re-supply them in friendly territory preferring them to buy supplies along the way. I gave them extra money for that. Once they arrived in the contested areas, I would consider dropping supplies to them. The procedure was for them to establish a command post (CP) where they set up the Delco radio so they could send Morse code messages back to my base camp. The Delco radio antenna was a long wire antenna and the teams preferred to string them up and leave them rather than put them up and take them down each day. The team leader, sometimes by himself and sometimes democratically in consultation with the team members, chose a drop reception team. As a result of area knowledge or reconnaissance along the way the team would have decided on safe locations to receive re-supply drops. The drop reception team worked its way from the CP back to the drop zone and waited for air to ground contact. The teams were instructed to choose drop zones in the safest area possible, where the enemy on the ground would not spot the parachute on the drop bundle, and the team would be able to unload the bundle, divvy up the load and move back toward the CP without being detected.

Once a team launched from base camp on a mission I tried to have my Thai operations assistants contact them by VHF radio on a regular basis. The average was about every three to four days. The teams carried walkie-talkie type radios called HT-2s that had crystals tuned to VHF frequencies in the range of about 118.1 to 129.9. The various aircraft available for making these air-to-ground contacts carried a VHF radio for use in talking to the airfield controllers and other aircraft. Frequencies such as 118.1, 119.1 and 121.5 were reserved for aircraft operations, so crystals were put in the HT-2's for other frequencies not usually used by the Air America and CASI aircraft and airfield controllers.

When a team wanted a re-supply drop, they requested it a few days before it was needed by telling the Thai operations assistant during one of the periodic air to ground contacts or by requesting it in a Morse code message. When I first arrived, the Thai operations assistants came to me to ask approval to set up re-supply drops. Within a short time, I told them to go ahead and handle the drops without coming to me for approval. The only time they did consult with me was when the team wanted something out of the ordinary in the drop bundle. Sometimes they wanted extra money, extra tobacco, extra salt or cloth material for use in bartering or to pay informants. Some teams operated among tribal people who had no use for Royal Lao Government money and considered commodities not readily available in the mountains, such as tobacco, salt or cloth, more valuable than paper money.

A drop bundle was a large reinforced cardboard box in which we put the supplies to be sent to the team. We sent them rice, various types of food, money, additional Delco radio batteries, tobacco, salt, ammunition, extra maps, new HT-2 batteries, a new radio if one of the two HT-2's was inoperable, or a new Delco radio if needed. I was able to manage the roadwatch program so that I had enough money to buy a variety of good quality food for the teams. In both the base camp and on the missions roadwatch teams were well fed with a variety of good quality food. We had live pigs and chickens, plenty of glutinous rice, good water, and a variety of fresh vegetables, while the soldiers in the irregular battalions and regiments were supplied by a more bureaucratic logistical system. The meat was already butchered and thus not always fresh while Team 300 meat was slaughtered as needed, an important consideration in a very hot climate with no refrigeration available. The battalion sized irregular units' vegetables were bought in quantity, transported, and stored and thus not fresh while Team 300's vegetables were much fresher. Often an irregular unit only had one vegetable, one type of meat and rice to eat, while Team 300 had a variety of vegetables, a variety of meats, rice and spices. I never lacked for volunteers to join the program, the money was better than in the battalions, the food was superior and I did not send them into combat, but rather wanted them to avoid combat and collect intelligence. Even when I wanted them to capture North Vietnamese Army soldiers or guide air strikes, the odds for survival were better than if they had to participate in combat operations.

We filled the drop bundles with the supplies for a particular team and then attached a parachute to the bundle. The drop bundle with parachute was loaded into the Porter where there was a rectangular hatch in the floor in the middle of the cargo area behind the pilot's seat. The hatch had two doors that opened downward when a ring was pulled. If the Porter was not carrying cargo, there were six seats in the cargo area over top of the hatch. When the drop bundle was loaded in place over the hatch in the cargo area, the pilot and Thai operations assistant took off to make the drop. The Thai operations assistant knew where the team would be and made contact with them to ask them to give the safe signal. The safe signal might be red cloth panels in a pre-arranged pattern, or a smoke grenade of a certain color. Re-supply drops in relatively safe areas were done during early to late afternoon and smoke might be used for signaling, otherwise the drops were made at dusk and only cloth panels were used for signaling. During my second year in Laos, I insisted the teams use signal mirrors as much as possible. With the drop bundle positioned over the hatch in the floor of the Porter, the pilot decided on how he would make his approach, which often was a steep dive followed by a steep pull up. At just the right moment, the pilot reached back and pulled a release that opened the hatch door and let the bundle drop out of the aircraft. A perfect drop resulted in the parachute deploying for only a second or two before hitting the ground.

Al Schwartz was one of the more colorful Porter pilots flying in southern Laos, if not in all of Laos. He was an ex-dive-bomber pilot, extroverted, full of colorful stories and well liked by most of the special operations case officers. I did not usually go with the Porters to make drops, so I do not remember why I was with Al flying out to an area in the vicinity of Kong My (PS-7). Al was in the usual left hand seat and I was in the right hand seat with one of the Thai operations assistants kneeling on the deck right behind us. The operations assistant made contact with the team and they put out red cloth panels in the shape of an L, which was the correct letter. They were on top of a large rock outcropping surrounded all around by tall leafy jungle trees. The only place to put the drop bundle was right on the rock outcropping, a target about thirty feet in diameter. I don't suppose you have to fly around in an area like that to appreciate the difficulty of trying to drop a large box attached to parachute from an airplane and have it hit such a small target. If it floats past the target, it falls into the jungle and becomes quite hard to retrieve. Telling me to hold on tight, Al flew into position to make a steep dive at the rock outcropping. The dive pushed my stomach up toward my throat and I gripped the sides of my seat and just tried to gut it out (no pun intended). At just the right moment in the dive Al began a steep pull up, reached back keeping one hand on the stick between his legs, and pulled the ring that allowed the hatch in the middle of the deck behind our seats to open up. The bundle tumbled out, the chute deployed staying open only a few seconds and the bundle hit the rock. The team scrambled about to avoid being hit and recovered the bundle before it went over the side. All during the drop the operations assistant was in the back holding on for dear life while the hatch dropped open leaving a gapingly open rectangle in the middle of the deck. As soon as the bundle was clear and the aircraft leveled off he moved quickly to pull the trap door shut. We climbed up and out of the drop zone area and headed back to Lima–11 (Pakse Airfield). Just another typical day at the office. I also have to say that Continental Air Services, Incorporated (CASI) pilots did not get as much publicity in the various books and other publications about the "Secret War in Laos" as Air America pilots did. However, I flew with CASI pilots, mostly in Porters, more than with Air America and I found the CASI pilots to be highly skilled, brave and very professional. I staked my life on their ability every day I flew with them since we flew in most weather conditions and over all terrain, enemy held or not. I would say the same thing about Air America pilots, the difference is that I usually flew in a small aircraft with CASI pilots while with Air America I was more often a passenger on a larger aircraft without as much direct contact with the pilot.

A view of the American housing compound in Pakse, Laos
Photo courtesy of Lloyd Duncan

The roadwatch headquarters building at Kong My (PS–7)
Photo by author

Roadwatch headquarters on PS–38
Photo by author

Roadwatch soldiers in formation at PS–47
Photo by author

The author and two Thai operations assistants at roadwatch headquarters on PS–18
Photo by author

The author at his desk in roadwatch headquarters on PS–18
Photo by author

INFILTRATING CAMBODIA

———◆◆———

"Bring me back reliable information."

–Inscription on a clay tablet, 1370 B.C., with instructions
from the Hittite prince to his envoy bound for Egypt; cited
in Haswell, Spies and Spymasters (1977).

For my first assignment, Ray, the Pakse Unit chief of operations, assigned me to be the PS–38 roadwatch case officer and to handle the Guerrilla Battalion working in Guerrilla Zone II. PS–38 was the designation for the major up-country site in Guerrilla Zone-II on the Bolovens Plateau.

"Tom, you'll be working with Dunc, he's the senior case officer at PS–38. There's only one other case officer working out of PS–38, Khamsing the commando/raider case officer. Your teams are based at PS–7 south of PS–38 almost to the Cambodian border."

I was working up-country by the end of February 1970 and just beginning to figure out what my job was and what I was supposed to be doing when Norodom Sihanouk was ousted from power in March 1970.

A new government, led by Lon Nol, came to power in Cambodia. During the regime of Norodom Sihanouk, the North Vietnamese Army had free access to the port of Sihanoukville on the west coast of Cambodia where they unloaded war materiel for use in the Republic of Vietnam. From Sihanoukville the cargo traveled by truck, on what was named Route 110, east across Cambodia to the border with the Republic of Vietnam where it was delivered to their forces fighting there. When Lon Nol took over the country he declared the North Vietnamese Army could no longer use Cambodia to transship men and materiel to the Republic of Vietnam. It became readily apparent that neither the CIA nor the new Cambodian government had any on the ground intelligence sources in the northern part of the country. The American intelligence community concerned with Indochina needed current information in northeast Cambodia along the border adjacent to Laos and would need time to develop the means to collect such information. CIA headquarters placed a requirement on Vientiane

Station to try to fill the gap until other methods of intelligence collection could be brought to bear on this target. Udorn Base gave Pakse Unit the mission to collect intelligence in northeast Cambodia using special operations intelligence teams.

Ray called me into his office and said, "Tom, Ambassador Godley wants intelligence from northeast Cambodia. Your teams from PS-7 live near Cambodia, get a few of them ready and get us some intelligence."

I launched five intelligence collection teams toward the Cambodian target area by June 1970 and until the end of September 1970, no less than five and as many nine teams were out on mission to northeast Cambodia. Royal Lao Government forces held an outpost on Khong Island in the Mekong River at the Lao-Cambodian border. The Dooley Foundation operated one of its facilities on the island and there was an airstrip designated L-07 (Lima Oh-Seven). Even though we usually launched the PS-7 teams from our main site at PS-38, Khong Island represented a safe haven, just across the Lao-Cambodian border from which the teams could walk into Cambodia and to which the teams could rally if they ran into trouble.

When the requirement was first levied on Pakse Unit, it seemed a good idea to use roadwatch teams from PS-7 (a small site in the village of Kong My). The PS-7 roadwatch teams were Lao Theung tribesmen living in a village in southern Laos near Cambodia. The border was about fifteen kilometers southeast of Kong My or twenty kilometers directly south of the village. They readily accepted roadwatch missions to the Ho Chi Minh Trail to the east of their village but they would not accept intelligence collection missions into Cambodia. They felt comfortable in the mountainous area around Kong My but traveling all the way to the Cambodian lowlands south of Khong Island was just unacceptable. This was a common problem with Kong My tribesmen. They would do their best in areas they were familiar with, but they did not want to venture away from those areas. Not much thought was given to this, we just assumed they would accept missions into Cambodia south of Khong Island or to the area near Ban San Keo, Cambodia because it was not that far from their mountainous home area. They wouldn't do either.

I had given my Thai operations assistants orders to start getting PS-7 teams ready. However, when I asked about their progress they did not have good news.

Somneuk said, "Tan Chanh, we have to sit down and talk about this with Somsit and Thong."

I asked him, "Why, what's the matter?"

"These tribesmen from Kong My refuse to go to Cambodia. You can try to make them but they will probably lie about their locations or report a clash with the enemy and request exfiltration."

After some discussion, we finally settled on teams made up of lowland Lao from PS-38. We flew them from Pakse (L-11) to Khong Island (L-07) and from there they were supposed to walk into the target areas in Cambodia. Running roadwatch and intelligence collection teams in Laos required the case officer be constantly vigilant. Generally, very few teams could be counted on to complete their missions honestly all the time. Good teams fabricated a mission and then returned to being honest, or fabricated parts of a mission while doing other parts to the best of their abilities.

The lowland Lao and Lao Theung tribesmen did not hold the same values as Americans. Their value system allowed them to do what was necessary to survive. If the Americans sent them on a mission that threatened to get them killed, they avoided danger and survived. When they returned from such missions there was no lost honor in lying to the Americans about the mission.

Under these circumstances, a case officer had to have methods to verify team activities while they were out on mission. One of these methods was to fly over the teams at 7,000 to 10,000 feet and talk to them via very high frequency (VHF) radios. The teams carried hand held VHF radios called HT-2s tuned to similar VHF frequencies used by the aircraft. The teams carried CW (continuous wave) radios for sending intelligence reports via Morse code. The teams used the VHF radios to arrange re-supply drops and to talk to the Thai operations assistants about their progress into the target area. In addition to talking to the teams via VHF radio, the over-flights were also used to require the teams to signal their locations to the aircraft.

I had adopted the technique of using a survival mirror to signal the aircraft. Previously, the teams were required to use cloth panels or smoke grenades. While the teams did not refuse to take the panels and grenades, they often wound up not using them. The cloth panels were hard to see unless the aircraft dropped to an altitude that was vulnerable to ground fire and could compromise the team's position. When an aircraft flew at low altitudes, it was easier for an enemy ground observer to guess the team's position. The higher the aircraft the more difficult it was to guess where the team on the ground might be. The smoke grenade was even more dangerous because the smoke was traceable directly to the team's location. The reflection from the sun flashed upwards from a mirror, however, was very easy to see no matter the altitude of the aircraft, could be aimed directly at the aircraft and was absolutely no danger to the team. An enemy ground observer could not see a mirror flash directed up toward an aircraft. At first, there was some doubt that mirrors could be used in the rainy season because of clouds, but it turned out that many days in the rainy season it was cloudy only when it rained and it usually rained the same time each day. If we scheduled over-flights for the time of day it usually did not rain, there was a good chance there would be no clouds. There were days of all day overcast, but we did not need to verify team locations every day. The mirror became my team location verification tool of choice.

Unfortunately, higher authorities decreed there could be no over flights over Cambodia. They were worried that there would be political repercussions if an aircraft went down in Cambodia. They did not consider that no aircraft had ever been shot down doing air-ground radio contacts and that position location was critical to mission authentication. We could not over fly the teams - period. We didn't know it at the beginning of the Cambodian intelligence collection operation, but the teams did not feel safe at all, as they tried to move south into Cambodia. They felt conspicuous, they were not familiar with the terrain, they had no idea where they could hide, and the terrain was flat and lacking the hiding places they were used to in the denser foliage of hilly or mountainous Laos. Nevertheless, the teams began to report that they were infiltrating to the target areas and setting up command posts from which they could go out and meet villagers. We had no way to verify these locations. The teams then reported that it was unsafe to receive re-supply drops near their positions. We were approved to make night re-supply drops into Cambodia but only up to 10 kilometers inside the country. We also could not use American Porter pilots. There were a few Thai Porter pilots and we had to use them. In case a Porter was shot down there would be "plausible denial" that Americans were in Cambodia. Therefore, when the teams reported they felt safer receiving re-supply drops back closer to the border area it suited our operational restrictions.

In reality, what was happening was that the teams were not going into Cambodia at all. They were stopping at the border and staying in Laos. When a re-supply was scheduled, they were willing to go over the border to receive it and then they would return to Laos. With the drops being made at dusk it was difficult to verify just where the drop reception unit really was. The teams discovered a large supply of refugees from Cambodia who had fled north to the Lao border. Some of the refugees lived on the Cambodian side and some on the Lao side. There was no Cambodian or Lao authority to interfere with them. The teams would interview refugees until they found some that came from their target area. They would then obtain information about the target area and report they had obtained it inside Cambodia.

Since we could not use any of our position verification techniques, which all required daytime over flight, we had to rely on the polygraph. When the teams returned from their missions, we polygraphed the team leaders. The polygraph operator began detecting fabrication. There was a flurry of cable traffic among Vientiane, Udorn and Pakse finally resulting in the decision to declare all the missions as compromised. In Pakse, we heard stories about Ambassador G. McMurtrie Godley going to meetings and talking about "his" intelligence collection teams in Cambodia. Before the fabrication was detected, we were heroes. We had responded to a new requirement quickly and had intelligence collection functioning in Cambodia when there was no other source available. It was very discouraging to have to send out burn notices[24] on all our Cambodian reports.

I was very interested in knowing as much about the enemy order of battle as I could as a way for me to better evaluate the intelligence my teams were reporting. Enemy order of battle was just about the only type of intelligence the teams collected. In my pursuit of this knowledge, I came to know Al, the senior southern Laos order of battle analyst in Udorn. Al was more than happy to work with me because very few, if any, other case officers were interested in his work. They wanted the results but were not interested in much else. I asked questions, took his requirements for more information and was always interested in talking to him when he visited Pakse or I visited Udorn. Months after we had to "burn" all our intelligence reporting on Cambodia from the teams, Al told me that as he began to receive intelligence from other collection platforms he would post it to his index card system. When he did, he often found he already had entries on units or commanders reported by the teams but now reported by the new collection platforms. He believed that the teams had not been fabricating their intelligence, just not reporting that it was coming from refugees at the border rather than sources deep inside Cambodia. What the teams were learning from the refugees was, in many cases, accurate information. They had not just dreamed up information to report to us. Unfortunately, since the teams fabricated the source of their information the reports had to be burned. I wonder how their reports would have been treated if they had merely reported they were getting the information from refugees at the border. My experience with the Lao idea of saving face leads me to think they would not have been able to admit they would not go into Cambodia and thus, their fabrications were culturally necessary.

Ultimately, I learned a valuable lesson that I used for the rest of my time in Laos. I became much more dedicated to running operations that were

---

[24] A burn notice was a report sent out to the original recipients saying that the CIA had determined that the original report had to be disregarded.

worth being run and that could have a variety of verification techniques built into them. I did not want to run operations if the operational reward was not worth the effort. Thus, I slowly began to reduce the number of pure roadwatch missions until I eliminated them. If an intelligence collection operation were to be run it had to have a measurable payoff to it, such as, it had to result in military action that could be verified by an American officer of the CIA or the U.S. pilots operating from Vietnam or Thailand, or in the case of the Ravens, from Laos. If the teams were going to receive cash, they would need to deliver verifiable intelligence or combat results. As you will see, this meant I wanted to use the roadwatch–intelligence collection teams to capture North Vietnamese Army soldiers, intercept North Vietnamese Army communications, recruit North Vietnamese Army soldiers to report to us from inside enemy held territory, or guide bombing operations on North Vietnamese Army positions. Such operations had not been done in Laos with roadwatch teams but the Cambodian mess encouraged me from my first few months in Laos to look for better operational goals and better means to authenticate them. I believed no one could argue the authenticity of a team's work if the product was a live North Vietnamese Army soldier. The ultimate product would be the intelligence that derived from his interrogation, but his capture by my team would be the *sine qua non*. The same could be said for intercepting coded North Vietnamese Army communications. Some one else might decrypt the messages to extract the ultimate intelligence product, but once more, my teams' work would be the *sine qua non*. I was not interested in sending teams to sit on an observation post and watch trucks or troops walk or drive by, nor in having a team go out and try to ambush a truck or a small number of enemy soldiers, nor having a team go out and interview villagers and report information on what the villagers might know about enemy activities, nor having teams go out and try to observe enemy activity and report on it. All of these operational goals, which were the goals for roadwatch teams when I first arrived, were too difficult to verify and the results not worth the effort. There were larger CIA sponsored irregular units, battalions and regiments, trying to attack the enemy and fight with him. There were U.S. Air Force air assets based in Vietnam and

Thailand trying to kill the enemy. My role, I believed, was to collect intelligence that would allow military assets to attack the enemy with greater efficiency or to collect reliable intelligence that would contribute to better tactical or strategic decisions. From this early intelligence collection activity in Cambodia until my departure, I tried to do that.

THE BATTLE FOR PS-26

---◆◆◆---

"I think you had better tell all this to my intelligence staff.
I don't go much for this sort of thing. You see, I just like fighting."

–General George Patton to a British intelligence officer
briefing him on the ULTRA decrypts of German messages,
1942; quoted in Winterbotham, Ultra Spy (1989).

Intelligence collection was my first priority, but in a war zone, operating in forward sites, sometimes in the middle of enemy controlled territory, it was easy to get involved in combat operations.

All my life I had been subject to motion sickness of all kinds, car, sea and air. Thus, it was just as well I did not understand how much time I would log in small airplanes such as the Pilatus Porter. It did not take long to get my first Porter ride "up-country." As soon after my arrival in Pakse as I was ready, I belted myself into one of the four seats in the cargo area right behind the pilot and co-pilot seats. Taking off from Pakse's airport, Lima One-One (L-11) was routine. The paved runway was quite long enough for a Porter's take-off. From overhead Pakse was a blur of light reflecting off tin roofs, red clay roads, the brown soft ribbon of the muddy water of the Mekong and Sedone rivers, green tropical vegetation and the hard black ribbon that was Highway 13, which ran from Vientiane, Laos to Phnom Penh, Cambodia to Saigon, South Vietnam. Pakse was hot and humid but as soon as we reached the normal cruising altitude of about 7,000 feet, it was comfortable, if not just a little chilly. Whenever we had to fly at 10,000 feet to be safe from the reach of anti-aircraft guns it became downright chilly. A long sleeve shirt or jacket was usually enough to ward off the chill but bare arms could become uncomfortable if a flight lasted more than an hour.

It only took a few minutes after reaching cruising altitude for the view below to become entirely green. In the dry season, there was a dull, grey haze on the horizon and grey or white smoke rising into the air from the burning of the rice paddies. The Lao were a simple people to whom it made no sense to suffer the backbreaking labor of manually clearing stubble from rice paddies. It was simpler to just set them ablaze and wait for the fire to do the work. Instead of an overall green carpet, you saw a stippled brown and green landscape looking out beyond the jet fuel driven prop. In the wet season, the pilot often took us up above the rain clouds and we flew until the pilot judged we had flown long enough to be out over the Bolovens Plateau. Near Pakse, the scene below the aircraft and out on the horizon was a wet green. Approaching the Bolovens Plateau all we saw was the clouds below and out front of us, looking like white and grey cotton balls of varying sizes all packed together with no space in between to see the ground. When I was the new guy and always flew in the back, I did not truly understand our bravery in trusting our lives to the Continental Air Services Porter pilots. In fact, it is only now years later, that I would label what we did with the pilots as brave. Back then, we did not think about it that way at all. We were somewhere above six, seven or eight thousand feet with an unknown depth of cloud below us, obscuring the ground, which was about three thousand feet above sea level. No one knew the altitude of the cloud cover over the ground. While some pilots might radio the site to talk to one of our English speaking Lao interpreters to ask for an estimate of cloud ceiling, most of them merely looked for a hole in the clouds and blindly dove into it corkscrewing toward the ground with the intention of pulling up on reaching the lower limit of the clouds. It never occurred to me to ask if the clouds ever touched the ground making it impossible to pull up before driving the aircraft into the ground.

The sites on the Bolovens Plateau reminded me of the symbol used on military maps to denote an airfield, a circle with a line dissecting it. The larger sites had runways over 3,000 feet in length that looked like 100 to 120-foot wide red gashes in the green. The runway at PS-38 was packed hard but it was not level, a gently rolling undulation. I watched many a C-130 and C-123 aircraft land at PS-38, as well as a variety of small aircraft like Porters, Cessnas, Beechcraft-Barons, OV-10 Broncos and all manner of helicopters. The Porters flared out of their corkscrew descent in the wet season or just lazily glided in during the dry season. They quickly reversed prop to come to a stop within 400 feet or so, if necessary, and then taxied over to the site headquarters building where we opened our seat belts and jumped to the ground. Often the Porters then took off again to complete other missions during the day before finally returning in the later afternoon to pick us up and fly us back to Pakse, another day at the office completed.

PS-38, one of CIA's principal sites on the Bolovens Plateau about 95 kilometers from Pakse near the eastern edge of the plateau, had a small satellite site, named PS-26, right on the edge of the karst, which was about 1,000 meters (roughly 3,000 feet) high. Friendly forces defended it on all sides that faced the Bolovens Plateau but not on the eastern side since that side was a steep drop 3,000 feet to the valley below. The karst was so steep and such an unfriendly climb no one responsible for the defense of the site believed an enemy could attack from that side. Nevertheless, the North Vietnamese Army somehow climbed the karst wall, assaulted PS-26 and chased off its defenders.

The loss of PS-26 presented a serious problem as it gave the North Vietnamese Army their first position on the Bolovens Plateau. If we allowed them to hold it, they could use it as a base of operations for further attacks on our sites. Our military planners decided the enemy had to be pushed off the Bolovens Plateau. The regular army units of the Lao government, Forces Armée du Royaume (FAR), had no real stomach for offensive combat and they could hardly defend anything either. Our irregular units were better fighters than the FAR, although that was a relative term as the Lao, in general, were regularly outfought by the North Vietnamese Army when we asked them to stay and defend positions. Since the captured site was a wide-open target, U.S. Air Force slow (propeller driven) and fast (jet aircraft) movers were called in to blast it whenever they were available. Lao T-28's also took turns bombing the site. Even though FAR was not much of a fighting force, Gen. Phasouk Somly, the MR-IV commander, decided he wanted in on the action and sent a unit to join the irregular units being organized for the counter assault.

None of the Lao units, FAR or irregular, was interested in assaulting the North Vietnamese Army held site until it had been thoroughly bombarded. In addition to the aerial bombing, Gen. Phasouk sent a 105mm howitzer to PS-38. A Lao Captain, named Keota, who had trained at Ft. Sill, Oklahoma and spoke reasonable English commanded the howitzer crew. In reality, he did more than command the gun crew, he was the only one who could plot the barrages. Since Dunc, the senior PS-38 case officer, had taken over the irregular units with which I was supposed to work, and my roadwatch teams were either out on mission or on leave, I had time to devote to other activities. I was fascinated by the 105 mm gun and went out to watch as it was delivered by aircraft and then dug in pointing at PS-26. The PS-38 runway could handle C-130's so it was not a problem for them to load the 105 in an aircraft in Pakse and deliver it to PS-38. The gun was out in the open with a clear line of sight to PS-26. It was not dug in or protected in any way. The gun's maximum effective range was about 11,200 meters (almost seven miles). The gun could easily hit PS-26 but the North Vietnamese Army did not have any mortars or guns that could reach PS-38.

I quickly made Captain Keota's acquaintance and he was happy to have a Sky[25] officer working with him. I quickly took up the job of spotter using a pair of binoculars that had been lying around in our office building. As the captain fired off targeting rounds, I watched where they landed.

I gave him adjusting directions, such as "left 100 meters" or "down "50 meters."

Since the site was on a small hill, I was zeroing the rounds in on the crown of the hill. Once I was happy with the placement of the targeting rounds, the gun crew could fire a barrage.

"Left 100. Now down 50. OK, looks good, fire for effect."

We were having a good old time enjoying our ability to place our artillery fire on the hill when one of my operations assistants, Somsit, came to me and said that one of the HT-2s on our site was receiving what he thought was Vietnamese transmissions. We knew that the North Vietnamese Army captured a lot of equipment from us and were happy to use our HT-2s whenever they could get more than one on the same frequency. I knew that and was intrigued by this information and asked Somsit to bring the radio to me.

---

[25] The Lao often referred to the CIA personnel as Sky. This was because everything we gave them, supplies, ammunition and even us, came down from the sky.

During my one year Army tour in the Republic of Vietnam, I had tried to learn as much Vietnamese as I could and was at least familiar with how it sounded. I listened to the HT-2 and knew right away that it was, in fact, Vietnamese. I asked Somsit if we had anyone handy who could speak Vietnamese. He eventually came back with a carpenter who had been working on PS-38. Since the carpenter spoke both Vietnamese and Lao, I asked Somsit to have the carpenter listen to the radio and then tell him in Lao what was being said. The carpenter listened and then spoke to Somsit. Somsit then translated to me. It seemed that the transmissions were coming from PS-26. Since we had been rather accurately hitting the crown of the hill with our 105 mm rounds, a Vietnamese was ordering the men on the hill to move off the crown and down to the base of the hill. I spoke to Captain Keota, commanding the gun crew and doing the plotting, and told him we thought the enemy was moving all his men to the bottom of the hill.

"OK, down 100."

"Down 50 more and right 50."

OK, fire for effect."

No sooner did our bombardment begin than the radio came alive with Vietnamese chatter. The carpenter listened and then spoke to Somsit. Somsit listened and then spoke to me. I listened and then told Captain Keota to adjust fire back to the top of the hill and again fire for effect.

There was a lull while the crew adjusted the gun and then once the bombardment began the radio rattled with Vietnamese. We went through another similar cycle as we adjusted to the North Vietnamese Army commander moving his men back down to the base of the hill. I had no idea what the North Vietnamese Army commander must have been thinking as he moved his men up and down on the hill to escape our one gun artillery bombardment and as soon as the men moved the 105mm bombardment followed them.

As the radio sputtered with Vietnamese, I asked Somsit to tell me what was being said, as I wanted to stay right on top of the enemy. Somsit acted sheepish and said the carpenter would not tell him what the North Vietnamese Army commander had said.

I told Somsit, "That's foolish. We have to know so we can keep hitting the enemy with our rounds."

Somsit spoke to the carpenter at length and then turned to me. The carpenter had thought it unseemly to tell me what the enemy soldier was saying. The Lao have a serious cultural tradition of preserving face. Part of that tradition was that it was not acceptable for a lower ranking person to criticize a higher-ranking person or even to relay to the higher-ranking person something that might be perceived as disrespectful. I became frustrated with the carpenter's reluctance to relay to me what was being said and insisted that Somsit find out what the North Vietnamese Army commander had said.

Finally, Somsit said, the North Vietnamese Army commander seems to be shaking his fist at us and saying to the effect, "You god damned, fucking no good Americans!"

We fired our one-gun barrages whenever aircraft were not available to pound the hill. The battle continued over several days and mostly due to the aerial bombardment, the hill slowly turned from all green to all brown. It was totally denuded of greenery. Bombing or artillery began to raise clouds of brown dust. Between General Phasouk's FAR troops and our irregulars, we were not able to force the North Vietnamese Army off but eventually the North Vietnamese Army withdrew from the hill. With all vegetation gone from the hill, it had become an impossible position to defend. We had won a small victory but we did not succeed in preventing the North Vietnamese Army from eventually taking positions on the Bolovens Plateau and threatening the key towns of Paksong and Pakse.

Of course, positive results do not always have to come from battlefield victory. CIA led irregular forces, Royal Lao regular forces, and Royal Lao and U.S. Air Force aircraft were tying down significant numbers of North Vietnamese Army forces and keeping them from being sent on into South Vietnam. In addition to having to commit troops to defend the Ho Chi Minh Trail, the North Vietnamese Army also had to commit forces to fighting Lao forces as the North Vietnamese Army tried to seize and hold enough Lao territory to create more security for their logistical supply line from North Vietnam into South Vietnam.

Royal Lao Air Force T–28 bombing NVA position on PS–26
Photo courtesy of Ken Thompson

PS–26 after the enemy's withdrawal
Photo courtesy of Glenn Ettinger

REMOTE SENSORS
AND BEACONS

———◆———

"Here, find the hat."

–Unknown CIA case officer

A CIA case officer is part of a chain of command and has to be willing to receive orders and follow them. Every field operative knows that often those orders come from people who don't know how things work in the field and who make decisions as much for political reasons as good sound on the ground judgment. I wanted to direct useful intelligence collection operations but sometimes we were ordered to conduct operations we knew would not work.

The American military has a preferred model of what a soldier should be and the Lao did not, in any way, measure up to the American preferred model of a combat soldier. It was not surprising then that there was a constant effort to come up with technical methods for the Lao irregulars to collect intelligence that did not expose them to risk or force them to try to live up to American ideals. If you read any of the interesting books about American led special operations in Vietnam, Laos and Cambodia you quickly understand the difference. However, we did not have the luxury of sending Americans along with the Lao and had to produce results by sending the Lao out by themselves. Naturally, we had much less combat success than American led special operations units, such as, MACVSOG. However, when you consider we could never send Americans along, the success we did have was astonishing.

CIA headquarters components were always looking for technical methods for intelligence collection in the Lao jungle environment and they even came up with a remote sensor that roadwatch teams were supposed to take all the way to an active road on the Ho Chi Minh Trail and plant in the middle of the roadbed. Not long after taking over the PS-7 roadwatch teams at Kong My, I was told I would have to send a team to the Ho Chi Minh Trail to emplace this remote sensor. TSD, the Technical Services Division, was the entity within the CIA that designed and built a variety of devices to support clandestine operations. The character Q, in the James Bond novels, worked for the British intelligence branch that does the sorts of things that TSD does. The remote sensor contained an audiometer, seismometer and a magnetometer. Thus, it was designed to detect the ground tremors as something like a truck rumbled past, or even a soldier walked by. If that something were a truck or other type of vehicle, the metal could be detected and recorded.

The remote sensor included computer technology for storing the data it collected and the ability to communicate with a companion device flown overhead in an airplane. The data could be uploaded to the device in the airplane upon establishing communication between the two devices. Under normal circumstances, roadwatch case officers were under pressure to verify that the roadwatch teams were actually going all the way to a position where they could observe the Ho Chi Minh Trail. There was no guarantee that many were really doing it. Even with the remote sensors, however, the likelihood that a case officer was going to get a team to go all the way to the middle of the actual trail was nil. It was one thing for a team to establish an observation post overlooking the Ho Chi Minh Trail, quite another for the team to go all the way to the actual roadbed. Teams routinely reported that the team member carrying the remote sensor had accidentally dropped it on a rock, into a river, lost it because of being ambushed or had successfully planted it and had no idea why it was not working. Of course, if the team said it planted the sensor, we had no way to figure out why it was not working. There was no method available for determining if a team planted a sensor out in the jungle or if they planted it at all.

Discussing this with my operations assistants, they expressed doubt that any team would be able to plant a sensor successfully. They thought a team would be willing to carry the thing out into the jungle but they were very doubtful that the team members would be willing or able to creep to a position adjacent to an in-use enemy truck track and then spend the time it would take to dig the device into the ground. If the team was not discovered and attacked while making the placement, they would be too fearful to actually try. The Thai operations assistants said that while the teams might be willing to sneak into positions that allowed them to observe enemy activity on the Ho Chi Minh Trail from a distance, they would not have the courage to go to within 25 meters of the actual road. The teams believed the traffic along the roads was such that the enemy would come along and discover them before they could make a placement. If they were not discovered by the troops using the roads, security forces patrolling the area would discover them.

I spent some time trying to lobby the chief of operations into letting me forego such an operation. He finally got tired of the debate and told me to write up a cable to send to CIA headquarters telling them all the reasons why such operations would not work. Any such cable had to be sent to Vientiane and Udorn first and if they agreed, we could then send it on to CIA headquarters. We were astonished to receive a reply from Vientiane that actually said that we could forget about refusing to run a remote sensor planting operation as someone at CIA headquarters had ordered a large number of the sensors and most of them were still sitting on the shelf unused.

Since using a team to put in the remote sensor was a relatively cheap way to put them to use no one in Vientiane expected CIA headquarters to agree with us and cancel the remote sensor implant operations.

I seized on the idea that I could dissuade CIA headquarters if I showed them it was actually an expensive operation. I gathered all the costs that would be involved, not just the payments to the teams, as that was cheap. An operation like this would involve two helicopters, one to carry the team and one as cover in case the first helicopter went down and the crew had to be rescued, a Porter to carry the case officer and operations assistant so that the case officer could coordinate the whole operation. On many infiltrations and exfiltrations, we also positioned strike aircraft in case the helicopter-landing zone was hot. All of these aircraft operated at an hourly rate. I had become familiar with these costs from listening to Ray as he went about the business of directing operations. The cost of the operation would then be doubled as you had to budget for going out and picking up the team at the end of the emplacement operation or in case they were attacked and had to abort the mission. If the sensor were successfully placed, its battery would eventually run down and we would have to run another operation to put in another sensor, or if management were really crazy, ask the team to go in, find the sensor and dig it up and replace the battery. I had the costs up to a significant amount of money for a full cycle of initial implant, battery replacement and sensor recovery.

At this point, one might wonder why we spent so much time and effort to place this remote sensor when its technology limited the amount of time it would function to the time the battery would last. There was no way, however, that Vientiane Station management was going to buy into telling CIA head-quarters we didn't want to run a remote sensor implant mission. The next cable from Vientiane, ignoring our well-reasoned arguments, told us a technical officer would be visiting Pakse to train a team for the mission.

I was not a happy camper, but I decided I had to cooperate fully with the technical officer. He was a congenial guy and easy to get along with so I figured it was best to help him out all I could which would also insure that my team was trained as well as it could be. I assigned Somsit to interpreter duty for the training and decided to observe the training while Somsit worked with the technical officer. They went through the first hour of training and then took a break. Somsit came to me and told me he did not think the training was going very well. The remote sensor consisted of a central processing unit (CPU), a signal transmission module, and two sensors connected to the CPU by long cables. During the first hour, the technical officer had been describing the sensor to the team using the technical English terms for the various parts and explaining what function each part had. Somsit said he could hardly understand the concepts himself no less translate the technical terms into Thai or Lao.

Somsit was primarily a Thai speaker who had not fully mastered Lao, which he considered an inferior language to Thai. However, in this case, Somsit, who was a university graduate, admitted that not only were there no words for the technical terms in Lao, but he did not even know if there were any Thai words for them either. To illustrate the point, I used to try to learn as much Lao as possible from my operations assistants. One day when I was quizzing them on various Lao words one of them asked me why I wanted to learn Lao, which was such a primitive language, compared to Thai. I asked for an example.

He said, "Take the Lao word for airplane. They use the word 'nyon' ."

He said this with an obvious sneer, so I asked, "Why is that so bad?"

He replied to that, "Well, it means engine, they call all such things, like cars, airplanes, trucks, just engine."

Reasonably impressed by the primitiveness of that, I asked, "OK, so how do the Thai say airplane?"

He triumphantly responded, "In Thai we say 'hua bin' ."

Not being familiar with the words, and wanting to know how much more technically savvy this was, I asked what it meant.

The reply, with a knowing and superior look on his face, was "It means flying boat." To which I could only agree that "flying boat" was much more technically correct than just "engine."

With my understanding of just how technical both the Thai and Lao languages were, I decided to volunteer to take over the training and went to talk to the technical officer about it. He was very relieved and more than happy to have me take over. While technical officers were usually quite accomplished in the various technical fields and their application to clandestine operations, they were not case officers or trained in operations. Case officers, on the other hand, usually did not take much interest in technical subjects nor were they interested in conducting training. To have me volunteer to take over the training was a big relief to the technical officer. I told Somsit I would not be using any technical vocabulary and to just follow along and translate what I was going to say.

"Sky put a spirit into this black box because Sky wants to count the trucks on the Ho Chi Minh Trail."

"However, Sky knows it is dangerous for the team to stay too close to the road and count the trucks itself. Therefore, Sky put a spirit in the box. If the team makes one trip to the road traveled by the enemy and places the spirit close to the road then the spirit can count the trucks and the team can withdraw to a safe place not too close to the road and enemy activity."

"However, in order to make the spirit happy so that it can do a good job of counting trucks and reporting the truck traffic to Sky, the team will have to conduct a spirit ceremony at the time it places the spirit near the road."

Let me pause here and explain that the Lao lowlanders and Lao hill tribesmen who made up the team members were all animists in one form or another. Some might profess belief in Buddhism but they were all practical enough not to exclude the possibility of help from any quarter that might wish to give it. I knew they had some, if not a lot of, belief in spirits and that spirit ceremonies were common events in their lives. In fact, they had all probably participated in a spirit ceremony prior to leaving their home villages to report in for this mission. In that case, the spirit ceremony was aimed at obtaining favorable protection from the appropriate spirits while they were out on their mission.

Since the Lao often referred to CIA personnel as Sky, I needed to put the training into a cultural context they could understand. They had never before heard that Sky had its own spirits, but why not? We had everything else and a lot they had never seen before. I decided to describe the remote sensor with terms like "head" for signal processor, "heart" for the central processing unit, "hand" for the sensor, and "arms" for the cables.

The training began again. I spoke to the team and Somsit translated.

"The black box with the spirit in it has to be buried in the ground and the spirit ceremony has to be performed while the spirit is being buried."

"The spirit will not be happy unless it is buried in just the right place. You must find a place that is near a road where the enemy drives their trucks and where the road is straight and flat for at least 50 to 60 meters."

"This spirit does not like water. It prefers vegetation and is happiest if it is buried in its box among some bushes or other broad leafy plants."

The reason for all this was that it was necessary, in order for the sensor to operate at maximum performance, that there be no curves in the road and that the trucks not be on an uphill struggle or a downhill run. Water was to be avoided so that it would not ruin the sensor's electronics and the bushes were needed to cover its antenna. There would not be much showing above ground but it would be better if they hid the antenna in the bushes.

I continued the training.

"This spirit ceremony must be memorized and performed according to my instructions or the spirit will not be happy and then it will not be able to report properly to another spirit that will be in a black box that the Nai Kou will carry in an airplane. The Nai Kou will fly out to the spirit's location and then let the one spirit talk to the other to learn what it had observed at its location near the Ho Chi Minh Trail."

First, after finding a good place to emplace the sensor, the team needed to make sure the sensor would be the proper distance from the road. The team would have a rope of a certain length that I would give them. They would have to use that rope with a rock tied on one end.

Somsit and I began again.

"I will give you a rope to use in the spirit ceremony. When you are near the road, you must creep as close to the road as necessary to be able to throw the rope, with a rock attached, across to the other side of the road. Next, the rope must be drawn back toward the team until the rock is in the center of the road."

I tied a knot at the end of the rope. This knot showed the distance from the road where the spirit ceremony had to be performed. It was also the proper distance for digging in the equipment.

"Next, you must dig a hole, as deep as the entrenching tool is long. This is for the spirit's head."

"Place the head into this hole. Then, stretch the arms out from the head parallel to the road."

"Dig one hole for each of the hands the same depth as the hole for the head."

"Next, dig a narrow trench for the arms, between the head and the hands."

"One last hole is for the spirit's heart. Dig this hole about one entrenching tool's length behind the head. When the four holes and the trenches are ready, put the spirit's head, heart, hands and arms into the holes."

"Last, pour the spirit water that I give you on the arms." The spirit water, actually a type of bug repellent, was necessary because the technical officers believed bugs might chew the wires while they were in the ground. The wires were the only part of the sensor that was vulnerable like that since the rest of it was metal.

"Fill the holes and the trenches with dirt and smooth everything over, taking care to use tree branches to disguise foot prints and signs of digging."

Having gotten through the explanation and demonstration of the Sky spirit ceremony I left it to Somsit to have them repeat the ceremony several times until they appeared to have mastered it. The team seemed to take this all in seriously and was quite solemn in carrying out the ceremony.

With the team trained and briefed on where Sky wanted its spirit buried, I arranged for an Air America helicopter infiltration. The team was safely unloaded at the selected drop zone and began their trek toward the target. It was a long distance and rough terrain. After about a week to ten days of monitoring their progress via Delco CW Morse code reports and air to ground VHF radio contacts, the operations assistants came in one day and said they had no contact with the team. After three days, the team was able to re-contact the operations assistants via air to ground VHF radio. They reported that they had run into North Vietnamese Army soldiers and gotten into a firefight with them. The team leader believed they were compromised and could not continue the mission as he had been wounded. He wanted me to send a helicopter to pick them up and take them back to base. When asked what had happened to the spirit box they said they had destroyed it, which is what they had been instructed to do. I was not sure they had really destroyed the equipment, but I had not been that much in favor of doing this anyway, so I was not going to make a big issue out of it. I requested an Air America exfiltration and extracted the team. They did have wounded, not serious, but such that they did need to be extracted. From time to time after that I paid lip service to organizing and sending in another remote sensor emplacement but I never actually put another team on a helicopter and sent them.

At some point during case officer training in those days, young case officer trainees heard the following story. A case officer in a foreign field station went out on a surveillance operation. During the course of the surveillance, he thought he might have been observed too closely by the opposition so he went into a clothing store and bought a hat to put on so his profile would appear a bit different. After the surveillance operation was over, he submitted his monthly expense accounting and listed the cost of the hat and claimed reimbursement for it. The finance officer called him in and berated him for trying to collect payment for the hat. The hat was a personal expense he was told. This did not sit well with the case officer as he felt he would not have bought the hat except as a way to try to keep from being compromised and thus compromising the surveillance operation. There was nothing he could do. The finance officer's decision was final. The next month, however, he returned to the finance officer's office, tossed his monthly expense report on the desk and said, "Here, find the hat."

Ultimately, most of what a case officer does is known only to him and the assets with whom he deals. There is always the threat that if one does something that is not approved such actions will be uncovered during polygraph examinations. There may not be a case officer alive, however, who has not submitted expense reports with hats hidden in them. That is how I felt about remote sensor emplacements. They wrote cables asking this and that about such operations, I wrote cables generating a lot of smoke and showing them reflections in a lot of mirrors, but in the end I never sent out any more teams to plant remote sensors. It was my way of telling CIA headquarters, "Find the hat."

The TSD technical officers also had a variety of beacons for use in Laos. Beacons may have been used successfully somewhere in Laos but I was not aware of it. The necessity for compartmentation being what it is, I had no need to know every detail of every operation in country, so maybe they were used successfully, however, that was not my experience. Now, I have to say, I like gadgets and would use technology without hesitation if I thought it would make an operation better. The problem with technology is that it has to be used by people who can adapt and improvise with it. Somewhere in Laos, there may have been people who successfully used technology but not at that time by the people I had working for me. Of course, I mean technology beyond tape recorders and radios.

Since we were always struggling with ways to validate the location of a team in enemy territory, TSD had proposed we use beacons. The idea being that the team would carry the beacon with them to set it up and turn it on when contacted by VHF air to ground radio. The beacon signal would be picked up by gear carried in the aircraft and we would know where the team was located.

Since my experience with remote sensor training, I wanted to be involved in the beacon training. I also wanted to see if I could successfully set up and operate the beacon. If I could not, then I could hardly expect my teams to do it. Even if I could make it work, that was no reason to think they could but I wanted to see what I could do with it before worrying about anything else.

I arranged to go to PS-18, our training site, with a technical officer and the beacon equipment. The beacon they wanted us to use consisted of a long wire antenna that had to be setup, connected to the little black beacon box and then turned on when the beacon-querying aircraft flew overhead. I could see that the beacon antenna was going to be a problem if it had to be set up in the confined spaces available in the jungle and no one would want to expose himself setting it up in a more open space. I was doubtful already but I kept my concerns to myself. Working in a wide-open space, the beacon antenna was set up and I connected it to its box and turned it on. Setting up the beacon antenna appeared to be the most difficult part of its operation. We had arranged for an aircraft, carrying the interrogation equipment, to fly over PS-18 and query the beacon. We only had a small window in time in which to turn on the beacon but that was more realistic than not. After spending time setting up the antenna, connecting it to the transmitter and turning it on several times, we waited until the aircraft was due to over fly us. After a few hours Grey Fox, the Pakse air operations officer, called to let us know the aircraft, a Beechcraft Baron, was on its way. We had a VHF HT-2 handheld radio, the same radio the teams used, so we went out to the beacon and stood by. Grey Fox had given the Baron pilot our VHF frequency so we waited for him to call us. When he called, we made contact and turned on the beacon. He flew over and then reported that he had not picked up the signal. He said he would fly back over us at a lower altitude and try again. Again, he reported he did not pick up the signal. Between having me to set the beacon up and the technical officer to check my setup and fiddle with the transmitter, we had much more than any team would have in the field if they tried to use the beacon and we could not make it work.

I had all the information I needed. I went back to Pakse and explained the whole thing to the chief of operations. I recommended we not try to use the beacon for validating my teams' locations. I was totally confounded when he actually agreed with me, but I went away happy.

CASH ON DELIVERY

———◆———

"Luck is the residue of design."

–Branch Rickey

By June 1970, I was trying every trick I could think of to motivate my men to try to capture a North Vietnamese Army soldier from behind enemy lines. I had learned that sending small teams out to try to spy on the activities of the North Vietnamese Army and count the number trucks or soldiers traveling north or south on the Ho Chi Minh Trail were ineffective activities.

Having reviewed all roadwatch intelligence reporting at CIA headquarters and having found it worthless and laying unprocessed under an analyst's desk, I had been seeking other ways to make use of the men assigned to my program.

On 10 November 1970, I was sitting at a small desk in the roadwatch and intelligence teams area when one of my Thai operations assistants came in with exciting news. He had just returned from an over flight of my teams out on mission. We conducted the over-flights from a Pilatus Porter PC-6 aircraft and called them "air-grounds" because we talked to the teams using the radio in the aircraft while the team on the ground used an HT-2 very high frequency radio.

"Tan Chanh, Thao Cho[26] reported that his team captured an NVA soldier."

"Somneuk, are you sure they really have an NVA?"

"Yes, they want you to come and get them with a chopper."

"OK, Somneuk, but I have to be sure. I'm going to request that Grey Fox let me use a Porter to go talk to the team. You and I will go."

I got on the Collins single sideband radio and, using the daily substitution codes, called Grey Fox, the Pakse air operations officer, to request permission to use a Porter to go out to talk to a team again. Grey Fox gave permission and

---

[26] Tan and Thao are Lao for mister and Chanh and Cho are given names, thus they were the equivalent of Mr. Bob and Mr. Bill. When one occupies a superior social position one addresses someone from a lesser social position as Thao, and vice versa, someone from a lesser social position addresses someone from a superior position as Tan.

I took Somneuk and flew out to the area where Thao Cho and Team Lime/307 were operating.

As we neared the team's area of operation, I told Somneuk to contact the team. Speaking in Lao, Somneuk began trying to contact the team.

"Team 307, Team 307, this is Nai Kou."

"Yes, Nai Kou, Team 307 here."

"Tan Chanh is here with me. He wants to know more about the prisoner you have."

As I gave Somneuk each question in English, he repeated it in Lao. I wanted to know, briefly, how the team had captured the prisoner and how Thao Cho knew he was a North Vietnamese Army soldier. It was then I learned the prisoner was a defector, which made no difference as long as he was really a North Vietnamese Army soldier. After getting enough details, to be confident it was really an enemy soldier, and to brief the chief of operations, I told Somneuk to tell Thao Cho to proceed to a helicopter-landing zone where we could pick them up. Thao Cho had a helicopter-landing zone in mind and gave us the map grid coordinates. Somneuk asked for a second helicopter-landing zone at least five kilometers away and Thao Cho gave Somneuk those coordinates, too. Somneuk asked Thao Cho how soon he could be ready and he replied he would be ready in about three hours.

I worried briefly about exchanging grid coordinates and other details of the capture in the clear over the radio, but the need to verify the facts and then get an immediate exfiltration outweighed the security concerns.

We flew directly back to Pakse where I alerted Grey Fox that we would need two helicopters (two pilots, two co-pilots and two crew chiefs) and combat air cover for an emergency exfiltration in two hours. I then went on to the Pakse Unit office, only about the equivalent of three to four blocks away from the Pakse airfield, and went straight to the chief of operations' office. I briefed him that Team Lime had a North Vietnamese Army prisoner and we needed to go out and pick them all up. He listened to my briefing and gave the OK.

I returned to the airfield and Grey Fox had two Air America helicopter crews in his office ready for briefing. Their H-34 helicopters were fueling. A

Raven pilot arrived because our chief of operations had informed him that I needed air cover for an emergency exfiltration. I gave the pilots a full briefing telling them we had a North Vietnamese Army prisoner and we had to pick up the prisoner and the roadwatch team that had captured him and bring them all to Pakse. I told them a little bit about how the team had captured the North Vietnamese Army soldier and that he was actually a defector. I felt the pilots would feel better knowing something about how the enemy soldier came into our custody.

One of the helicopter pilots asked about the team leader. I said, "Thao Cho is one of the best team leaders we have. He has been completely trustworthy and reliable on every mission so far."

The pilots were aware that it was just as possible that this might be the first mission on which Thao Cho turned sour, but they accepted my declaration of faith in the team leader. I then proceeded to give them the primary and secondary helicopter landing zone locations, the air to ground safe signal, which the team displayed using red cloth panels, the color of the smoke the team would pop, and the radio frequencies for the team. The Air America, Raven and Continental Air Services, Incorporated (CASI) pilots all agreed on a radio frequency to use among themselves apart from the radio frequency we were using with the team. I told the helicopter pilots the North Vietnamese Army soldier had to be blindfolded asking that the kicker on the helicopter that made the pickup make sure the blindfold was in place. We would fly out to the general area and wait for the Raven to tell us that cover had arrived. While waiting for the air cover, I would contact the team and make sure they were there, in hiding near the helicopter landing zone and ready to place the panels and pop the smoke. The team would not move to the helicopter-landing zone until instructed by the Nai Kou, Somneuk in this case. Once the team popped the smoke, the pick up helicopter would go in to get them. The Raven would be ready to direct air strikes on any enemy that might appear near or on the helicopter-landing zone. The air cover the Raven would have would be either local Pakse Royal Lao Air Force T-28s, U.S. Air Force or U.S. Navy assets flying missions over Laos. These American assets were sometimes jet aircraft and sometimes propeller driven aircraft. Upon making the pickup, the Air America helicopters would proceed to Pakse airfield, known as L-11 (Lima One-One).

As we approached Team Lime's location, I told Somneuk to go ahead and call Thao Cho on the radio.

"Team 307, this is Nai Kou."

"Yes, Nai Kou, 307 here."

"307 is everything ready?"

"Nai Kou, this is 307, all is ready."

"Team 307, this is Nai Kou, do you see any enemy?"

"Nai Kou, this is 307, there is no enemy in sight, all is ready."

I was sitting in the right side seat next to the Porter pilot in the left side seat. Somneuk was right behind us leaning between the two front seats so he could easily reach the microphone on the Porter's radio. I had flipped the radio to the team's radio frequency and as soon as I knew the team was ready, I flipped the radio over to the frequency for the helicopters and the Raven. I told them the team was ready, there were no enemy in sight and that I was going to instruct the team to pop smoke. I flipped the radio over to the team's frequency and told Somneuk to tell Thao Cho to pop smoke.

As soon as Somneuk did that and got an affirmative reply, I flipped the radio back to the helicopter's frequency. "Everything is a go, as soon as you spot the team's smoke go in and make the pick up. Is that a roger?"

"Roger, we see the smoke. Going for the pick up."

One helicopter went in and picked up the team while one helicopter stayed high as backup in case anything went wrong. The primary mission of the second helicopter would be to get the Air America crew. The helicopters would only pick up the team if everything were safe. Indeed, the team would probably have already taken off into the jungle if anything went wrong. Nothing went wrong and it was a smooth pickup.

As soon as both helicopters were well on their way back to Pakse, I called the helicopter carrying the team and asked them to verify that the team had brought aboard a blindfolded North Vietnamese Army soldier. They verified that and I settled back while the Porter easily beat the helicopters back to the airfield. We landed and waited for the helicopters.

Glenn, one of my colleagues and an irregular unit advisor, was at the airfield and asked me, "Did you really get an NVA?" His skepticism was an indicator of how difficult such an operation was and at the same time recognition for the success.

North Vietnamese Army Sergeant *Trinh Dinh Thu* became the first in an unprecedented number of North Vietnamese Army soldiers snatched or lured from behind enemy lines by Lao irregular special operations teams. The significance of this is that we did not wait to find enemy soldiers wounded on the battlefield or wait for them to surrender. Having teams go out and develop a plan to snatch a North Vietnamese Army soldier or identify one who wanted to defect and help him defect was not being done anywhere in Laos or Vietnam.

I reported into my sub-unit in Special Operations Division at CIA headquarters after my return home from Laos. This sub-unit was the "home base" for most special operations case officers but did not exercise operational control over them. When assigned to the Far East, you were the responsibility of that area division for the duration of your time there. The sub-unit might hear about you from time to time but would not know any of the details of your tour of duty. The chief, Wayne, asked me what I had done in Laos. I summarized what I had done and Wayne said it sounded like something that should be written up in an after action report. I said I would be happy to write it up and spent two weeks completing my report. During those two weeks I came across an article in *Studies in Intelligence*, CIA's classified in-house publication, titled "*Five Weeks at Phalane*"[27]. One of my colleagues and friends who had been assigned to the Savannakhet Unit had written the article, now declassified and available for review and reproduction at the National Archives in College Park, Maryland. While it was, in my opinion, a very interesting and

---

[27] Edwin K. Stockinger, "*Five Weeks at Phalane*", Studies in Intelligence 17, No. 1 (Spring 1973): Pages 11-19.

well-written article it was about combat operations not about intelligence collection. I thought to myself that if an article about combat could be published in *Studies In Intelligence* then my after action report should make the basis of an article about how special operations was used to collect intelligence.

I took a copy of my after action report and went to see the *Studies in Intelligence* editor. He looked it over and said he did indeed think it could be published but that it needed some editing. He asked me, "Would you mind if I edited it for you?" I replied, "That's fine with me." When he completed the editing and showed me the finished product it was quite different from my after action report but the facts were identical except for a couple of minor distortions which I pointed out and he corrected.

The article appeared in the Fall 1973 edition of *Studies in Intelligence* and was titled *"Cash on Delivery: How to Obtain North Vietnamese Soldiers for Intelligence in Laos."* It appeared under the pen name Robert A. Petchell. My article has also been declassified and made available, with redactions, at the National Archives. It is reprinted here.

NOTE: *At the time my article was declassified for release to the National Archives, certain team, North Vietnamese Army soldier, team leader and informant or villager names were redacted, i.e. blacked out. While the CIA did not require the redaction of those names from the rest of this manuscript, the CIA has insisted that they remain redacted in the reprint of my article[28]. Thus, to comply with the CIA's demands, the redacted names appear as aliases in italics in the reprint of my article, even though the true names appear in the remainder of the manuscript.*

---

[28] When I pointed out that the names that were redacted were the equivalent of Mr. Bob or Mr. Bill, the CIA told me I had to submit a Freedom of Information Act (FOIA) request to have the redactions removed. I explained everything but my request was still rejected.

How to obtain North Vietnamese soldiers for intelligence in Laos

CASH ON DELIVERY

Robert A. Petchell

Through the early years of the fighting in Laos, technology was the primary source of intelligence about the enemy, and it left something to be desired. The jungle canopy frustrated photography, sensors which counted trucks or marching units could not determine what they were carrying, and the enemy order of battle derived from communications intelligence was less than complete.

Human sources were needed to fill the gaps. Friendly sources were available, and did yeoman service on such missions as road watch teams and reconnaissance. A more useful human source, however, would be the North Vietnamese Army soldier. Pathet Lao sources were of minimal value - they had little access to North Vietnamese Army activities or plans, and were not sufficiently interested in North Vietnamese Army unit designations to provide adequate order of battle intelligence.

Five years into the war in Laos, North Vietnamese Army defectors or prisoners of war were rare.

What was needed was an aggressive program to provoke defection or to snatch North Vietnamese Army soldiers bodily from their environment. And for success in any snatch program, it would first be necessary to overcome the conviction of the average government soldier that all North Vietnamese were ogres 10 feet tall.

For assets, there were the Paramilitary Team Operations, a little-known companion program to the highly publicized Meo irregular battalions of General Vang Pao. The majority of these irregular guerrilla intelligence collection teams came from the area of Saravane Province and the Bolovens

Plateau region, where North Vietnamese Army troops were more vulnerable than they were along the main routes of the Ho Chi Minh Trail. At a considerable distance from their supply bases, their hold on the territory not consolidated, they bivouacked their troops in or near villages, and they sought supplies from the villagers. North Vietnamese Army support and service soldiers began to move through the area in small groups or alone, as couriers or foragers, or on reconnaissance. Later on, during 1971 and 1972, deserters began leaving North Vietnamese Army units in combat, trying to make their way home to North Vietnam or find asylum in the villages.

These villages, however – in contrast to the Ho Chi Minh Trail area where most of the villagers had left – turned out to be the friendly sea in which the 'fish" of the irregular guerrilla intelligence teams could swim.

Each of these teams normally had a team leader, a deputy, and a Morse operator, along with enough team members for an average total strength of eight men. At times, there were as many as twelve, or as few as two. Sometimes they wore uniforms, other times they wore native dress. They carried a variety of weapons, from AK-47 or M-2 carbines to Colt .45s and hand grenades. They used VHF portable voice radios and Delco CW radios (PRC-64s).

The teams were encouraged to remain in the field for at least 30 days per mission, and often extended to 60 or 90 days with light resupply drops. Members received a regular base salary–ranging in 1970 from $16 a month for a team member to $26 for a team leader–and additional mission pay of $1 for each day spent on assignment in the field.

The real incentive under this system was the mission pay. Salary could in effect be doubled simply by doing, or unfortunately by faking, a modicum of assigned work in the field. But where was there enough incentive to persuade the irregulars to lay one of those 10-foot North Vietnamese Army ogres by the heels?

The mission pay was intended to be payment for results, but it had the weakness, first, that it allowed no differentiation to recognize either quality or quantity of results, and second, most of the missions were of such a nature that it was difficult for the headquarters to verify the results claimed.

The Bounty System

Out of these difficulties, the case officer handling Paramilitary Team Operations in Military Region IV of southern Laos came up in 1970 with a simple
solution to bring rational cupidity to bear on primitive fear. He told selected
guerrilla teams that they would receive no daily mission pay, but instead could
share $1,000 for each live North Vietnamese Army officer delivered to the
base, $400 for each NCO, and $200 for each NVA private–Cash on Delivery.

It worked. The first reliable guerrilla teams who were offered this scheme
declined, preferring to remain on regular assignment and daily mission pay,
but pressure was maintained to cajole them into trying abductions in return
for the premium. The first successful effort, in fact, was by such a team on
another mission, which found the premium overpowering their fears when
they spotted an opportunity to bring in an NVA sergeant. After several such
successes by reliable teams, the case officer began calling in the more marginal
teams and putting them on abduction missions without any option – and
without mission pay. If they failed, they would be terminated, if they succeeded, they would earn the bounty and be allowed to return to regular
missions at mission pay.

In November 1970, Lao guerrilla intelligence teams were able to induce
the defection of a NVA sergeant, the first time in the Lao war that Royal Lao
Government soldiers were able to bring a NVA soldier under their control by
means other than his voluntary walk into an Royal Lao Government position
or his capture in a dazed or wounded condition on the battlefield. It was the
first successful aggressive operation specifically designed to pluck a NVA
soldier out of the NVA environment. It began like this:

Team Cranberry operated in an area five kilometers south of the southern
provincial capital of Saravane during September and October of 1970. Their
principal informant, Thao *Outhine*, had advised the team leader during their
last meeting prior to the team's withdrawal that it was possible to capture a
NVA officer. Team Lime, led by Thao *Keo*, a reliable and authenticated team
leader, was briefed and sent into the same area to collect intelligence and tried

to work with Thao *Outhine* on his capture plan. Thao *Keo* decided to brief every informant that Team Lime was interested in capturing NVA soldiers. This simple step paid an immediate dividend.

A former Royal Lao Government soldier, living about three kilometers south of Saravane and serving as an informant of Team Lime, knew of an NVA soldier who was living with a local Lao girl whose father was ethnic Vietnamese. The informant, Thao *Sengkham*, went to see the father and enlisted his aid in convincing the NVA soldier to defect to the Royal Lao Government so he could marry his girlfriend and live in Laos. Thao *Sengkham* and the father successfully did just that, and Thao *Sengkham* was able to lead NVA Sergeant *Trinh Dinh Thu* to the Team Lime command post, whence he was taken by helicopter to the Royal Lao Government military headquarters at Pakse. Unknown to Thao *Sengkham* was the fact that Sgt. *Thu* was not only vulnerable in his relationship to the Lao girl, but had deserted his unit during a Royal Lao Government Air Force bombing attack just a few days before Thao *Sengkham* proposed defection.

Team Lime thus concluded the first successful operation, and was replaced by Team Cranberry, led by Thao *Somdy*, who decided to re-contact Thao *Outhine* and go after a NVA soldier. He was confident that if Team Lime could do it, he could, too. It might be added that Thao *Somdy* was impressed by the $400 that Team Lime received to divide among six men for 20 days' work. For team members, this was more than three times the dollar-a-day mission incentive pay.

The First Abduction

Thao *Somdy* and Thao *Outhine* put their heads together and, after reviewing possible ambush sites, decided on a small trail Thao *Outhine* knew was often used by NVA soldiers traveling alone. After three days of waiting in ambush alongside this trail Team Cranberry got lucky on 2 January 1971. A single NVA soldier riding a bicycle approached the team, which was hidden in high grass on each side of the trail. One team member and Thao *Outhine*, stationed in plain view, tried to hail the soldier. When it did not seem that he was going to stop, the team member charged the bicycle and bowled over the NVA soldier. He was immediately joined by the rest of the team, who hauled the struggling soldier into the grass, trussed him up, and while one team member removed the bicycle from the scene, moved off to the Team Cranberry command post for successful delivery by helicopter. The captured soldier was Corporal *Nguyen Nhan Tiu*.

As a result of the defection of Sgt. *Thu* and the capture of Cpl. *Tiu*, intelligence analysts in Laos received the first reliable human source order of battle information on the 968th NVA Group, a command unit for military operations in Southern Laos. In addition, Sgt. *Thu* reported that a major effort would be made to capture all of the Bolovens Plateau including the key city of Paksong. The NVA did mount such an effort throughout 1971.

Meanwhile, Team Cranberry decided to remain in the field and try again. They had successfully pulled the first abduction of a NVA soldier in enemy-held territory, and their case officer was anxious to keep them working. The team was expanded from the eight men who had snatched Cpl. *Tiu* to a 20-man team, divided into a five-man command post and three five-man snatch units. Each snatch unit was augmented by from three to five informants, who were to spot vulnerable NVA soldiers and then participate in the abduction. The snatch units fanned out in three directions and by 15 January 1971 had accomplished their second abduction.

Pfc. *Hoang Van Ton* was assigned to work in a supply depot with 25 other NVA in Khanchom village, three kilometers northwest of Saravane. Two of Team Cranberry's informants lived in Khanthalat village, one kilometer south of Khanchom, and were acquainted with Pfc. *Ton*. Lao villagers were not allowed in Khanchom, but the informants knew that Pfc. *Ton* often traveled alone from Khanchom and always returned through Khanthalat where he stopped to visit his Lao friends. While six team members waited a few hundred meters away in the forest, the two informants went to await Pfc. *Ton* along the trail from Khanthalat to Khanchom.

As Pfc. *Ton* emerged from the village he spied the two and hailed them. They talked a bit and told *Ton* they wanted to walk with him to Khanchom to ask for rice. Pfc. *Ton* agreed and they all continued along the trail. Soon a third team member joined them and said he too was going to seek rice at Khanchom. At this *Ton* became suspicious, since it was very unusual for any Lao villager to try to beg rice from a NVA depot, let alone three of them at one time. The third team member, spotting *Ton*'s suspiciousness, gave the high sign in their tribal dialect, and all three pounced on him. Pfc. *Ton* kicked and fought, biting one Lao on the thumb, but was subdued, tied by the wrists and elbows with parachute suspension line and taken to headquarters by helicopter, together with a triumphant Team Cranberry.

There was little of intelligence interest from *Ton*'s interrogation, but his abduction was of great service operationally: it buttressed the argument that NVA soldiers were vulnerable to abduction or defection by a resourceful Laotian guerrilla team.

From Informant to Team Leader

Team Cranberry's departure left Thao *Outhine* behind, hoping to continue sharing bounties with any team as willing to use his information as Lime and Cranberry had been. He was disappointed, however, because for the next three months the teams were unable to make contact with him. He then spent the ensuing three months on the run, seeking the safety of a Royal Lao Government area. The North Vietnamese had learned of his informant role.

He finally reached Pakse, where he walked into Guerrilla Team Operations headquarters to volunteer as a team member. Recognizing his value in abduction operations, the case officer accepted Thao *Outhine* as a team leader, and trained him and a radio operator in the *modus operandi* of the guerrilla teams. Then Thao *Outhine*, now operating as "Team Pomelo", went back into the field in August 1971, and by 18 September had succeeded in capturing Sgt. *Trinh Thuy Long* of the NVA 9th Regiment.

Sgt. *Long* had been in combat at Paksong against Royal Lao Government forces when he decided to desert and return to North Vietnam. Heading north, he had covered almost 50 kilometers when he stopped to rest for the night in the village of Khiang Phoukhong. The village chief, a Team Pomelo informant, made his way to the team hideout and told Thao *Outhine* that an NVA soldier was going to spend the night at his house. Thao *Outhine* and his radio operator returned to the village with the chief, bringing with them an ample supply of lao-lao, the local moonshine. They proceeded to get the tired and emotionally distraught NVA sergeant thoroughly drunk by the time their supply ran out, and invited him to another house to find more lao-lao.

As they left the chief's house, Thao *Outhine* and his radio operator draped their arms around Sgt. *Long's* shoulders as if to support the staggering sergeant, but halfway down the steps the friendly arms tightened into vise-like grips on his head and shoulders. They subdued him and delivered him to a helicopter landing zone. At headquarters, Sgt. *Long* provided important order of battle information about the 9th Regiment, then the principal NVA unit in heavy contact with Royal Lao Government forces near Paksong.

This was not the end of Thao *Outhine's* contributions. In January 1972 he successfully induced the defection of Sgt. *Phan Van Hoi*, a mechanic-driver in a transportation pool of the 968th NVA Group. Sgt. *Hoi* was an ethnic Vietnamese, but had been born in Vientiane and had talked to Thao *Outhine* of owning his own taxi some day - a capitalistic pipe dream from the Hanoi viewpoint. Thao *Outhine* urged him to defect with the argument that his birth in Laos would help him obtain Laotian acceptance, and that his dream was much more likely to come true in a free Laos than in a Communist North Vietnam. *Hoi* bought the pitch and defected.

The Capable Brigand

The most successful Lao guerrilla team leader ever to stalk the NVA on abduction missions was probably Than *Bounlert*, the leader of Team Tomato. His past performance was inauspicious: returning overland in January 1971 from a roadwatch mission along the Ho Chi Minh Trail, he had refused to make the necessary signals for evacuation, and was taking a month to make his way back to base at an unproductive dollar-a-day per man. He was then advised by radio that the ruse would not earn any extra mission pay, and that he would probably be fired. *Bounlert* "resigned" instead, returning to his home village after telling the team members to report him killed in action. He then sent his wife to claim an indemnity for survivors of team members killed in action.

The case officer flatly informed the wife that he did not believe Thao *Bounlert* had been killed, and that the indemnity would not be paid. While a glum *Bounlert* was pondering his next move, he heard about the bounties offered for NVA soldiers, and the successes of Teams Lime and Cranberry. He reasoned that if he could catch an NVA soldier, he could rehabilitate himself. With the aid of another former team member, he set out to redeem his job.

NVA 2nd Lt. *Pham Huu Khang* of the F31 Reconnaissance Company and 1st Lt. *Tran Ngoc Khanh* of the 3rd Battalion, 968th Group returning from a reconnaissance, had stopped to make camp for the night near Thao *Bounlert*'s village. As *Bounlert* and his assistant hid and watched, 1st Lt. *Khanh* began to bathe in a stream, while 2nd Lt. *Khang* followed nature's call into the jungle. They followed 2nd Lt. *Khang* and caught him literally with his pants down. Under the circumstances, it was relatively easy to subdue, gag, and hog-tie him. They then turned their attention to 1st Lt. *Khanh*, who was still bathing, and managed to subdue him. *Bounlert* then secured the arms of both prisoners, but left their legs free for the 50-kilometer overland hike to guerrilla team headquarters.

On 28 April 1971, Thao *Bounlert* and his partner appeared at the base, leading the two bedraggled NVA officers by neck ropes. *Bounlert* announced that he would deliver them only to the guerrilla team case officer. 1st Lt. *Khanh* was a very truculent prisoner and refused to talk, but the 2nd lieutenant had no such scruples and outlined the complete order of battle of the NVA military command for all of southern Laos. He also reported an NVA plan to conduct a major offensive in May 1971, which took place and resulted in the loss of Paksong.

Thao *Bounlert* was an instant hero, albeit marked as a rogue and brigand and a man who would have to be carefully handled. The case officer refused to pay Thao *Bounlert* mission pay for his failed roadwatch mission, which he had the nerve to ask for, but did agree to pay the monthly salary he had missed from February to April 1971. He was told, however, that the only way he could continue to work as a guerrilla team leader was capturing NVA soldiers on a C.O.D. basis. Thao *Bounlert* pleaded and wheedled but could do no better and accepted. It was on his second mission that he achieved one of the more imaginative abductions.

Team Tomato was operating near a village about eight kilometers south of Saravane, employing a net of informants who were seeking vulnerable NVA soldiers. On 4 July 1971 an informant reported to Thao *Bounlert* that four NVA soldiers had arrived in their village to buy buffaloes. Two soldiers had gone out of the village on the buying mission, while two soldiers were staying in the village chief's house. The informants reported that these two were lax in their personal security and could be taken. The two NVA soldiers were Pfc. *Thai Van Thanh* and Pfc. *Dinh The Dung* of the Production and the Logistic Companies of Binh Tram 38, a major logistical unit of the Ho Chi Minh Trail complex.

A Bridal Party

Thao *Bounlert* with five team members, six informants, and Nang *Songsak*, the daughter of one of the informants, rounded up pigs, chickens, and lao-lao and headed for the village to announce that Thao *Bounlert* and Nang *Songsak* wanted to be married. It is a Lao custom that weddings be conducted at the village chief's house and that there be a feast and drinking before and after the wedding. Thao *Bounlert*'s plan was to pack the village chief's house with his men and then jump the two NVA soldiers. The ruse worked. After beginning the pre-wedding festivities, Thao *Bounlert* invited the two soldiers to join the party.

One soldier, Pfc. *Dung*, spoke Lao and was happy to join in, while Pfc. *Thanh* who spoke no Lao sat warily by, AK–47 rifle across his lap, not participating. They had a pre-arranged signal that if Thao *Bounlert* poured whiskey for the soldiers three times, the third pouring would be the signal to grab the soldiers. As the team leader poured the third drink for Pfc. *Dung*, the deputy team leader slammed Pfc. *Thanh's* rifle to the ground and kicked it away while Thao *Bounlert* seized Pfc. *Dung*. The team quickly tied up the two prisoners, cautioned the bewildered village chief to maintain silence over what happened, and left the hut, the bride, and the village.

Unfortunately for Thao *Bounlert*, his propensity for thievery did him in. He had kept for himself a large part of the $2,400 he received for the four prisoners, and paid his informants piddling amounts for their help. They were so dissatisfied that when he appeared near their village for his third try, the informants turned him in to the NVA authorities. He was last seen being led eastward toward an NVA prison camp.

The Cash on Delivery program, from the first successful defection in November 1970 through January 1972, provided nine NVA prisoners or defectors. During this same 15-month period another case officer, encouraged by the successes, organized a similar program and contributed six more prisoners. A successor case officer subsequently obtained eight more NVA soldiers through guerrilla intelligence teams.

Teams Lime and Cranberry had indeed initiated a useful program for providing a continuing supply of NVA human intelligence resources.

I had launched or trained, before I left, the teams that captured the eight North Vietnamese Army soldiers brought in after I departed Laos. My successor did not capture any North Vietnamese Army soldiers after those operations had run their course. He had arrived in Laos and been assigned to be my successor with at least a month of overlap. I told him, on the first day, I was not going to just stack arms and turn over the operations to him thirty days early. I said I would be running everything until the day I went to the airfield and boarded the aircraft to begin my journey home. That, it turned out, is what I did. We actually got along well and he seemed happy to let me have my way. Either you can give me full credit for those eight or you can say we should share the credit because I launched the teams and he supervised the delivery of the prisoners into Royal Lao Government hands. I will share the credit and say I inspired the first successful operation and had a hand in the capture of a total of 17 North Vietnamese Army soldiers at a time when no one else, except fellow case officer Khamsing, who had copied my modus operandi, was bringing them in.

The full roster of the nine North Vietnamese soldiers captured or induced to defect by my teams follows below. The date each one arrived in Pakse, the identification of the team and the team leader that brought him in, the North Vietnamese Army soldier's name and his unit, and the date and title of some of the field intelligence reports resulting from each North Vietnamese Army's debriefing are included in the list.

- 10 November 1970 – Team Lime/307 – Thao Cho
  SGT *Trinh Dinh Thu* – 46th Battalion/Group 968
  Intelligence Report: 12 November 1970 "Major Offensive against the Bolovens Plateau & Paksong"

- 2 January 1971 – Team Cranberry/316 – Thao Sengchanh
  CPL Thai Van Tiu – F30 Heavy Weapons Company/Group 968

- 15 January 1971 – Team Cranberry/316 – Thao Sengchanh
  PFC Tran Nhan Ton – Storage Unit/Ban Kanthalat

- 28 April 1971 – Team Tomato/204 – Thao Bouathong
  2LT Phan The Khang - F31 Reconnaissance Co./Group 968
  Intelligence Report: 1–3 May 1971 – "Major Offensive in May"
  Intelligence Report: 6 May 1971 – "Creation of Front Y"

- 28 April 1971 – Team Tomato/204 – Thao Bouathong
  1LT Hoang Huu Khanh – 2nd Company/3rd Battalion/Group 968

- 8 July 1971 – Team Tomato/204 – Thao Bouathong
  PFC Nguyen Ngoc Thanh – Production Company/Binh Tram 38

- 8 July 1971 – Team Tomato/204 – Thao Bouathong
  PFC Tran Van Dung – Logistics Company/Binh Tram 38
  Intelligence Report: 14–21 Jul 1971 – "BT 35 and BT 38"

- 18 September 1971 – Team Pomelo/328 – Thao Ouy
  SGT Pham Van Long – 3rd Company/1st Battalion/9th Regiment

- 28 January 1972 – Team Pomelo/328 – Thao Ouy
  SGT *Phan Van Hoi* – NVA Truong Son Command/Trans. Pltn.
  Intelligence Report Non Dissemination: "Offensive in Quang Tri"

At the time I was writing my after action report for my branch chief in Special Operations Division, I had the opportunity to review cable traffic from Laos and made informal notes on the North Vietnamese Army soldiers reported captured by or defected to "roadwatch" teams, that is, specifically teams belonging to the Team 300 project operating from PS 18. Following is what I believe is a list of the eight North Vietnamese Army soldiers brought in by Team 300 after I departed Laos. I did not make any notes on whether any intelligence reports resulted from their interrogations or debriefings.

- 10 March 1972 – Captured
  SGT Vuong Thuyet Bai – C26/9th Regiment

- 16 March 1972 – Captured
  CPL Nguyen Thanh Xuan – 25th Engineer Co/Group 968

- 16 March 1972 – Captured
  CPL Nguyen Xuan Thu – 1st Battalion/39th Regiment

- 25 April 1972 – Defected
  CPL Tong Viet Dai –309th Artillery Battalion/Group 968

- 5 May 1972 – Captured
  CPL Cao Ba Can – BT 46/Group 471

- 22 May 1972 – Defected
  Senior Lt Lo Van Can – Hqs Company/Group 968

- 27 July 1972 – Defected
  Lt Nguyen Hong Tho – Hqs Company/Group 968

- 28 August 1972 – Captured
  Staff Sgt Do Van Chin – 3rd Battalion/39th Regiment

These snatch or defection operations began because I often asked other case officers, "What would be a valuable objective for my teams other than roadwatch?" The answer I often received was, "capture a North Vietnamese Army soldier." This captured my imagination – pun intended. From my early days in Laos, I looked for ways to make the operations of my teams valuable and verifiable. While North Vietnamese Army soldiers had been captured in Laos on the battlefield, either dazed or wounded, no North Vietnamese Army soldier had ever been purposefully snatched from behind enemy lines. I wanted to do this. I believed the interrogation of a captured North Vietnamese Army soldier would yield useful intelligence.

Since I already knew the reporting of roadwatch and riverwatch teams was not really getting any attention back at CIA headquarters, I was looking for new and better ways to use the teams for intelligence collection. In addition to the roadwatch mission being ineffective, I was also struggling with the valida-tion and verification problem. Running operations that did not produce valuable intelligence and were difficult if not impossible to verify did not seem to be the best use of my time. I wanted to produce good intelligence and I did not want to have that intelligence challenged as fabricated, which happened when I tried to run operations in Cambodia. I studied the situation and decided that if my teams could capture a North Vietnamese Army soldier and that soldier gave us intelligence during interrogation, then the end result of the team's collection effort would be worthwhile.

Getting the teams to agree to go out to capture North Vietnamese Army soldiers was a huge obstacle. The teams were intimidated by the idea. They could not imagine how it could be done. They had often taken off and run away when confronted by enemy troops. The general opinion was you would wind up dead if you tried to stand up to battle hardened regular North Vietnamese Army soldiers. I worked with my Thai operations assistants to try to think up ways to convince the teams to try it. I believed that if we could get just one success it would snowball in to many more, notwithstanding the fact that snowballs were a very alien concept in Laos.

Finally, Hom, one of my Thai operations assistants, suggested to me that if I could offer a bounty for a captured North Vietnamese Army soldier he thought there were team leaders who would be tempted to try. I went to Ray, the chief of operations, and asked him if he could get authorization to pay rewards for capturing North Vietnamese Army soldiers. Ray said he thought there was a reward system in effect and he would check into it and let me know. A day or so later, Ray told me we were authorized to offer $1,000 for a North Vietnamese Army officer, $400 for a non-commissioned officer and $200 for a private soldier. When I brought this information to the Thai operations assistants, they thought they could work with those figures. During a normal mission, all the members of a team earned $1 per day-mission pay. The pay scale for monthly salary for the teams was, Team Leader $26 per month, Deputy Team Leader $24 per month, Radio Operator $22 per month, and Team Member $16 per month. Thus, a team leader remaining in the field for one month would earn $30 daily mission pay plus $26 monthly salary for a total of $56 for the month. The rest of the team members would be earning $54, $52 and $46 per month. A small team of 2-5 members, capturing a North Vietnamese Army officer, could earn a substantial payday if they could pull off a capture within a one-month mission. A five-man team capturing an officer within one month would split $1000, getting $200 each. Even the capture of a North Vietnamese Army private soldier would mean an extra $40 for each man – something that apparently appealed to some of the men. Perhaps that sort of money is not appealing to an American who has nothing if not plenty of opportunity to better himself and increase his income, but a Lao soldier did not have that sort of opportunity to dramatically increase his income. The bounties were significant incentives for my soldiers.

I felt that the men's lack of confidence was the biggest obstacle but with no successes to point to, I did not know how to go about motivating them. My Thai operations assistants, at my urging, were constantly encouraging the team leaders to try grabbing a North Vietnamese Army soldier. I went to Hom and told him what the bounty would be. Hom and I spent a lot of time talking to team leaders trying to encourage them to try a snatch. Finally, one of the former LS–171 team leaders, Thao Cho (we all pronounced this Joe even though the general transliteration of the letters of his Lao name was written Cho) told Hom he wanted to try it. I knew Cho's combat and mission record and he was an exemplary soldier. I had inherited him from the Team 300 operations out of LS–171 and he was well thought of by his CIA case officers, Heng and Noy, and by Viroj and Niphon, the Thai operations assistants who had worked with him at LS–171. I decided to let him go on the mission while collecting daily mission pay (one dollar per day for each soldier on the team). My operations assistants were confident that if any of the team leaders could do it, Cho could. Team Lime successfully induced a North Vietnamese Army soldier to defect to the team. I should note here that "Thao" in Lao meant mister, so we were calling Cho, Mr. Cho. If a person was in a superior position to another, the superior person referred to the other as "Thao." The person in the inferior position called his superior "Tan." Thus, Mr. Chanh was Tan Chanh when addressed by a subordinate person but Thao Chanh when addressed by someone who was his superior.

I made a major production out of paying Thao Cho and his team in front of all the men in camp. The rest of the team leaders and men saw the $400 dollar payment and realized it was possible. I had Hom and the other Thai assistants sit down with any team leader who would listen and go over how Team Lime had succeeded. Every time a team brought in a North Vietnamese Army soldier, we added that story and the Thai operations assistants would go over the ever–longer list of success stories with the team leaders. We repeatedly reviewed the successful stories and the accumulation of reward payments with the teams. I imagine the reward amounts appealed to the team leaders just as selling Cadillacs instead of Chevys appeals to some car salesmen. A team could go out on mission, qualify for the daily mission pay and if they could make a capture they could really clean up. Of course, I made it plain I had to believe they were really trying. I would not pay daily mission pay if they were faking it. I told them I would find out and I believe my past actions were proof enough for them. My reputation helped for these snatch operations but later it almost got me killed.

An example of my mission validation efforts happened during the first rainy season after my arrival in Laos. One of the teams on a riverwatch mission had been required to take photographs during the mission. The team came back with photographs of enemy dugouts on the north–south river they had been watching. When the Thai operations assistant debriefing the team brought the completed debriefing to me, I read it over and then called the team in and told them I wanted to review their mission with them.

"Somsit, ask the team leader to show me on the map exactly where this photograph was taken and tell me what time it was taken."

I had noticed that the photograph clearly showed shadows so I wanted to use the time to orient the photograph. The team leader said he they took the photograph in the late afternoon. Since the sun would be in the west I could orient the photograph so the shadows in the photograph would be in line, as they should in relation to a setting sun, but they lined up making the river east–west rather than north–south, as it should be.

"Somsit, tell the team leader he's lying. Tell him he must tell me the truth."

At first, the team leader remained adamant that he was telling the truth, however, I asked Somsit to once more explain how the team had actually brought me the proof that they in fact had not been on a north–south river.

Somsit said to the team leader, "Here look at your map. Now, look at the river where you say you took the photos. This river runs from north to south."

Somsit pointed to a place on the map next to the river, "You say you were here and the time of the photograph was in the afternoon. The sun sets in the west, so if you are telling the truth then the shadows in the photograph must be this way."

I handed Somsit the photograph and he placed it on the map and positioned it so that the river ran north to south and so the shadows would be made from a sun setting in the west.

Somsit said, "Look the shadows in your photograph are not correct if you took this photo where you say you did. In fact, the shadows in the photograph can only be as they are if the river was really running east to west."

Faced with the evidence they had provided themselves and now understanding that I would not be convinced otherwise, the true story finally came out. They had taken the photographs in a safe area using their friends and a local boat. It would not have been in my long-term interest to refuse to pay them anything at all so I decided not to pay them for a portion of the mission thus reducing their total mission pay. There were a number of instances such as this where, between the Thai operations assistants and me, we established that teams had not done what they said.

Team intelligence operations was a popular form of employment instead of battalion combat operations, even though it was well known among the population of Lao irregulars that their work would be closely monitored and validated. Working in an irregular battalion meant you were going to get into combat with the North Vietnamese Army while working in my team operations meant you were supposed to avoid combat with the North Vietnamese Army unless you had numeric superiority and the element of surprise. You ate well while in base camp and you received drop bundles by parachute every ten days or so that were well packed with a variety of items. By the time the team intelligence operations base camp was located at PS-18 the irregular battalions were receiving rations of rice, a vegetable and meat. Unfortunately, meat and vegetables were subject to spoiling in the tropical heat and lack of refrigeration. At PS-18, the team intelligence operations base camp commander, Sergeant Vouk, received a monthly allowance from me to buy rice, vegetables, chickens, pigs, salt, spices and whatever else he needed. Since he bought live animals, the meat was always from freshly killed stock. Sergeant Vouk was wise with the money and was able to buy enough chickens and pigs that he began to raise new stock. Chickens produced eggs and when enough chickens had been grown, a few were killed for food. A pig could be kept long enough to fatten up for a special feast. Sergeant Vouk also bought a variety of vegetables while the food buyers for the battalions bought one vegetable in bulk. Since he was honest and not out to make money from the food allowance he was able to budget his money and buy a variety of salt and spices so that different Lao dishes could be prepared. It was not lost on the Lao irregulars that our base camp was well run. We did the same for the drop bundles we parachuted to them. I instructed the Thai operations assistants to make sure the bundles included a variety of food, spices and other things to make life on mission a little more comfortable. Making life more comfortable for a Lao or Lao Theung tribesman was not that difficult, as they were not used to having too much anyway. The fact that we did make it so was what was important.

At the end of my tour in Laos, this cash on delivery program of encouraging the roadwatch and intelligence collection teams to capture or induce the defection of North Vietnamese Army soldiers was the most successful intelligence producer in MR-IV using special operations methods behind enemy lines. MACVSOG, at this time, was using either U.S. led indigenous teams or all-U.S. teams and did not successfully bring in many live prisoners. The best they could do was shoot an enemy soldier and hope he lived long enough to be interrogated.[29] To be fair, they were operating in a much more hostile environment, however, I doubt the U.S. military could have ever been convinced that all-indigenous teams would ever be successful on their own. Moreover, the teams formulated their own plans for the capture of the North Vietnamese Army soldiers. I was not able to provide any close control of what they were doing. The first I knew of what they were doing was when they came back with a prisoner and I debriefed them on how they did it. I made sure that

---

[29] Barry Lando, *The Secret War of SOG*, Washington Post, August 12, 1973 quoting an Army Special Forces officer, "For years we agonized over ways to take prisoners without losing them or bringing everything down on top of us. We'd wind up using a pistol or a grease gun with a silencer, aim for some non-vital part, and hope the guy wouldn't die before we got him out."

each new story of a successful capture or defection was added to the others and told to all the team leaders by my operations assistants. I do not believe that any American led or all-American units ever captured or induced the defections of this many North Vietnamese Army soldiers during the Vietnam War. This was a significant achievement by all-surrogate indigenous units.

DEATH OF A
NORTH VIETNAMESE ARMY
POLITICAL OFFICER

———◆◆◆———

"You can't always get what you want, but if you try sometimes
you just might find you get what you need."

–Mick Jagger and Keith Richards, "You Can't Always Get What
You Want", from the Rolling Stones' 1969 album "Let It Bleed."
The unofficial anthem of intelligence collectors.

T he Cash on Delivery program was working well. I was pushing the good team leaders to try snatch operations and I was using it as method for weeding out bad team leaders or giving them the opportunity to redeem themselves.

I had inherited one particular team leader from the LS-171 roadwatch program whose missions troubled me. I was convinced that he was a fabricator who did not go anywhere near enemy territory on his missions. I took special interest in his debriefing when he returned from his next mission. He had accomplished little and had taken an excessive amount of time going out to the target area and even more time returning to base camp during the mission. After the debriefing was completed, I decided that I could not totally satisfy myself that he was fabricating even though he had established a habit of working missions that accomplished nothing and took a long time to complete.

I did not want to keep sending him out on roadwatch missions if he was fabricating, as it would be a bad example to the other team leaders. The men in the roadwatch project would know sooner than I would what he was really doing. I decided I needed to run him on a mission I could validate. I told him I was terminating him as a regular team leader and he would not be able to go on any more roadwatch missions but if he wanted to try to capture a North Vietnamese Army soldier I would let him go on that mission.

"You will be reinstated as a team leader if you capture a North Vietnamese Army soldier", I told him.

Thinking he was going to be able to bamboozle me one last time, he said he would try.

I told him, "I will only give you hand grenades, .45 caliber pistols, maps and two radios."

Further, I said, "I will only make re-supply drops to you if you mark your position by flashing a mirror at the drop aircraft. The re-supply drop positions have to be in enemy territory."

I continued, "There will be no re-supply drops while you are in friendly territory. You will have to obtain food from the local villagers. You will get no mission pay unless you capture a North Vietnamese Army soldier. If you do capture an enemy soldier you will get the mission pay plus the reward for the captured soldier."

He was unhappy to hear this and tried to negotiate with me to give him some money for buying food, or better weapons, or to make re-supply drops in friendly territory. I refused to change the terms of his mission and he finally agreed to go on the mission. I told Hom that I did not think he was going to be successful but the cost of pistols, hand grenades and radios was not much. I was willing to risk them against the chance he might be successful.

As the days passed while he was supposedly walking through friendly territory on his way into enemy held territory his rate of speed was very slow. He kept making excuses for why it was taking so long and then asking for re-supply. Every time one of my operations assistants came back from air-ground radio contact with the teams, they would tell me his latest excuses and request for re-supply.

I told them to tell him, "No re-supply."

This went on for so long I was getting quite annoyed. I could not believe this team leader thought he was some how going to convince me to change my mind. I prided myself on being a no-nonsense case officer who could not be easily deceived.

After going through two months of this, I finally told the operations assistants. "Tell him he is terminated."

In the past, a terminated team might be able to recoup some money by not turning in their weapons and other equipment and then selling it all. With only hand grenades, pistols and radios, the team leader was not going to get much from their sale. I figured I had heard the last from this team leader.

Nevertheless, Somneuk, the Thai operations assistant doing air-grounds one day, came back quite excited.

He said, "The team reported they have killed a North Vietnamese Army soldier. They have some important documents to give you and you should send a helicopter to pick up the team."

I laughed, "Somneuk, I'm not a fool. This is just the team leader's way of tricking me into giving him an easy ride back to base camp."

Tell them, "Walk in and if the documents are worth something I'll pay them what they are worth to me."

Once again, I did not expect to hear anything more from this team leader.

About a week later, the team leader walked into the base camp. When my chief operations assistant, Hom, brought me the captured items he was carrying, I was flabbergasted. Hom was holding a Soviet Tokarev pistol and a military shoulder bag, stained with blood. In the shoulder bag were what appeared to be genuine North Vietnamese Army documents. I had learned in my time in Laos that my teams had absolutely no ability to obtain something like a Tokarev, a North Vietnamese Army officer's sidearm, without having done something like seize it from that officer. There was also no way that one of my teams could come up with one North Vietnamese Army document no less a whole shoulder bag of them. I could not believe it. I grabbed Hom and began to debrief the team leader myself using Hom as my interpreter.

While the team leader would not admit it, I became increasingly convinced that he had undertaken the mission with the intention of trying to deceive me. As the weeks had gone by and none of his ploys or deceptions produced any re-supply, he had become increasingly depressed and his team members were becoming progressively unhappy. When he was informed that he was terminated and should make his way back to base camp on foot he was really upset. He and his team passed through a village west of Saravane, a Lao city our CIA irregular forces had recaptured from the North Vietnamese Army and were trying to hold. The team's normal practice was to try to panhandle food from the villagers. Lao villagers tended to be friendly to other Lao peasants. My teams dressed like peasants in civilian clothing and usually hid such things as pistols, hand grenades, maps and radios before approaching local villagers. While schmoozing the villagers for food, they would also inquire about North Vietnamese Army and Pathet Lao troops in the area. Such queries were normal. The typical Lao citizen, traveling overland, did not want to stumble into North Vietnamese Army or Pathet Lao soldiers. They did not want to be near an enemy camp that might be bombed. If the North Vietnamese met able-bodied men while they had supplies, they might try to dragoon the men into porter duty. Local villagers were sympathetic to fellow Lao who did not want to run into the enemy.

The team learned that five North Vietnamese Army soldiers were in the village during the course of obtaining some food and drink and inquiring about enemy presence in the area. One of the enemy soldiers was in the hut of a local woman. This North Vietnamese Army soldier traveled through the village on a regular basis. He had arranged an accommodation with this woman. It was known in the village that he obtained sexual favors from her when he visited the village. The other four North Vietnamese Army soldiers, his bodyguards, were down at the nearby stream washing. After hearing this information, the team leader and the team members conferred and decided that they had stumbled on to a chance to capture a North Vietnamese Army soldier just as the "Nai Kou" was always encouraging them to do. They had not had the discipline to try to plot out how to do this on purpose but now that the opportunity was at hand, they decided to take the risk and try. They were able to sneak up close to the hut where the North Vietnamese Army soldier and the local woman were conducting their sexual tryst. They waited outside. When the enemy soldier came out of the hut, they tried to overwhelm him. A fight ensued and he fought them as best he could. In the course of the fight, the team leader seized the soldier's pistol while the soldier began shouting to his four men for help. The team leader did not speak or understand Vietnamese but now during his debriefing he reported that he could deduce what was going to happen. The North Vietnamese Army soldier shouted, his men grabbed their weapons and ran toward him firing in the air to frighten the men trying to abduct their leader. My team leader panicked and decided to flee. He turned the North Vietnamese Army soldier's pistol on him and shot him dead. He then removed the shoulder bag from the dead body and with his men ran away from the village and the four would be North Vietnamese Army rescuers.

The team then successfully escaped the village without any casualties and hid themselves until the air–ground aircraft flew over them and they reported their success and requested helicopter exfiltration. They were extremely chagrined when they were told that they had to walk to base camp and that no helicopter would be sent for them. Since they had no other alternative and they thought they might be paid for the pistol and the documents, they walked.

I could not believe it. I had one Lao operations assistant who was ethnic Vietnamese and could read, write and speak Vietnamese. I called for him and started going over the documents. It became readily apparent they were genuine and needed to be fully translated as soon as possible. Eventually it turned out that the dead North Vietnamese Army soldier had been a battalion political officer, the equivalent of a lieutenant colonel. He was making his rounds from unit to unit to gather the communist party members in each unit to brief them on the impending plans to attack and retake Saravane. The documents included the complete written plan for the attack and hand drawn maps. We knew it was accurate because the North Vietnamese Army had attacked and retaken Saravane a few days before just as outlined in the documents. If I had ordered a helicopter exfiltration, we would have had the plans before the attack. That is not to say we would have been able to defeat the North Vietnamese Army but an intelligence officer dreams of obtaining the enemy's plans before they are carried out. An intelligence officer cannot make the field commander's decisions but he can provide the field command-er with the necessary intelligence to make a good decision if that commander is capable of it.

It turned out that the documents provided a small amount of additional information of intelligence value and that was something to take away the sting of failure. Hindsight being more accurate than foresight, I wish I would have had some reason to go ahead and run a helicopter exfiltration of that team. I was very caught up in validation and did not spend much time considering whether there was any chance the team had what it clamed to have. The team leader had such a bad record of trying to skate by I like to think no one else would have believed him either. I took some solace in the Tokarev pistol. It was in good condition and even had bloodstains on the grip. It would make a fascinating war souvenir, especially with the story that would explain my possession of it. I held on to it until the end of my tour and then I took it to Udorn to my friend, Ken. He knew a U.S. Air Force field grade officer who was returning home about the same time I was. Ken said this officer was a good guy. He would ask him to take it home for me and I could reclaim it once the officer and I were both stateside. As civilians, CIA personnel could not get a war souvenir through U.S. Customs, but U.S. military personnel could. It seemed the only way to get the Tokarev home so I gave it to Ken to give to the officer. I never saw the pistol again, so much for the myth of "officers and gentlemen." This certainly did nothing for the reputation of Air Force officers, or at least for this particular "officer." This bit of thievery might even tend to sour one's outlook on all Air Force officers, but not for me. In my experience, any CIA officer who served in Laos knew the bravery and dedication of the Air Force officers who flew as Raven forward air controllers and all the other rotary and fixed wing combat pilots. The fact this particular thief was serving in Udorn meant he was probably just another sorry, no-account REMF (rear echelon mother f----r).

THE NORTH VIETNAMESE ARMY'S MOLE

"There is one evil that I dread, & that is their Spies...I think it a matter of some importance to prevent them from obtaining Intelligence of our Situation."

–George Washington in 1775; cited in Andrew,
For the President's Eyes Only (1995).

The CIA's objectives in Laos were primarily conducting combat operations and collecting intelligence. An often forgotten requirement is to learn what the enemy is doing to collect information about our activities and us.

One day the chief of operations called me into his office. He told me, "Roger (the case officer running interrogation center operations) wants to take two weeks of annual leave. Can you take on his duties for him?"

I agreed and for the next two weeks I spent a lot of my time at the MR–IV Interrogation Center. I had an excellent crew of Thai operational assistants who had been around a long time and were experienced and dedicated to the work. I would be able to leave them on their own and just check on them from time to time. All of my roadwatch and other intelligence collection operations were running routinely and nothing out of the ordinary was scheduled for the two weeks. There was always the chance something unexpected would pop up but I felt I could deal with it, if it happened.

As I reviewed what was going on in the interrogation center I was briefed that a newly arrived North Vietnamese Army prisoner of war was not being cooperative. The prisoner of war's name was *Le Quang Nhi*, and to be honest, I do not remember the details of his capture; I think a regular FAR unit had brought him in. While the U.S. military has a long history of not cooperating with the enemy when captured and only giving name, rank and serial number, our experience with the North Vietnamese Army was that many would talk without reservation after capture. To be sure, from time to time a hardcore communist was captured and would not talk but that was more rare than common. Despite what many anti-CIA people may want to think, we did not torture or beat prisoners. I cannot say that our liaison counterparts did not torture or beat prisoners when we were not around to prevent it, but I do not know of any CIA officer in Laos who ever participated in or allowed the mistreatment of enemy prisoners. I felt it was crude and unnecessary. North Vietnamese Army soldiers were either going to be hard-core and never talk or they would eventually cooperate, all you had to do was enough to determine if the prisoner was truly adamant against cooperation or not. When I learned we had an uncooperative prisoner, I decided I would see what I could do to get him to cooperate.

I brought in Hom, one of my top three Thai operations assistants, and asked him to conduct additional interviews of the prisoner named *Le Quang Nhi*. I wrote out a series of questions designed to uncover the prisoner's area of expertise and gave them to Hom. I told him, "Hom, go into the interrogation room and use my list of questions to see what you can get from the prisoner."

Hom was intelligent and clever and I knew he would improvise from the list of questions if need be. Hom tried for two days to get *Nhi* to cooperate, but we were getting no where when Hom mentioned to me that he had noticed that the prisoner was very clean and was fastidious about staying clean. Hom thought the enemy soldier might be obsessed with cleanliness. We were keeping the prisoner in a cell by himself where we fed him three meals a day and provided him with a bucket to relieve himself and soap and water for bathing. Whenever he used the bucket he could call for the guard, it was removed, and a fresh bucket sent in to the cell to replace it. He was able to wash himself after using it and get fresh water. Hom and I discussed how we would make it difficult for *Nhi* to maintain his cleanliness.

We decided that Hom would tell *Nhi* at the next session that *Nhi* was not being cooperative and therefore the interrogation center commander was probably going to order that *Nhi*'s privileges be reduced. *Nhi* asked what that meant and Hom replied, "To begin with you will no longer get to wash yourself more than once per day. The bucket will only be removed once per day. If your cooperation does not improve, further reductions in privileges will have to be made."

Hom told *Nhi*, "Think this over and decide if you will cooperate more fully answering my questions."

We left him alone for twenty four hours and then Hom visited him again. Hom told him, "All you have to do is cooperate and answer all questions truthfully and your privileges will not be reduced."

Remarkably, the prisoner told Hom he would cooperate. The threat to remove some of his privileges had encouraged him to cooperate fully.

Once we had his cooperation, I began to work with Hom providing questions to ask the prisoner. We always insured that North Vietnamese Army prisoners never saw Americans in the interrogation center. Eventually, we sent all prisoners to a POW camp near Vientiane and from time to time, the international media were allowed to meet with them and ask questions. We did not want them to be able to tell the reporters they had seen or been interrogated by Americans. Thus, Hom conducted the interrogation and I stayed in another room where I could not be seen. As the interrogation progressed and *Le Quang Nhi*'s information was passed on to me I had to leave the interrogation center and return to the Pakse Unit office to try to research his information and write up reports to be cabled to Vientiane Station and Udorn Base or eventually back to CIA headquarters in Washington.

Le Quang Nhi was a fluent Lao speaker. He had been born in Laos prior to 1962 and then moved with his family back to North Vietnam because of the 1962 Geneva Accords. Vietnamese born in Laos lived in Vietnamese enclaves but often learned Lao as a second language because the majority around them spoke Lao. When the war in South Vietnam heated up in 1965, with the introduction of major U.S. ground forces and the North Vietnamese Army wanted to expand its logistical network into Laos, they used ethnic North Vietnamese who spoke Lao to work in Laos. It was never clear to me at the time whether *Le Quang Nhi* was a member of the North Vietnamese Army military intelligence apparatus or just subordinated to it because of his Lao language skill. In any case, he worked with intelligence operators a good bit of the time. I also had the impression he was neither a hard-core communist nor a model soldier. It may have been this lack of a stellar character and record that kept him from being inducted fully into an intelligence unit but his Lao language ability made it necessary for them to use him on both logistical and intelligence activities. As his cooperation with us continued, it became apparent that he had been working in a commo liaison station that was part of a binh tram operating in the jungles south of the Bolovens Plateau.

The North Vietnamese Army logistical system, known as the Ho Chi Minh Trail, consisted of a series of consecutive logistical units named binh trams. In southern Laos in the vicinity of the Bolovens Plateau, we had identified Binh Tram 35 and Binh Tram 38. A binh tram was responsible for the logistical activity in a 50 to 75 kilometer long section of the Ho Chi Minh Trail. Within the binh tram, there were commo liaison stations. North Vietnamese Army soldiers permanently assigned to the binh tram area lived in these locations and carried out their duties from them. The soldiers assigned to a commo liaison station remained in place to provide support to the movement of personnel, soldiers or cadre, and to support communications, sometimes in the form of moving official dispatches and correspondence up and down the trail system. We came to understand that in some cases the cadre that moved along the trail might be communist officials on their way to or from Hanoi or special commando units infiltrating covertly from North Vietnam to, for example, Thailand to attack U.S. B–52 bases, or intelligence agents going to or returning from assignments. The binh tram area had to be secured and patrolled, the roads had to be camouflaged or repaired, cargo transporters and reinforcement troops on their way south had to be guided from one binh tram to the next, communications personnel operated radios and field telephones for coordinating activities within the binh tram and for sending reports on to Hanoi. These and a variety of other duties had to be carried out.

Le Quang Nhi, because he spoke Lao, was often assigned to go to Lao villages in the area seeking to buy supplies from the villagers, for example, rice. He also was assigned to guide special travelers moving along the Trail. He told us that one of his assignments was to guide and escort a high–ranking Malaysian communist official and his family who were walking from Malaysia to Hanoi so the official could attend several years of study in Hanoi. Another of his assignments had been to guide a "dac cong" unit on its way to Thailand.

North Vietnamese Army dac cong, also known as sappers, were commandos, what we call special operations, especially trained to covertly infiltrate and attack their targets. He also met the unit when it returned from Thailand and learned it had attacked a U.S. B-52 airbase. The timing of this event indicated the dac cong unit may have attacked Utapao air base near Bangkok. The commandos had been sent from Hanoi especially for this assignment and had passed through *Le Quang Nhi*'s unit on the way to the attack and on the way back. I wrote an intelligence report from his information describing the sapper unit, its weapons and equipment and that it had traveled from North Vietnam to carry out a mission in Thailand.

The information *Le Quang Nhi* was providing was fascinating. I had no idea the North Vietnamese Army was capable of having dac cong sappers walk from Hanoi to Thailand for an attack. Can you imagine the looks on the faces of American military men, even elite ones, if their commander told them they had to spend months walking through the jungle just to get to the target and when they were done, they would be walking back? I do not intend to demean the courage and bravery of our American special operations units but it is just a very different mentality. I was confronted with the need to stop thinking of the North Vietnamese Army in American terms, these were people who could plan months and years in advance just for a commando raid. *Le Quang Nhi*'s interrogation quickly introduced me to this new way of thinking.

Le Quang Nhi also told us that the Neo Lao Hak Sat (NLHS), which we considered the political arm of the communist Lao movement, was in fact a front for the North Vietnamese Lao Dong communist party, which was the actual power in communist Laos. *Le Quang Nhi* said that most high-ranking NLHS officials were in reality ethnic Vietnamese, members of the Lao Dong party and Vietnamese intelligence operatives. These men had been sent into Laos as far back as the late 1940s and 1950s to take Lao wives, start families and live in Laos until all of Indochina was united under North Vietnamese communism. They worked themselves up into Lao communist party district and provincial level positions. Most, if not all, of the Lao communist party members did not remember that these men were ethnic Vietnamese. Over the years, they had used the Neo Lao Hak Sat as a front. He also said that the North Vietnamese Army had infiltrated every Military Region in Laos by sending false defectors to each interrogation center. These false defectors had wormed their way into becoming trusted employees in each Military Region. The Lao military commanders considered them valuable sources on the North Vietnamese Army.

As I began to digest Le Quang Nhi's information, I began to wonder about our region, Military Region IV. I knew there was a former North Vietnamese Army officer who was the special advisor to General Phasouk Somly, the Forces Armée du Royaume (FAR) commander of MR-IV. The North Vietnamese Army defector spoke Lao and Vietnamese fluently and was usually around Gen. Phasouk and aware of everything going on in the military region. I delved into the Pakse Unit's records and found some information about him and then I wrote a cable back to CIA headquarters asking for a complete background on him. When I had all the information assembled, I asked the chief of operations if I could interview the former North Vietnamese Army defector working at the interrogation center. I framed my request for the interview as a request for me to learn more about the North Vietnamese Army from a former North Vietnamese Army soldier. In my first interview with him, I asked him to describe where he was before he defected and what he had been doing. This was my first area of interest because when I read what he had told the interrogator when he defected I did not recognize anything. The North Vietnamese Army order of battle he had reported was very obscure and nothing else that he had said was confirmed in anything we had learned about the North Vietnamese Army since his defection. To my surprise he told me a different story, very little of what he said now correlated with what he had said back when he defected. I did not let on that I was becoming very suspicious of him and I ended the interview cordially. I went back to the chief of operations and reported what I had learned. He was not very interested but did not discourage me. I said I was going to do more research and then another interview.

I took a trip to Udorn and consulted with the Udorn Base order of battle shop, especially our MR-IV expert Al. I also talked to Mitch, our signals intelligence analyst. I gathered as much information about order of battle in MR-IV as I could and returned to Pakse. I also reviewed with *Le Quang Nhi* what he knew about life in the jungle because he had lived in the same area as the defector, not quite overlapping each other. When I conducted the second interview, I concentrated on what it was like living in the jungle before his defection. Nothing that he told me rang true. It occurred to me that two things had happened since his defection. He never expected to be re-interrogated on the facts of his defection and had forgotten what he had told his original interrogator. Second, he had wholly fabricated what he told the interrogator, which held up at the time because we did not have much solid intelligence about the North Vietnamese Army. Over the years, however, the CIA and U.S. military intelligence had brought a variety of technical intelligence collection methodologies to bear on the North Vietnamese Army and had coordinated the dissemination of intelligence from captured documents and prisoner and rallier debriefings. We knew a lot more about the North Vietnamese Army and his choice to fabricate was now working against him. I remember hearing in a training course that if you are going to lie to cover yourself, tell as much of the truth as you can and lie only about certain key elements of your story. Now, his failure to do that trapped the defector. He had woven a wide and extensive web of lies.

I was now sure that, as *Le Quang Nhi* had told us, this was a North Vietnamese Army penetration of MR-IV, and he had done an excellent job of placing himself in the best possible position to be valuable to his North Vietnamese Army handlers. Of course, our lack of understanding of the sophistication and dedication of North Vietnamese Army intelligence and our lack of knowledge of the North Vietnamese Army contributed to our inability to evaluate his story. However, I was sure we had found him out and I wrote up an extensive report of what I had found and why I believed I had uncovered a North Vietnamese Army mole. Nothing was ever done about it. Who knows? Perhaps the stodgy traditional intelligence collectors in Vientiane Station could not believe that a special operations knuckle dragger could interview, analyze and uncover a mole. Maybe, no one in Vientiane thought a

North Vietnamese Army penetration of MR–IV headquarters was very important. Perhaps, as is often the case, counterintelligence was given short shrift. Or, maybe it was easier to ignore the whole thing and not let anyone be embarrassed by acknowledging that what was believed to be a third rate intelligence service had pulled the wool over our eyes for so long. Sometimes I wonder if retired North Vietnamese Army intelligence officers sit around drinking beer or rice wine or whatever and telling stories about how they ran circles around American intelligence. My only comfort is that they did not fool all of us, just the ones that mattered – the so–called "management."

As the months went by *Le Quang Nhi* became more and more cooperative and helpful. If I did not know that there was already one penetration of the interrogation center and if *Le Quang Nhi* had not helped us do some serious damage to the North Vietnamese Army, I might have to admit he was following a similar path worming his way into our operations. I took him into my roadwatch/intelligence operations to make use of his Vietnamese language ability and his knowledge of the North Vietnamese Army. I used him to help train my teams on what to expect from the North Vietnamese Army and how to avoid them. When I took over all responsibility for signals intelligence operations, I used him to help us translate decrypted messages. When we needed to draft a recruitment pitch letter, he helped us make sure we worded it properly. I am sure he was eventually very disappointed when communism triumphed in Indochina and I hope he made it to Thailand before the end.

OUR NORTH VIETNAMESE ARMY SPY

"I have found that good fishermen tend to make good intelligence officers. The fisherman's preparation for the catch, his consideration of the weather, the light, the currents, the depth of the water, the right bait or fly to use, the time of day to fish, the spot he chooses and the patience he shows are all part of the art and essential to success."

-Former DCI Allen Dulles, "The Craft of Intelligence" (1963).

C ombat operations in a war zone do not often provide the opportunity to contact an enemy soldier and recruit him to remain in place and send reports. Making contact and then setting up a method of sending reports are almost impossible. Thus, such a recruitment is an extraordinary achievement.

During the history of American participation in the war in Laos there were many North Vietnamese Army soldiers captured by Royal Lao Government regular and irregular military units, most of them often dazed or wounded on the battlefield. Such North Vietnamese Army prisoners of war were turned over to the Royal Lao Government interrogation center in the military region in which they were captured. The interrogation center in MR IV was a Forces Armée du Royaume operation under the command of the MR-IV Command- ing General, Phasouk Somly. However, CIA had a lot of influence over it because we provided significant funding to it. Since we provided most of the money, the Lao government allowed us to have a case officer working in the interrogation center. Lao military and political leaders were touchy about letting us appear to be running anything in Laos and always tried to insert Lao officers or officials into things so as to appear to run them. Many such FAR officers were mainly interested in how they could bleed off as much money for themselves as possible. They also did not tend to persist in their interest unless there was a lot of money involved. The case officers working with irregular battalions and later regiments had to endure persistent efforts by corrupt Lao officers because there were many ways to siphon off money. In my case, I did not have such problems. There was a FAR sergeant, a Lao Theung from the LS-171 area, assigned to be the de facto regular Lao military official working with the irregular intelligence teams, but he was not the type to try to steal money. Additionally, I kept an iron fist on the money I had to finance the operations I was responsible for running.

The CIA case officer in the interrogation center had to deal with FAR interference but he still could get a lot done. From the very first of the North Vietnamese Army soldiers my teams captured I consistently instructed the teams to blindfold the prisoner before they brought him to the helicopter exfiltration site so he would not see the helicopter or the crew. If possible, Grey Fox, our air operations officer, would send Thai crewed Air America helicopters to pick up North Vietnamese Army prisoners but they were not always available. The prisoner had to remain blindfolded all the way to the interrogation center so he would not see any of the Americans at Pakse airfield. Our hope was that he would only see the team members and the personnel at the interrogation center. My relationship to a North Vietnamese Army prisoner ended when we turned him over for interrogation. However, there was one particular case where I became involved again.

The first North Vietnamese Army soldier ever captured behind enemy lines by Lao irregular intelligence teams was *Trinh Dinh Thu. Thu* actually defected via Team Lime in November 1970 and as a defector, he proved to be very cooperative with the Lao authorities. The interrogation center case officer employed him to help by providing his knowledge of the North Vietnamese Army and acting as an interpreter between Lao interrogators and Vietnamese prisoners. Eventually he made it known to the case officer that there were North Vietnamese Army soldiers who would defect to us if they had the opportunity. He knew of one in particular, a friend of his, he thought would defect. He said that the two of them often sat and talked of deserting the war and fleeing to Laos. Both he and his friend were ethnic Vietnamese who had been born in Laos before its partition in 1962. At that time, a large number of these Vietnamese left Laos and moved to North Vietnam. Since most of them spoke fluent Lao, the North Vietnamese Army assigned them to duties that involved being able to speak Lao. In their case, *Trinh Dinh Thu* and *Phan Van Hoi* were assigned to a unit that traveled from village to village procuring food for the North Vietnamese Army. Because *Phan Van Hoi* had mechanic skills, he and *Trinh Dinh Thu* dreamed of buying a cyclo (a 3-wheeled vehicle often used as a taxi) and starting a taxi business. *Trinh Dinh Thu* wanted to be the driver and *Phan Van Hoi* wanted to be the mechanic.

Based on this information, the interrogation center case officer, Roger, came to me to propose we run a joint operation to try to recruit *Phan Van Hoi*. He and I discussed the proposal in detail and decided to use one of my teams to deliver a recruitment pitch letter to *Phan Van Hoi*. We would use Team Pomelo, whose team leader was Thao Ouy. Thao Ouy had been primary informant for Team Lime, the team that had brought in *Trinh Dinh Thu*. It became obvious to me that Thao Ouy had the intelligence to become a team leader and I encouraged him to come to Team 300 headquarters. When he did, I recruited him to join Team 300 to be a team leader. Thao Ouy had all the contacts necessary in the area where *Thu* and *Hoi* had served together and would be able to deliver the letter to *Hoi*.

We spent many hours in discussion with *Thu* to devise a letter that would convince *Hoi* it was from his friend *Thu*. The letter also needed to convince *Hoi* he could safely join *Thu* in Laos to pursue their capitalist dream. The final element of the letter was a proposal that *Hoi* not defect right away but rather that he remain in place and report North Vietnamese Army activities to Team Pomelo for at least six months. During that time, he would earn money for his reporting that would enable *Thu* and *Hoi* to buy their taxi. First, we drafted the letter in English. Next, I had it translated into Vietnamese for *Thu* to write in his own hand. *Thu* aided the activity with suggestions to make the Vietnamese seem as authentic as possible. I was familiar with the problems of directly translating one language into another and I insisted that my Thai operations assistants work with *Thu* to turn English phrases and word order into the way a true Vietnamese speaker would write. Once we had the letter ready and the team briefed for the mission we only needed Vientiane Station permission to launch the team on the mission.

Usually irregular intelligence teams conducted action operations or collected information by observation or talking to villagers and peasants. Such activity was well beneath the notice of the traditional case officers in Vientiane who believed their operations tended to be more in tune with the tradecraft of Paris or Berlin than with the knuckle draggers running up-country special operations. We were about to show them up, however, as they had never been able to recruit a North Vietnamese and run him in place. We firmly believed they were either a bit jealous or totally incapable of believing we could recruit a North Vietnamese Army agent in place because from the first cable to Vientiane proposing our operation they did nothing but get in the way. Their questions and comments clearly showed they had no idea how to run special operations behind enemy lines. Moreover, they tried to hold our operation up to the measure of a traditional operation - apples and oranges, really. We wanted to get on with it and they wanted to dither over meaningless details, but that is usually how it was as special operations usually attracts an aggressive can-do type of case officer.

We had no idea why our chief of operations, Ray's successor, decided to toady to them but he did. We had one or two false starts. We would be down at the Pakse airfield (L-11) thinking we had the go ahead and getting ready to put the team on the helicopter when the air operations officer would tell us to stand down. Each time we had to stand the team down and go in to the office to write a cable to answer some new silly question from Vientiane. Finally, we actually had the team on the helicopter with the rotors turning when the deputy chief of operations came roaring up to the helicopters in a jeep to tell us we had to stand down once again. I was very angry because it was just not good practice to put a team on a helicopter ready to go and then pull them off and have them hang around for days wondering when they might actually go. Roger, the interrogation center case officer, was livid. The deputy chief of operations had to threaten us to get us to return, as he realized we were intent on just ignoring him and sending the team off. Roger and I jumped into a jeep and drove to the office ready to do battle over this meddling. The discussion between Roger and the chief of operations quickly deteriorated into a shouting match. The chief of operations turned it into an issue of being disrespectful with Roger countering by telling him he was not being respectful to Roger. When the heat died down, we wound up writing one more cable answering Vientiane's simpering questions.

Finally, with all questions and issues resolved, we received Vientiane's approval to proceed and we infiltrated Team Pomelo. The team moved into the target area and made contact with their informants. They told their informants they wanted to locate a particular North Vietnamese Army soldier and described him. Eventually one informant told the team he had located *Phan Van Hoi* and the team leader decided to give the letter to the informant to deliver to *Hoi*. The team reported all of these developments via encrypted Morse code messages back to me. I spent several days waiting for something to happen while the informant had the letter and waited for *Hoi* to reappear in the village. When *Hoi* did arrive in the village, the informant gave him the letter. After reading the letter, *Hoi* asked the informant to take him to the team leader. Since *Hoi* spoke Lao, there was no communication problem. After some discussion, *Hoi* agreed to remain in place and report to the team. When this message came in I shared it with Roger and we were ecstatic. We had done it. We had a North Vietnamese Army soldier recruited in place to report to us via Team Pomelo. We would have given the Vientiane case officers the bird if they had been available to see it.

Our glory was short lived, however. Within a few days of getting *Hoi*'s agreement, *Hoi* appeared at the team's location and told them he had to get out immediately. He said that North Vietnamese Army soldiers had come to his unit looking for him and he was afraid they wanted to arrest him. He believed he had been compromised and would not stay any longer. He wanted the team to take him out of the war zone. We were suspicious that *Hoi* had gotten cold feet and just wanted to get out. During the debriefing of the team, however, my operations assistants determined that the team had been very lax in talking to the villagers and had told them that they had persuaded an enemy soldier to report North Vietnamese Army activities to them. The Thai operations assistants were convinced that the word had gotten around the village and a villager who wanted to curry favor with the North Vietnamese Army had turned informant and betrayed *Hoi*.

Once *Hoi* was safely in Pakse, we interviewed him in the Royal Lao Government's MR–IV interrogation center. I had been the primary case officer for the infiltration of the team into the area where *Hoi* was located and had been responsible for everything until we delivered *Hoi* to the interrogation center.

Roger, as the case officer assigned to manage the interrogation center, was now responsible for debriefing *Hoi*. The interrogation center was a Royal Lao Government facility operated by the Lao army, however, since the CIA provided all the money and equipment to run it we had some say in what went on there and Pakse Unit assigned a case officer to be in liaison with it. Having learned the value of centralized facilities for the exploitation of captured documents and the interrogation of prisoners or debriefing of defectors in Vietnam, the CIA sponsored such facilities in all the military regions of Laos. Roger and I got along well and while he was the primary case officer, I was involved in helping him with *Hoi*'s debriefing. As the debriefing of *Hoi* proceeded, we learned that *Hoi* was actually a communist party member. That meant that he attended meetings in his unit conducted by party cadre. The non-party soldiers were generally excluded from such meetings. *Hoi* told us that it was the practice of the North Vietnamese Army, prior to the commencement of any major offensive, to have communist party political officers hold meetings with the party members of all units to brief them on the extent and purpose of the upcoming offensive. Thus, *Hoi* had attended such a meeting where the upcoming 1972 Easter offensive was discussed.

Roger and I immediately understood the importance of this intelligence. There was a lot of speculation about an Easter offensive but the main requirement was to determine whether it would be an all-out offensive designed to hit and withdraw, as Tet 1968 had been, or would it be designed to take and hold specific territory, and if the latter, which location or locations would be the targets? *Hoi* told us that his unit's party members had been briefed that the 1972 Easter offensive was to be an all out effort to seize and hold the former imperial capital, Hue, in Quang Tri province. We did our best to compose the report, titled "Offensive in Quang Tri", and cabled it off to Vientiane for review and further dissemination to CIA headquarters. *Hoi* arrived in the interrogation center in January 1972 and the Easter offensive did not kick off until 30 March 1972. I departed Laos in early February 1972 believing we had scored an intelligence coup. We had filed an intelligence report describing what the enemy intended to do well before the date of the event.

W. R. Baker, a military intelligence analyst assigned to the 525th Military Intelligence Group in Danang, has written in the "Military Intelligence Professional Bulletin:"

"Like the Battle of the Bulge, the 1972 Easter Offensive in Vietnam has often been referred to as an 'intelligence failure,' mainly because it caught the United States and South Vietnam completely by surprise. A look beneath the surface, however, reveals that U.S. and South Vietnamese combat commanders were aware of significant changes in the posture of the North Vietnamese Army (NVA) and had access to many indicators of an impending NVA offensive."[30]

"The Easter Offensive caught the Allies by complete surprise needlessly so. While the indicators of attack were numerous, U.S. and South Vietnamese commanders ignored them in favor of a more reassuring position: that the NVA could not and would not attack before the end of March. Their failure to use HUMINT to the fullest extent possible also contributed to the Allied forces being caught off guard. The "intelligence failure" during the Easter Offensive was less a failure to collect intelligence than it was a failure to exploit obvious indicators."

Upon departing Laos, my wife and I took our time traveling from Vientiane to Bangkok to Athens, Greece where we spent a few days sightseeing. From Athens, we went on to Rome, Italy for a few more days. In Rome, we decided to cut our mini-vacation short and head on home since my wife was pregnant with our first child and she was not feeling up to any more sightseeing. Back in the U.S., I took home leave and was still not back to work by Easter time. Watching the news on television and reading the newspapers, I heard the constant questions, prior to the beginning of the offensive, about what the North Vietnamese Army intentions were. I was confident our military commanders had been warned because of the report we had filed in February.

I reported in to CIA headquarters the week after Easter and was eager to find out how valuable our report had been. I asked in Special Operations

---

[30] Lewis Sorley, *Vietnam Chronicles: The Abrams Tapes 1968-1972*, Texas Tech University Press, 2004, for information about how much MACV knew about the impending offensive .

Division and no one knew anything about it. They suggested I go visit the Lao Desk and ask them. I took that advice and visited the Lao Desk but no one there had heard of the report either. Their suggestion was that I go visit the Vietnam Desk and ask them since the report dealt with an event that was to occur in Vietnam. I finally learned what had happened from the Vietnam Desk.

When our report had arrived there, since they were the "action desk" for reports dealing with Vietnam, they had decided not to disseminate the report to the intelligence community and thus, to MACV. The CIA commonly called this an "ND" for non-dissemination. Our report had been "ND'd" and I could not understand what had happened. The intelligence was important, it told MACV the precise target of the offensive and that the goal would be to take and hold Hue. The Vietnam desk officer sanctimoniously offered this explanation. "The report was from a defector and it is policy not to disseminate such a report unless the defector has been polygraphed." The Vietnam desk had ND'd the report - tossed it in the trash as worthless, because *Phan Van Hoi* had not passed a polygraph.

I was beside myself. I could not believe some lard-ass bureaucrat in Langley would just toss the report. Why wouldn't they publish the report with a qualifying comment that the source was not established as fully reliable? To this day, I have no idea what the answers to my questions are. However, if W.R. Baker's assertion of an intelligence failure in relation to the 1972 Easter offensive seems believable, then here is one factual anecdote indicating how such a thing could happen. The CIA had been in possession of a report detailing exactly what MACV needed to know and had tossed the report in the trash. Knowing now what happened during the offensive, the report was completely accurate.

Previously, the story of how *Phan Van Hoi* came to defect had not been fully told. My article in Studies in Intelligence, "*Cash on Delivery: How to Obtain North Vietnamese Soldiers for Intelligence in Laos*" included mention of *Hoi's* defection to Team Pomelo but not these details of his later activities on our behalf.

FIND, FIX AND DESTROY

—◆—

"On the battlefield of the future, enemy forces will be located, tracked and targeted almost instantaneously through the use of data–links, computer–assisted intelligence evaluation and automated fire control. With first–round kill probabilities approaching certainty, and with surveillance devices that can continuously track the enemy, the need for large forces to fix the opposition physically will be less important. I see battlefields that are under 24–hour real or near–real time surveillance of all types. I see battlefields on which we can destroy anything we can locate through instant communications and almost instantaneous application of highly lethal firepower."

–General William C. Westmoreland, U.S. Army Chief of Staff, speech to the Association of the U.S. Army, 14 October 1969

G en. Westmoreland's remarkably prescient statement was a little more than 30 years ahead of his time. Not that there were not other such activities, possibly as early as Gulf War I in the early 1990s, but special operations units in Afghanistan fulfilled his prophecy to the letter in the war in Afghanistan at the beginning in 2002.

At the beginning of the "Global War on Terrorism", which began in September 2001, the American military's subsequent actions in Afghanistan brought new publicity to the use of special operations in denied areas. The use of small teams consisting of Rangers, Seals, Delta Force or others of this type of specially trained soldier in conjunction with the U.S. Air Force and U.S. Navy's advanced smart bomb technology may turn out to be an advancement in warfare equivalent to the long bow, gunpowder, the machine gun, the tank or the airplane. The combination of global positioning systems, laser guidance, detailed maps, radar, J-Stars, and moving target indicators make the delivery of bombs by the United States Air Force and the United States Navy the most deadly and accurate ever.

During the "Secret War in Laos" CIA made good use of on-the-ground spotters who could direct U.S. Air Force forward air controllers to lucrative enemy targets, both troop concentrations and ammunition storage areas. When the enemy attacked our irregular guerrilla battalions trying to hold their positions, more often than not, our battalions had English-speaking officers who could talk to the Raven Forward Air Controllers (FAC). We also sent out large sized patrols to find the enemy. When these patrols were involved in firefights with the enemy, the Raven FACs, with English speaking backseaters, would show up and coordinate aerial bombardment of the enemy.

Early in my two-year assignment, I was looking for new and better ways to make use of the teams I was directing. I wanted valid intelligence we could use to take action against the enemy. Small teams of 3–6 men had established that they could travel into enemy controlled areas and make contact with the villagers to collect information. Sometimes the teams traveled to villages where they had relatives or friends. Other times they just took advantage of being able to get cooperation from local villagers because the villagers were Lao peasants, too. The Lao are a friendly people and have a tradition of providing aid and comfort to people traveling through their villages. I felt a team could go to villages in enemy controlled areas and develop sources of intelligence on the North Vietnamese Army's locations and activity. The sources might be witting of what they were doing or the teams might elicit information while the villagers remained unwitting of the team's true purposes.

The concept of operations was that once a team acquired intelligence about an enemy location it would have to go find the enemy location and then covertly move to a position where it could remain in observation of the location. The team might get their witting informant to take them to the vicinity of the enemy, or it might get directions from an unwitting informant. A team could tell the unwitting informant it wanted to know precisely where the enemy was so it could avoid them. The team then could go off and find the enemy location without the informant. The teams moved relatively freely through the denied area because it was in the interest of the North Vietnamese Army to allow traffic to and from their area to Royal Lao Government controlled areas.

The roadwatch teams had experience with intelligence collection missions but I needed a way to collect actionable intelligence. It was not enough to just collect information and let it molder without taking action on it. Eventually I came up with an idea based on using a quality team leader and mirror signaling devices. I had flown over the teams in a Porter while my operations assistants conducted air to ground radio contacts with them. I required that my operations assistants have the teams flash their mirrors at the air to ground Porter as frequently as the terrain and sunshine allowed. The operations assistants marked their 1:50,000 scale maps with the location of the mirror flashes and we recorded the map grid coordinates in our log of the teams' missions. Flying over the jungle, it was a revelation to me how easy it was to spot the mirror flash. It is one thing to "know" something should work and it is quite another to actually see it work. If a team flashed its mirror at the Porter it was a difficult, but not impossible, problem to plot the team location on the map. After all, you are looking at a rolling sea of green with few recognizable locations to use as references. My idea was that I wanted a team to go into an area and not just collect information on North Vietnamese Army activity, but also go and find the enemy locations. Up to this time, we just collected and compiled the information and passed it on to the irregular guerrilla forces but they did not usually act on it. The irregular guerrilla forces were usually located in base camps on the Bolovens Plateau. They would have had to load into helicopters and been flown out to attack the enemy. They were just not that type of military unit. Without a combat force to take action on the intelligence, it was going to waste.

I felt that I could use a team leader like Thao Sengchanh, team leader of Team Cranberry/316, to make use of the mirror signaling capability. Upon receiving information on an enemy location, I wanted them to recon the area to find the enemy and then secretly move into a position where they could observe them. I emphasized that they did not have to be close. It could be as far away as made them feel safe, but I wanted them to estimate the distance and use a compass to determine the azimuth, or compass direction, from their location to the enemy. Once a team was in such a position I would request that a Raven FAC fly over the team and contact them by air to ground very high frequency (VHF) radio. Ravens usually flew with a Lao speaking backseater who would talk to the team and then tell the Raven pilot what the team had reported.

The operation consisted of the team flashing its mirror at the Raven and then giving the Raven the compass azimuth from the team's location to the enemy and the team's estimate of the distance. The Raven, flying at tree top level as they often did, would then fly over the location of the mirror flash in the designated direction. If the Raven could spot the enemy location, he could then call in strikes on it.

We were already partially prepared because the teams were getting used to using the mirrors to flash their locations, but compass azimuths and distances were another matter. My Thai operations assistants were doubtful that the teams could do it. Hom had once given me a graphic demonstration of the problem. We had been talking about roadwatch reports giving estimates of numbers of enemy soldiers moving along the Ho Chi Minh Trail. I was taking them at face value but Hom was dubious. I asked him why but he said it would be better to give a demonstration. He lined up 30-40 empty 55 gallon drums and then took three or four team leaders to a position about 100 meters from the drums. He asked each team leader how many drums he saw. The replies were astonishing in how inaccurate they were. Hom explained to me that estimating numbers of people in a group at a distance was an American concept that the Lao lowland and hill tribe people did not understand. They would never lose face and say they did not know so they would just guess a number. I told Hom I appreciated this insight into Lao culture but I still wanted to do this and we would just have to find a way to give the Lao an understanding of how to make the distance estimates. I said we would have to devise and conduct training that would teach them how to estimate distances and how to shoot azimuths with a compass. His reaction was one of the reasons I liked and respected Hom so much. He discussed the problem with the other Thai operations assistants, developed methods to teach compass use and distance estimation and then conducted the training. As it turned out, distance estimation was not important.

I chose Team Cranberry/316 under the leadership of Thao Sengchanh for the first mission for two reasons. I considered Sengchanh one of my very best team leaders and using him would give us the best chance for success. I also felt this mission would be a reward for him. He had taken on the North Vietnamese Army capture missions and succeeded but they were dangerous. Having done his share of the most dangerous jobs, this mission would be much easier. Sengchanh, demonstrating once more his cooperative attitude,

readily agreed to take the training and try the new mission. I made a nuisance
of myself asking Hom repeatedly how he thought the training was going and if
he thought Sengchanh could do it. Hom quietly and professionally conducted
the training and prepared Sengchanh and his team for the mission. When
they were ready, we sent them off to walk into the target area. They wore
normal clothing, which was a mix of civilian clothes and military fatigues, and
carried radios, maps, money and .45 caliber pistols and hand grenades. They
would use the money to buy food or meals and to pay informants.

We monitored the team's progress by air to ground radio contacts as they
infiltrated enemy controlled territory, found a safe location and set up their
command post hidden in the jungle away from the target villages. It was
common for Lao villagers to travel from Lao government controlled territory
to their former home villages and back. This was as much to the benefit of the
Pathet Lao and North Vietnamese Army as to us. It left open a way for the
communists to travel back and forth, collect intelligence and obtain supplies.
Once the team's command post was set up, the team members walked into
their former villages. They visited their relatives and friends and conducted
themselves as if they were on a typical visit. When they found relatives or
friends they trusted, they interviewed them for information about enemy
activity. For this mission, when they learned about an enemy troop or supply
location they asked the informant to take them as close to the enemy location
as they thought was safe and close enough to be able to observe the enemy.
Since Sengchanh was the one who knew how to read the map, handle the
compass and make the distance estimates, he would go along to the enemy
location. Having identified where the enemy was, Sengchanh would then wait
for the next Porter air to ground contact so he could report he had a target.
The Thai operations assistant returning from the air to ground told me Team
Cranberry/316 had a target and I contacted the Ravens, briefed them and
asked them to contact the team. As the operation developed, Sengchanh
understood that once he reported a target he had to remain at the observation
post until the Raven arrived, then flash his mirror at the Raven's aircraft and
give him the compass azimuth to the enemy position.

I had a good enough reputation with the Ravens that the first time I briefed them they took the first opportunity to fly out and contact the team. This was to prove a revelation. The Senior Raven, Frank Kricker, Raven 40, took the first report, flew out to the general location, saw the mirror flash, listened to the azimuth and distance and then flew over the team's location in the indicated direction. What he saw was an enemy bivouac of about one hundred men. He quickly arranged for strikes and guided them right on to the enemy location. He was rewarded with enemy ground fire and once the strikes were put in, secondary explosions; a sure sign that damage was being done. It is one thing for a Raven to roam about the countryside trying to locate the enemy and it is quite another to be directed right to them. The Ravens quickly realized they only had to fly over the team's location, as revealed by the mirror flash, in the indicated direction. They did not need to know the distance because they had to observe the enemy themselves anyway and if enemy were there the Raven would see them. It did not take long for Raven 40 to become addicted to Team 316. Over a period of approximately sixty days, he had numerous successful strikes on targets given to him by Sengchanh. I had only sent Sengchanh out for thirty days, but he requested permission to stay on and I was happy to let him do it.

One day Sengchanh reported that he had information that the enemy had a large storage area half way up the side of a Bolovens Plateau karst inside a cave. Sengchanh told the Thai operations assistant he doubted the informant's information but was going to pursue it anyway. Sengchanh spent extra time scouting the area and was rewarded for his diligence when he found tank tracks leading toward the karst. He was now confident there really was an enemy supply depot there. By this time, Raven 40 and I were quite willing to believe Sengchanh so I briefed him on Team 316's latest information and Raven 40 went out to take a look. Flying just above the treetops, as Ravens usually did, he flew as close as possible to the karst and saw what looked like a cave mouth. There was no sign of enemy activity and he was certainly too high and moving too fast, at tree top level, to see tracks on the ground. Given Team 316's record of accomplishment to that date,

Raven 40 was willing to call for a strike on the cave and requested aircraft carrying laser guided smart bombs. When the strike aircraft arrived, Raven 40 fired a white phosphorus (WP) rocket at the mouth of the cave. Since he did not score a direct hit on the cave mouth, he radioed a correction to the strike aircraft. A two-aircraft team then dropped the laser-guided bomb. Back then, two aircraft were needed to drop a single laser-guided bomb. A weapons officer in the back seat of one F-4 Phantom used a hand-held laser to illuminate a target. A second F-4 Phantom dropped the laser-guided bomb on a glide path that enabled its sensor to pick up the laser spot. When released, moveable vanes on the bomb could adjust the bomb's path to the target but the bomb had to be heading to the target in order to hit it. Paveway laser guided bombs were used briefly against bridges and other high-value targets before President Lyndon Johnson's 1968 moratorium on bombing North Vietnam. After that, they were used in Laos against small bridges and cave entrances. Later advances allowed a single jet to both illuminate a target and drop a bomb. I did not ask Raven 40 what size bomb was used but in those days, the most common size laser guided bomb was a 2,000 pounder. A bomb that size would have kicked up a lot of dust even if there were nothing there, however, the F-4s guided this bomb right into the mouth of the cave. When relating these events to me that evening at the daily operations meeting, Frank was quite animated because of this success-ful strike. He said it was the most amazing thing he had ever seen. Not long after the bomb disappeared into the cave opening, the top of the karst literally blew off. He said he had never seen such secondary explosions and fires. Bomb damage assessment (BDA) later determined that we had unco-vered a major North Vietnamese Army tank park, fuel and ammunition storage depot. Normally, we had not often seen the North Vietnamese Army put a large amount of fuel and ammunition in one place. We can only surmise they thought they had found the perfect hiding place. Who would think they could get tanks, fuel and ammunition halfway up the side of a 1000-meter (3,000 feet) karst? We did not, but Raven 40 was willing to guide a bomb into the cave based on Team 316's excellent record of results.

The North Vietnamese Army must have been very surprised when their hidden lair was discovered and even more so when a bomb flew right into the mouth of the cave.

Every evening, when we met for the end-of-day operations meeting at Pakse Unit headquarters, Raven 40 wanted to know what Team 316 was doing and if they had any more targets. I, of course, was eager to pass him any and everything I had. For almost three months, we reveled in our ability to collect intelligence, pass it from the jungle to the Raven forward air controllers and on to strike aircraft and then blow the total shit out of the enemy. For the time and place, the blend of Team 316's intelligence collection and willingness to guide the Ravens to the targets, my direction of Team 316, my Thai operations assistants' guidance and coordination of Team 316's activities, and the Raven FAC's bravery and expertise in calling in U.S. Air Force strike aircraft or RLAF T-28 strikes all combined for very successful use of air power against the North Vietnamese Army. My only goal for these missions was to have a Raven FAC tell me he had delivered a strike based on the team's information and had seen secondary explosions and secondary fires. I was prepared to tell the teams they only had to succeed in identifying one target that resulted in secondary explosions and secondary fires to receive full pay for a mission. However, Team Cranberry/316, preferred to stay in the field and guide numerous successful missions, for which they proved themselves one of the best teams I had during my two years in Laos.

The basic elements needed for the successful application of air power in ground operations are good intelligence, target acquisition and accurate delivery of ordnance. In the early 1970s, we used surrogate special operations soldiers such as Lao hill tribesmen to gather intelligence. We acquired the targets by having trained a team to use that intelligence to find the actual enemy locations and then mark its own position and provide direction and distance to the target and pass that to the Raven FAC backseater so he could relay it to the Raven pilot. Finally, U.S. Air Force aircraft delivered bombs to specific locations after the Raven FAC marked them with white phosphorous (also known as WP or "willy pete") rockets.

By 2001, special operations soldiers on the ground using a combination of global positioning systems (GPS), laser guidance, detailed maps, radar, J-Stars, and moving target indicators were locating and acquiring targets while the U.S. Air Force delivered massive bombs from jet aircraft and bombers to devastate enemy positions in Afghanistan just as we had devastated that North Vietnamese Army tank, fuel and ammunition depot in a cave off the side of the Bolovens Plateau in Laos.

The techniques of Afghanistan 2001 did not evolve directly from Laos 1971. Afghanistan 2001 is American military might deployed at its deadliest while Laos 1971 was Lao irregular team soldiers and the innovation of an individual CIA special operations case officer. However, what it does show is that long-established special operations concepts only require adaptation and improvisation to overcome immediate circumstances.

OPERATION SHOTGUN

---

*Just because something doesn't do what you
planned it to do doesn't mean it's useless.*

-Thomas A. Edison (1847-1931)

I gained a lot of knowledge and experience during my first year in Laos. I knew that sending teams to try to watch the Ho Chi Minh Trail to count trucks or soldiers was not an effective use of their talents. Eventually, I developed an alternative plan, to place a team where it could observe enemy activity and give it the capability to call in U.S. air strikes. The combining of intelligence collection with the capability to take action on the information was very appealing.

Central Intelligence Agency (CIA) case officers working in support of the Lao irregular units deployed against the North Vietnamese Army believed those units would not be able to resist the North Vietnamese Army without a large amount of close air support. A key ingredient for close air support was the ability of the supported ground unit to talk to the pilots controlling the bombing and strafing runs. When Royal Lao Air Force (RLAF) Lao piloted T-28s flew close air support the Lao T-28 pilots or the Lao backseaters flying with the American Raven forward air controllers could communicate with the ground units. However, when American piloted aircraft arrived to provide close air support there could be communication only if one of the Lao troops on the ground could speak English. Not many Lao officers spoke English. Many of them spoke French, but the American pilots did not. Some Lao officers had attended U.S. Army training courses in the United States and spoke English well enough. They could talk to American pilots. The Ravens tried to fly with English speaking backseaters who could talk to the Lao on the ground, but there were times when the Ravens flew without backseaters and there were times when FAC's from Vietnam or Thailand, such as call-signs NAIL or COVEY, gunships, such as call-signs STINGER or SPECTRE, or the F-4, F-100 and A-7 fighter-bomber pilots needed to talk to the ground units and they could not because they had no access to English speaking Lao backseaters or to English speaking Lao officers on the ground.

At one point early in my tour, the chief of operations asked us to identify candidates to receive English instruction. The idea was that we should send bright, intelligent young Lao volunteers to English language school so that we could send them out with our irregular units when there was no Lao officer who could speak English. These young men were to become "forward air guides" or FAGs. They would learn enough English to be able to talk to the American pilots and coordinate the bombing and strafing in support of the ground units.

It proved much harder than we thought. It took quite a bit of time to train a Lao to speak English well enough to function on the ground in combat. One of the English language school graduates had been a radio operator in the Team 300 roadwatch project. The FAG program was not going well and he had no assignment to a ground unit. I asked Ray if I could have him back for roadwatch operations. I had my own ideas on how to use someone like this and I took him and trained him in a manner similar to Team Cranberry/316, that is, to spot targets and give as accurate an azimuth and distance to the target as possible.

I had success with Team Cranberry/316 because we always gave their targets to Ravens who had backseaters who could talk to the team on the ground. Now, I wanted to be able to spot targets and direct American piloted aircraft to hit them. I would use my roadwatch soldiers on the ground for intelligence collection and then use American firepower from the air to hit the targets we identified. The activities in Saravane Province, north and east of Pakse, dominated the combat situation in MR-IV. The North Vietnamese Army was driving tanks and trucks through the Toumlane Valley into the province. Most of the truck movement was at night and the only way to detect it was for aircraft to fly over the valley looking for it. There were too many known targets in Laos and Vietnam for American pilots to spend any time flying around the Toumlane Valley looking for vehicle movement. Neither was it possible for an aircraft to fly from Thailand or Vietnam, spend time looking for targets, bomb them and return to base. The best, most efficient use of the aircraft was to have identified targets for them to fly to, bomb and then return home. I needed a Team Cranberry/316 with an English speaker.

Route 23 through the Toumlane Valley was the primary road for North Vietnamese Army vehicular traffic into Saravane Province. The valley narrowed at a point where there was a high bluff overlooking the road. I decided to put my intelligence collection operation on top of that bluff. I did not need the various skills of a typical team, but rather just security for my English speaker whom we had trained to spot targets. Usually forward air guides on the ground had one-word call signs. I wanted mine to have a name that would be easy for the Lao soldier to pronounce so I decided to give him the call sign "Shotgun." My operational plan was to deliver Shotgun and his security detail by helicopter to a place from which they could securely walk undetected to where the observation post (OP) would be. There would be a command post (CP) where they would spend the daylight hours sleeping, eating and hiding from the enemy. The command post would also be the location for the Delco CW Morse code radio for communicating daily situation reports (sitreps) to my roadwatch operations base at PS-18. In the late afternoon, at dusk, they would move from the command post to the observation post and be in position to observe Route 23 on the valley floor. I insisted that Shotgun and his security take a signal mirror so they could signal from their command post. I wanted to be sure that they put their command post in a position that was believable. There was less chance they would try to fabricate their activities if the command post was in an appropriate location. Once Shotgun manned his observation post he would have a VHF radio for speaking to the American pilots. The United States Air Force flew Airborne Battlefield Command & Control Center (ABCCC) aircraft over Laos 24 hours per day, one in the north and one in the south. In the daytime, the call sign of the ABCCC aircraft in the south was "Hillsboro" and at night, the call sign was "Moonbeam." As far as I knew, there were two different C-130 aircraft and crews flying 12-hour shifts each. Shotgun was to call Moonbeam with his VHF radio to pass his targets. With everything in place and ready to go, I went to Ubon, Thailand to brief the U.S. Air Force there about Shotgun.

I had been to Ubon months earlier to talk to U.S. Air Force officers of the 16th Special Operations Squadron, 8th Tactical Fighter Wing, Ubon Royal Thai Air Force Base, about the significantly high numbers of truck kills they were claiming. In Pakse, we were skeptical about the high numbers. Our thoughts were, "how could they be destroying so many"? Either they were destroying every truck the North Vietnamese Army drove every night or there were many more trucks out there than we could imagine. The U.S. Air Force officers showed us film from cameras on board the AC-130 Spectre gunships. The cameras were recording the Spectre missions each night. We watched the film and could see the road and small white rectangles moving on the road. They explained that they were using heat-seeking equipment and the white rectangles were the truck engines. As we watched, there was a sudden high-pitched ripping whine and simultaneously, bright lancing streaks of light that struck each white rectangle. As the streaking lights struck the white rectangles, they exploded in quick succession. The U.S. Air Force briefing officer explained that the AC-130 Spectre gunship was firing rounds that were heat-seeking ammunition that could penetrate the truck engines. The film seemed to provide indisputable evidence that the U.S. Air Force was indeed destroying the numbers of trucks they claimed.

On this trip to Ubon, I spent several hours with U.S. Air Force officers explaining the Shotgun operation and telling them that I expected to be able to give them definite targets. I expected the U.S. Air Force to brief the Moonbeam C-130 crews on Shotgun so that when he called them they would respond. My expectations were much too high. I soon realized that the Moonbeam crews had no idea who or what Shotgun was and did not want to deal with him. Shotgun began telling my operations assistant, during daytime air to ground contacts that he was seeing many trucks and tanks every night but when he called Moonbeam, there was no response. Shotgun was getting frustrated and so was I. The Pakse Unit headquarters building had a wide variety of communications capabilities. One of them was a radio, in a rack the size of a large refrigerator that was capable of VHF transmission. It turned out that I could receive Shotgun's VHF transmissions from his hand held HT-2 radio in the Pakse Unit headquarters building on that rack-mounted radio, even though the distance from Pakse to Shotgun's position was approximately one hundred kilometers on a straight line. One evening, after the daily operations meeting, I went to the big VHF radio and called Shotgun. He responded and I asked if he had any targets. He said there was a convoy of trucks in the valley and I should get Moonbeam to bomb them as soon as possible. I told him to stand by and then switched frequencies and called Moonbeam. I was using the call sign Statehouse that Moonbeam would know was CIA. I explained that I had a team with an English speaker in position to observe Route 23 in the Toumlane Valley and that the team was reporting a truck convoy. I asked them to send aircraft to look and told them the pilots could talk to Shotgun to get further details to help their strikes. Moonbeam said he would see what he could do. To be fair, Moonbeam was coordinating a large number of aircraft among a large number of targets or requests for close air support. My request for him to support Shotgun was just one of many that he had to prioritize. In any event, no aircraft ever arrived.

From the point of view of arranging successful air strikes on the trucks and tanks Shotgun was reporting, the operation was not successful. However, the general reporting of a roadwatch type asset from the high bluff overlooking Route 23 through the Toumlane Valley into Saravane Province did result in more focus on the threat. Shotgun was making Pakse Unit more aware of the numbers of trucks and tanks that the North Vietnamese Army was moving south into Saravane Province. I remember a Raven coming in one day to tell us he could not believe what he was seeing out there. It was dry season and the roads in Saravane Province were hard and dusty. He said it looked like something out of a World War II movie about North Africa. He had seen Soviet made T-34 tanks, with radio antennas bent in the wind, raising clouds of dust as they barreled along the road.

THIS IS THE
MONTHLY REPORT
OF BINH TRAM 35

———◆———

"In 1901, when the French Navy began its first experiments with communication by radio telegraphy, the French carried out the tests in the Mediterranean rather than the Channel, presumably to lessen the possibility of eavesdropping by the Royal navy. But not only did the British pick up the record of the French tests at a listening station on Gibraltar, HMS Pyramis closely tracked the French squadron and secured a complete record of the French messages. Apparently this was the first instance of radio intelligence interception."

–Bradley Smith, "The American Road to Central Intelligence",
in Jeffreys–Jones and Andrew, Eternal Vigilance (1997).

L ewis Sorley[31] has described how MACV, under the command of General Creighton Abrams, analyzed significant intelligence being obtained from intercepts of the North Vietnamese Army's (NVA) General Directorate of Rear Services (GDRS) radio communications. According to Sorley, General Abrams, who had assumed command of U.S. forces in Vietnam from General William Westmoreland in 1968, had come to understand that the North Vietnamese Army did not follow the usual procedure of moving troops and supplies into position first with more supplies to follow as the logistical tail. Abrams understood that NVA military operations led with its logistical nose positioning all supplies before moving in troop units. It was also well known in MACV that the NVA used the Ho Chi Minh Trail to send men and supplies from North Vietnam through Laos and Cambodia into South Vietnam, therefore, one of MACV's high priority intelligence targets was to gather information on the number of troops and the amounts and types of ammunition and supplies traveling from north to south. It was, in fact, a long standing requirement, but it was not until November 1967 that MACV began to intercept NVA GDRS communications. It was several more months after that until MACV began to understand what it had and then begin to analyze the data.

The intercepted messages gave MACV information about the flow of men, not only the numbers moving down the Ho Chi Minh Trail but also where the troops were going and when they would arrive. Since the NVA always moved ammunition and supplies into position and then moved the troops in when

[31] Lewis Sorley, *A Better War: The Unexamined Victories and Final Tragedy of America's Last Years in Vietnam*, Harcourt Brace & Company, 1999.

the logistical preparations were complete, intercepting these messages provided excellent intelligence in support of MACV.

In Laos, the CIA, for its part, had been running intelligence operations against the Ho Chi Minh Trail to count troops and identify types and amounts of ammunition and supplies by trying to position small teams of Lao irregular soldiers to observe the Ho Chi Minh Trail. The teams' objective was to count troops and trucks, boats and pack animals and report their observations to their case officers. In the chapter titled "Roadwatch", I described how these "roadwatch" reports had been accumulating under a desk in the CIA's Directorate of Intelligence and how I participated in a two week effort to analyze the accumulated data and see if it were possible to make some useful sense out of it all. Of course, merely observing troops, trucks, boats or pack animals moving north or south told you nothing about the final destination of the troops, supplies or ammunition.

Under Westmoreland, MACV conducted the Vietnam War using search and destroy military operations and counting enemy dead, the so-called "head counts." Supposedly, the more North Vietnamese Army and Viet Cong killed the closer we would be to forcing them to quit and winning the war. CIA's roadwatch effort was intended to give intelligence analysts in Washington a way to gauge how the war was going. If you kill enemy soldiers and capture or destroy materiel but the flow of men and materiel continues at replacement rates, you are not winning. CIA also thought it could provide real time information to assist MACV in bombing the troops and supplies moving along the Trail. The HARK-1 was issued to roadwatch teams to improve their reporting. It had symbols on it for soldier, truck, boat, etcetera. When the team observed four trucks it pressed the truck button four times and the information would be transmitted from the HARK-1 radio device to a CIA radio receiver in an orbiting aircraft for further transmission to the USAF in Udorn, Thailand. At some point, as described by Ted Shackley[32], the CIA in Laos thought the roadwatch teams could transmit timely information about

---

[32] Theodore G. Shackley, *Spymaster: My Life in the CIA*, Potomac Books, 2005.

troop or truck movement that the USAF could use to target air strikes. If that was the case, the HARK-1 was nowhere to be found in Pakse when I arrived. One might assume that if it had been truly effective for guiding air strikes it would still be in use in early 1970.

Pakse Unit's roadwatch special operations teams were the primary small teams used for intelligence collection. Before my arrival, roadwatch and action (truck and troop ambush) operations were the dominant missions. From time to time, the teams were also given radio intercept or field telephone wiretapping missions.

Pakse Unit, in addition to having special operations case officers from Special Operations Division of the Directorate of Operations, had one Science and Technology, Office of Special Operations (OSO) officer assigned to it in 1970. The OSO officer was responsible for all Pakse Unit wiretapping and radio intercept operations. In the 1960s and 1970s, the CIA often conducted signals intelligence (sigint) operations that required case officers on the ground using clandestine tradecraft targeted on low powered transmitters, for example the tactical radio transmissions of North Vietnamese Army military units in Laos. The OSO officer maintained the wiretapping and radio intercept technical equipment, hired and employed local inhabitants to assist him with the equipment and the code breaking, and maintained coordination with the OSO officer in Udorn. The Pakse chief of unit, Carl, decided that when the OSO officer was due for replacement he would let him depart Laos and replace him with me. I was already providing the manpower for the wiretapping and radio intercept operations by sending my teams out on those missions. All I had to do was take over responsibility for the intercept operations assistants, the equipment, the code breaking and the liaison with the Udorn OSO officer.

I had already reviewed the activities and production of my teams participating in radio intercept and field telephone wiretapping and was not impressed because all of it consisted of conversations in Lao, purportedly intercepts of Pathet Lao transmissions. I felt that our Lao speaking team members could fabricate Pathet Lao conversations. However, if we targeted

North Vietnamese Army conversations the Lao teams would not be able to fabricate messages in the Vietnamese language. A team of Lao soldiers could not fabricate enemy messages because they could not imitate the North Vietnamese language, the military jargon and the message content even if they had access to a Vietnamese speaker who could help them manufacture an intercept tape.

Neither did I believe a team could gain the cooperation of a real North Vietnamese Army soldier in order to fabricate messages. Since I was now responsible for all Pakse based intercept operations, I would be choosing the targets for my teams rather than just supplying my teams for the targets and missions chosen by the OSO officer. I wanted the teams to find North Vietnamese Army rather than Pathet Lao targets for the radio intercept and wiretapping but I did not have much luck, at first.

After I took over signals intelligence operations, Pakse Unit received a cable from Udorn Base telling us we were not doing well in the collection of low power, tactical, voice communications. Udorn also mentioned that, overall in all Southeast Asia, there was a lapse in coverage of North Vietnamese Army GDRS communications. We did not know it then, but it appears that South Vietnam based U.S. signals intelligence had lost its last remaining position for intercepting GDRS messages. Because this Udorn cable praised Long Tieng Unit's successful interception of North Vietnamese Army tactical communications and criticized Pakse's efforts, Pakse Unit did not receive this cable very well.

The GDRS used the Soviet R-401 radio relay equipment, known by the NATO designation "Mercury Grass", operating in the 60-70 megaherz (MHz) frequency range, to transmits its messages. The North Vietnamese Army used this radio relay equipment as a multi-channel tactical radio in their rear area logistical nets, and as a supplement to tactical wire communications systems. It was versatile field radio equipment, usable either as a terminal or as a relay station and was similar in concept to the AN/TRC-24[33] radio relay. Using this

---

[33] The AN/TRC-24 is a transportable VHF/UHF-FM radio set which operates in six frequency bands, 50-1875 MHz. Various antennas are used as required for the different frequency bands.

"Mercury Grass" equipment, the North Vietnamese Army was sending its monthly logistical reports to Hanoi by encoding them and then sending them over the radio for relay from binh tram to binh tram until they arrived in Hanoi. As mentioned previously, in 1967 South Vietnam based U.S. signals intelligence operators had discovered they could intercept "Mercury Grass" transmissions from certain mountains and hilltops near the Ho Chi Minh and Sihanouk Trails. Up to 1971 these intercept operations were successfully capturing enemy logistical messages and providing very significant intelligence to MACV.

Until Udorn sent out this cable criticizing the radio intercept operations in Pakse, I was just punching my time card in relation to signals intelligence. The cable praised the radio intercept operations at Long Tieng[34] and wrote something like the intercept operations in Pakse did not compare well. It suggested that we try sending out teams to specifically search for radio transmissions in the 60–70 megaherz (MHz) frequency range of "Mercury Grass" radios. "Mercury Grass" was the NATO designation for this type of World War II radio the Soviets had given the North Vietnamese. I felt the criticism of our radio intercept operations was uncalled for because the operating conditions were quite different. In the Long Tieng area, they were able to put teams on mountaintops immediately overlooking the North Vietnamese Army operating in the valleys. There were many mountains and many North Vietnamese Army units moving through the valleys. In the Pakse area, we operated from the Bolovens Plateau, which was about 3,000 feet in elevation, but the enemy was another 50 kilometers away operating along the Ho Chi Minh Trail. Long Tieng Unit was intercepting low power tactical radios that were best intercepted by being right on top of them or in line of sight of their transmissions. To do that in the area of the Ho Chi Minh Trail we would have to put a team on a hill along or near the trail. We could not insert a team by helicopter because all the mountains or hilltops were in the middle of enemy held territory. The enemy could easily spot helicopters dropping off soldiers

---

[34] Long Tieng, also called Lima Site 20A, or 20-Alternate, was the headquarters for CIA operations on the Plaine des Jarres led by Hmong general, Vang Pao.

on hilltops and then attack them. Neither could we convince a team to walk to a hilltop in enemy territory. If nothing else, American bombing on the trail would place a team in peril of being killed either en route or while in place.

I did not like being goaded into running an operation because of unfair criticism, but I decided to try targeting the "Mercury Grass" frequencies. There was a small hill not far from Pakse, named Phou Batiane. I could safely insert a team by helicopter and it could remain there in relative safety. At this time, I did not know the "Mercury Grass" radios were low power. The only thing they told us was that we should place the intercept equipment on the highest possible location. We had an intercept radio, the Zenith manufactured AN/PRR-15, especially designed for scanning frequencies so I organized a small team of three men, trained them specifically to intercept transmissions in the "Mercury Grass" frequency range and placed them on top of Phou Batiane. I named them Team Termite but did not give them a number, to distinguish them from roadwatch teams, which always had names and numbers. The intercept radio was an expensive piece of equipment but we had nothing more than a simple Sony audiocassette recorder for recording whatever we might find.

The team was on the hilltop for about two weeks. I sent my intercept operations assistant out by helicopter every few days to visit them and see how they were doing. After about two weeks, he came back with a box of audiotapes. He said the team had been recording steadily for a few days and thought they had something. I told him to start reviewing the tapes and let me know what he thought. He was of Lao/Vietnamese origin and could read and write both languages. He came back the next day. He was a serious young man, laconic and not given to much demonstration of emotion. Nonetheless, I could tell something was up. He explained what the team had discovered.

As the team scanned the "Mercury Grass" frequency range they heard a voice speaking in Vietnamese, calling the equivalent in American military terms of "Red Dog 3, Red Dog 3, this is Black Tiger, come in."

The team heard this, did not understand the words but recognized it as being a military radio-calling pattern in Vietnamese. Eventually "Red Dog 3" answered "Black Tiger", but then the voices ceased. At first, the team did not understand what was happening. Being familiar with military radio procedures, they suspected that one identity was calling another and when an answer was received, the two identities were switching to another pre-arranged frequency. As soon as the calling was answered by a new voice and both voices disappeared, the team immediately began scanning the rest of the frequency range. It was not a very wide frequency range so it was relatively easy to cover it quickly. While the first few attempts were not successful, they eventually found the two voices engaged in continuous conversation. They then recorded them, even though they had no understanding of Vietnamese. The team realized they had to find the new frequency very quickly or they would not be able to record the entire transmission. It helped that the frequency range was short. They also helped themselves by turning on the tape recorder when they heard the initial calling and kept it on until they found the second frequency.

The intercept operations assistant could only translate the first few sentences of each conversation but they were electrifying. What he had to say next excited me even more. After establishing contact the calling entity would say something like this, "Following is the monthly report for Binh Tram 35." What followed were groups of four numbers. This was an intercept holy grail.

Along the Ho Chi Minh Trail, from Hanoi to the Republic of Vietnam, there was a series of binh trams. A binh tram was a logistical unit responsible for a 50 to 75 kilometer section of the Trail. If we could intercept the monthly report for one binh tram, we would know all that had passed through it from Hanoi to the Republic of Vietnam. Some of the war materiel and men passing through it would wind up in the Republic of Vietnam and some of it would not, but that was for the analysts to figure out. The primary goal of roadwatch intelligence operations in Laos was to collect intelligence on the flow of men and materiel into the Republic of Vietnam. Now, instead of just counting the number of troops or trucks, we had our hands on a significant source of that intelligence.

Operations like roadwatch, merely counting enemy trucks and troops, were a waste of time. This, however, was a potential game winning home run. All of my excitement was dashed, however, when Udorn replied that until the code was broken they could not be sure if what we were getting was truly valuable and they had no resources to spare to work on breaking out the messages.[35] We would have to do it ourselves even though we did not have the codes or code breaking experience. In addition, we had no idea which particular code the enemy was using. I did not think much of the Udorn radio intercept operations officer for having goaded us into running this operation by criticizing us, and then when we might be successful, refusing to give us proper support. This sort of thing really annoyed me but also made me that much more determined to solve the problems and show him up.

Thus began a six-month long struggle. We would receive code sheets but they would not be the right ones. We would get a valid code sheet, begin to break out messages, but then the North Vietnamese Army changed the codes. That locked us out until we received code sheets for the new code. All the while, my cables to Udorn were ignored and I had to send "Please Reply Ref" cables asking for replies.[36]

Finally, I had a large 36 by 24 by 24-inch box full of 60 and 90-minute audiocassettes but I was getting ready to depart Laos and return to Washington, D.C. I decided to take the box with me on my way out of country. I would have to go through Udorn and Vientiane on my way out so I decided to take the box of cassettes to my friend and former training partner Ken, who was staying on for another two years, and explain the situation. I knew that if Ken saw what we had he would raise hell until someone paid attention. I dropped the box on Ken's desk and explained the whole history of the operation and my frustrations with not getting the proper resources to help in

---

[35] Although it was not apparent then, it seems the Udorn signals intelligence (sigint) officer was not aware of the RVN based sigint operations so highly prized by MACV and was only interested in sigint possibilties in Laos. This is not surprising given the requirement for compartmentation of intelligence operations.

[36] At one time in the CIA, a "Please Reply Ref" cable caused trouble for the office that was not responding. Management came down hard on subordinate units that did not reply to cables in a timely fashion. In this case, some of the replies would be snippy and would try to impose ridiculous bureaucratic requirements on us.

breaking out the messages. Ken said he would take care of it and I went on home, secure in the knowledge Ken would resolve the problems.

After returning home, taking some home leave and returning to work at CIA headquarters, I visited the Lao Desk and nosed around to see what was going on in Pakse. One of the things I learned was that after my departure Ken had raised a big furor over the box of cassettes. At some point, they added the proverbial "2 plus 2" and someone figured out we had discovered a location from which "Mercury Grass" transmissions could be intercepted. South Vietnam based signals intelligence units had learned that CIA assets in Laos had the ability to intercept "Mercury Grass" transmissions and they wanted to exploit that. They wanted our team to continue to operate on the hill near Pakse while they prepared to replace us. They eventually did but then learned that they could not relay the messages to their processing location without boosting the signal along the way. They needed to put equipment halfway between the collection point and the processing point to boost the signal for a successful relay. The military asked our team to go back to the hill outside Pakse and again do the intercept work. They were still in the process of setting up the signal boosting equipment when the war ended and the peace agreement would not let them have friendly assets on the hill near Pakse.

From about 1965 until 1973 when the cease-fire in Laos was established the CIA management rode the dead horse of the roadwatch program never making the decision to dismount. They continued to address the problem of determining the flow of men and materiel by counting enemy troops and trucks. Meanwhile South Vietnam based signals intelligence units were intercepting and breaking North Vietnamese Army logistical message traffic reporting the monthly flow of men and materiel from North Vietnam into the Republic of Vietnam. It remains for the appropriate signals intelligence agencies to declassify that story. How did they do it? What was the intelligence? How did they disseminate it to the policy and military decision makers? How did the decisions makers use it?

It would also be interesting to learn why the CIA continued the roadwatch program while other intelligence collectors were successfully acquiring much more about the flow of logistics into South Vietnam than the roadwatch program could ever hope to acquire. Even if the South Vietnam based signals intelligence program was so compartmented that no one in the CIA field command in Laos knew about it, didn't someone in CIA headquarters realize that the intelligence objectives of the roadwatch program were being met and more by something else? Perhaps by the time the South Vietnam based signals intelligence program had achieved success the CIA was so focused on its combat military objectives in Laos it was failing to properly supervise its intelligence collection programs.

HIS BROTHER'S KEEPER

———◆———

"As an American asked to serve, I was prepared to fight, to be wounded, to be captured, and even prepared to die, but I was not prepared to be abandoned."

–Former POW Eugene "Red" McDaniel

Obtaining information about Americans missing in action in Vietnam or Laos was a high priority requirement in 1970-1972. A Continental Air Services pilot asked me to try to learn the whereabouts of a missing Air America employee. I agreed and took his request and gave it to one of my teams.

All wars result in soldiers becoming missing in action (MIA) or prisoners of war (POW). The Vietnam War (1965-1975) was certainly no exception. The activities of civilian intelligence officers in a war zone present unique problems when those intelligence officers are missing or captured. Mostly an organization like the CIA does not want to acknowledge that it has been using civilians for espionage and thus will not admit such activities or will delay such admissions. This can be complicated when the enemy captures civilians who have been working in a war zone but have not been involved in intelligence activities. The enemy is also in a position where it does not want to reveal details of how it captured someone or that it even has possession of a civilian. As of this writing, Eugene DeBruin has been missing in Laos since 1963. It has been proved beyond a doubt that he was captured – his captors released a photograph of him in captivity. Yet, the communist government of Laos refuses to admit that he was captured and the communist government of Vietnam refuses to help the U.S. government in its dealing with the communist Lao.

The communists have said, "It was a long war, many were killed or went missing, how could we possibly know who they all were or what happened to them?"

There are two things to remember about the North Vietnamese. First, the North Vietnamese communists thoroughly infiltrated the communist Lao movement and controlled it top to bottom, something I describe in more detail in the chapter titled, "The North Vietnamese Army's Mole." Second, the North Vietnamese Army not only had records of every bicycle used on the Ho Chi Minh Trail, it kept a tally of all the poundage those bicycles carried and it knew the names of every bicycle rider and how much he carried - and it had those records from the French Indochina War beginning in 1945 to the end of the Vietnam War in 1975. John Prados has written[37], "One Favorit bike, frame number 20220, held the record for hauling loads totaling more than 100 tons in a two-year interval. The individual record for a bicycle load, made in 1964 by bo doi Nguyen Dieu, was 924 pounds. The record previously set, at Dien Bien Phu, had been 724 pounds." How could any reasonable person believe that people with such anal-retentive tendencies did not know the name and disposition of every POW that fell into their hands? The POW's were sources of intelligence, and even more, they had high propaganda value. If an American died without falling into their hands, we might believe they did not know anything about him. However, if an American was a POW, of the Pathet Lao or the North Vietnamese Army, they knew.

Eugene DeBruin arrived in Laos in 1963 as an employee of Air America. He was a "kicker" or air cargo handler on a C-46 when the enemy shot it down and captured him one month after his arrival in Laos. A kicker flies in the cargo bay of such aircraft and pushes the bundles of cargo rigged with parachutes out of the aircraft. His aircraft was on a rice-dropping mission when the enemy shot it down. What was Air America and what was it doing dropping rice to villagers in Laos in 1963?

From time to time, the CIA needs to be able to cover its activities behind a commercial front. In such instances, CIA might go to an existing company and request its cooperation. In such a case, the company secretly employs one or more CIA officers. Sometimes the CIA needs the services of a commercial company and decides that it is better to establish the company itself rather than try to get an existing company to help. In CIA parlance, a company it

---

[37] John Prados, *The Blood Road: The Ho Chi Minh Trail and the Vietnam War*, John Wiley & Sons, New York, 1999, p 85.

controls is known as a "proprietary." A proprietary might be wholly staffed by CIA employees or it might only have a few CIA employees in certain positions while the rest of the proprietary's employees are not witting of the company's true sponsorship. Air America was such a proprietary. Many of Air America's pilots, mechanics, administrative and other personnel were unwitting of CIA sponsorship, at least in the early days. After a while, non–CIA Air America personnel had to have their heads in the sand if they were not aware of the company's true sponsorship. I was one of the many CIA employees sent to Laos with Air America as my cover. Eugene DeBruin was one of the many hired to work directly for the proprietary. It is an interesting question, however, as to whether he was just an employee of an airline providing services to the CIA or whether he was, in fact, an employee of his government. A distinction that will take on much more importance later on in this story of Eugene DeBruin and his fate in Laos.

Eugene DeBruin had been a "Montana smokejumper." Early on, the CIA hired some ex-smokejumpers as employees, while hiring others as employees of Air America, unwitting of CIA sponsorship. Eugene was hired to be a cargo handler on C-46 and C-47 aircraft. These old workhorse planes were used extensively to haul cargo from airfield to airfield and for dropping supplies by parachute. One of my operational sites, which I visited often in Pilatus Porters, was PS-7 close to the Cambodian border in southern Laos. On one trip I told Grey Fox, the Pakse Air Operations Officer, that I would stay at PS-7 for a couple of hours and asked to be let off and picked up later in the day. PS-7 was equipped with a single side band radio with which I could talk to Grey Fox, or indeed all the way to Vientiane if necessary. Additionally, I had a VHF radio known as an HT-2. The pilot took off leaving me alone, deep in the jungles a long, long way from any place safe. I was not particularly worried and I went about my business. I was in the thatched roof hut we used as our headquarters and that housed the single side band radio when I heard a long series of heavy thumps. I looked out the "windows" of the hut and saw villagers running toward the airstrip. Curious, I went out toward the airstrip, too. There were sacks of rice all over the strip. Some were broken open but most were intact. An Air America C-46 had "bombed" PS-7 with its monthly ration of rice. Our irregular assets at PS-7 would pick up the double wrapped rice sacks and put them in storage for later issuing to the villagers, but blown open sacks were considered fair game for anyone in the village who could get to them and scoop up the rice before our guys got to them.

Anyway, Gene DeBruin, less than one month in country, had gone out on a supply drop mission and the C-46 he was crewing was shot down. I first heard Eugene DeBruin's story from Lee Gossett in early 1971, about eight years after the shoot down. Lee was a Pilatus Porter pilot for Continental Air Services, Incorporated (CASI). I knew Lee from flying with him whenever he was in Pakse. The CASI Porter pilots rotated from unit to unit. I was not particularly aware of what their rotation schedule was or how long they stayed. I just knew that a pilot like Lee would fly for us for a while and then be gone until the next time his rotation brought him to Pakse. Lee was very professional. He inspired confidence and was very likeable. We were sitting around up-country at PS-22 one day when Lee asked me to look at some materials he had. He handed me information about Eugene that Jerry DeBruin, Eugene's brother, had prepared. It detailed Eugene's story as related in the previous paragraphs. I read it with interest. There was significant emphasis from CIA headquarters in Washington on American POW's and we had a high priority requirement to gather intelligence on whether they were in Laos and where. Lee knew that I handled all of the roadwatch assets in MR-IV and that I could have my teams take the material out with them and distribute them to villagers. A case officer working out of Savannakhet had helped Jerry DeBruin make up small, plastic covered cards in the Lao language that asked for information about his brother Eugene.

I was more than willing to help Lee and Jerry but I wanted to do more than just send the cards out and distribute them.

I told Lee, "I'll give one of my teams specific requirements to collect information about Eugene."

Lee and Jerry's proposal was that I send the cards into areas where Eugene was known to have been. I really only had one team that regularly operated in such an area. Team Papaya/305 was one that I had inherited from CIA officers, Heng and Noy and the LS–171 roadwatch operation. Heng and Noy told me that Bounlert, the Papaya team leader, had been one of their very best. They felt he was more courageous than most and had been honest and reliable.

Heng told me, "Bounlert had a problem on his last mission when I was still handling him. On a mission to the area of Moung Nong[38], an area well known to Bounlert because he was originally from there, one of Bounlert's agents told him about a prison camp near Moung Nong and said the camp held 12 American prisoners. I put a camera in the next parachute re-supply drop with instructions for Bounlert to give the camera to the agent and ask the agent to take photographs of the camp and the American prisoners. Bounlert already had a camera and when the new one arrived, he decided to keep the new camera for his team's use and give the old one to the agent."

This made sense to Bounlert because he felt he would put the new camera to better use in a wider variety of tasks while the old camera was only going to be used to photograph the camp. Unfortunately, Bounlert did not take into account that he had already used the camera to take photographs of several of his agents in the area. The agent went back to the area of the prison camp with the old camera but the North Vietnamese Army arrested him. They developed the film and found photographs of the prison camp as well as of various inhabitants of the area. The North Vietnamese Army interrogated the agent and learned that the individuals on the film were his sub-agents. The North Vietnamese Army executed the agent. Heng had seen an intercepted North Vietnamese Army message that disclosed the agent's fate and what was on the roll of film. Bounlert was out on mission when the North Vietnamese Army message was intercepted and did not immediately learn what had happened from his error giving the agent the old camera. Heng and Noy were concerned that this incident might affect Bounlert's ability to perform as well as he had in

---

[38] Muang Nong was a village near the intersections of Routes 92, 920 and 921, all key parts of the Ho Chi Minh Trail. It was also on a parallel just a short distance south of Hue in South Vietnam.

the past. In fact, Bounlert had lost all of his current informants. Since it was common for team leaders like Bounlert to use family and friends as agents it was highly probable that Bounlert's actions had caused harm, not only to the agent, but to the sub-agents as well, all of whom were probably close to him.

I was going to send him out on his first mission subsequent to the disaster of losing all his informants. When using Lao Theung, that is, mountain tribal soldiers, they were usually only effective in their home areas, thus it was incumbent on me to send Bounlert back to his home area or not use him as a team leader. I felt that his previous excellent record was enough reason to trust him and see if he could rebuild his informant network. Besides, we did not have any other men who were team leader material from that area, so it was send Bounlert or give up on missions to Moung Nong.

I worked out an extensive list of questions about Eugene DeBruin with Lee Gossett. I then worked with my Thai operations assistants to carefully get the questions translated into Lao and directed the operations assistants to go over the questions with Bounlert to be sure he understood them all. I felt confident that if we could obtain any intelligence about the alleged prison camp near Moung Nong, Bounlert and Team Papaya/305 would be able to do it.

In any job, a person wants to do well and be recognized by his superiors. I could have just taken this on because it was part of the job, or I could have worked hard at it because there would be recognition for having collected intelligence against one of our high priority requirements. A case officer always looks good if he can produce well-received intelligence, but I made an emotional investment in this effort to uncover information about the fate of Eugene DeBruin. At this point, 1971, Eugene was missing for 8 years. I thought this was excruciating for his family and it must have been hell for him. I could not possibly know his fate would remain unknown for more than 46 years (as of this writing) and may never be known.

I got together with Niphon and Viroj, the two senior LS-171 operations assistants, and discussed the requirement. I told them, "I want the team to put a major effort into uncovering information about Eugene DeBruin."

Most of the time, I briefed my operations assistants and they briefed the teams, but from time to time, I took a special interest in a particular mission and wanted to brief the team myself. I explained the special interest we had in finding prisoners of war, gave them Jerry DeBruin's materials and explained that I wanted the materials distributed to villagers. I also gave them a list of questions, requirements in intelligence jargon, about prisoners of war in general and some specific questions about Eugene DeBruin. I tried to make them understand this was very important to me. I did not offer any additional money, as that would have been a bad precedent to set, but it still made a difference to them that I, "Tan Chanh", personally briefed them and asked them to do something special. It gave them a little more face, definitely a good thing to do if I wanted an extra effort. I did not know that when Bounlert and Team Papaya/305 did uncover and report information about Eugene DeBruin the information would languish in a twilight zone created by CIA people who had no understanding of special operations in Laos nor how intelligence information was reported and DIA people who had no understanding of how the CIA functions. Moreover, all of them were willing to "understand" in their own parochial ways and never knew what they did not know or whom to ask to get the real story.

Briefly, Eugene DeBruin was shot down on 5 September 1963 while aboard a C-46 dropping rice to a Forces Armée du Royaume (FAR) position in Savannahkhet Province. One author, writing about MIAs in Laos, has alleged that this mission was illegal. One wonders how a rice drop requested by a Royal Lao Government army unit in Laos might be considered illegal, even in the mind of some fuzzy-headed liberal loony, especially since Air America had contracts with the Royal Lao Government to do just that sort of thing, that is, deliver supplies and transport people in Laos. While the pilot and co-pilot died in the crash, five crew members survived by parachuting from the aircraft before it hit the ground. Eugene DeBruin, three Thais and one Taiwanese were captured after landing on the ground. They were held in various prison camps in the area until May 1964 when the five escaped but were recaptured in a few days. In July 1964, while being held in a prison camp in Savannahkhet province, the Pathet Lao photographed the five and distributed the photo widely in Pathet Lao propaganda publications. Eventually, Jerry DeBruin, Eugene's brother, obtained a copy of this photo. This was the first concrete evidence for Jerry that his brother had survived the shoot-down.

In June 1966, the five Air America prisoners plus U.S. Air Force pilot Duane Martin and U.S. Navy pilot Dieter Dengler were in the same prison camp, Ban Houai Het camp near grid coordinates XD 3089. They all initially escaped, but all but one was recaptured. Dengler was picked up by helicopter 23 days after the escape had begun. Later, one of the Thais was liberated from the Mahaxay prison camp by a Lao irregular commando/raider unit from Savannahkhet in the only known successful POW rescue of the Vietnam War. No Americans were in the camp when the rescue was made. Dieter Dengler and the Thai, Pisidhi Indradat, were sources of information about Eugene DeBruin for the time they were all in the same prison camp. Dieter Dengler's life and his experiences in Laos were the subject of a 1997 documentary film by a German filmmaker, titled "Little Dieter Needs to Fly."

For the next 46-plus years, Jerry DeBruin has not had any further concrete evidence about the fate of his brother Eugene. There have been a variety of reports but nothing with the cachet of that photograph distributed by the Pathet Lao.

In March 1971, Team Papaya/305, while on mission with the materials I gave them about Eugene DeBruin reported that they had spoken to a villager who gave them information about Eugene after looking at his photograph. We cabled the information obtained by the team to Vientiane and Udorn, as that was the custom at that time. The Pakse reports officer was not sure the information rose to the level of being disseminable to the intelligence community on its own as an official CIA intelligence report. However, such information was often sent to Vientiane reports section in case they thought it did or in case it might be incorporated as a paragraph in an overall summary of POW sightings. Later, CIA personnel, who lacked knowledge of how things worked in a place like Laos, made much of the report not being directly disseminated. The lack of independent dissemination has transmuted into declarations that it was evidence that the report was considered a fabrication. Moreover, declarations have also been made that Bounlert was not trusted and was considered a fabricator. Far from it, I would never have sent Bounlert out with Jerry DeBruin's materials and my list of questions if I thought he was unreliable or a fabricator.

The next time I saw Lee Gossett in Pakse I gave him a copy of the information I had received from Team Papaya/305, as well as a copy of the questions we had given Bounlert for the mission. I felt that the raw information was not classified in any way and that Eugene's brother deserved to get the information.

In a strange turn of events, Lee Gossett visited Vientiane in June 1971 and was able to meet with Bob, a CIA officer assigned to the U.S. Embassy there. Lee had interviewed Bounlert using my Thai operations assistants, Niphon and Viroj. Lee had the information from the interview of Bounlert and a copy of the report from Bounlert's debriefing after the mission with him. Bob had Bounlert's report in his hand across the table from Lee and asked what specifically Lee wanted to know. Lee purposefully asked Bob questions for which he already had the answers.

Bob said, "We don't have any information on that." Lee knew Bob was lying and after a few minutes having his time wasted, he left.

Needless to say, this created doubts in Lee and Jerry's minds about the honesty of the Vientiane officer. It also raised questions about why they would conceal any of the information.

I never kept a copy of the report but Jerry, of course, did. Here is what Jerry has held on to all these years.

"Eugene Henry DeBruin arrived at Muong Phine (XD 0927) in late 1966. On or about 3 January 1967 DeBruin was taken from Muong Phine and arrived at Moung Nong (XD 6010) on or about 5 January 1967. The Moung Nong prison contained only eight other Americans at this time. While in Moung Nong, DeBruin was strictly guarded by the North Vietnamese Army and he suffered very much. The North Vietnamese Army did not torture him but kept him imprisoned and gave him propaganda lectures. Pathet Lao

General Khamkong and North Vietnamese Army General Tao, who speaks English, were the only high ranking officers to interview him. The North Vietnamese Army often displayed anger towards the prisoners because of the U.S. bombing in their area. DeBruin was allowed to eat his meals with, and talk to the other Americans but the villagers had no knowledge whether he ever received letters or packages. DeBruin never escaped from Muong Phine or Moung Nong, because he was strictly guarded. In early January 1968 Ong Lui and six North Vietnamese Army soldiers took DeBruin and eight other Americans away. The villagers did not know Ong Lui's rank and said he was not from that area, but probably came from NVN to get the prisoners. The villagers were told only that DeBruin and the others were being taken away for training. End of report."

I can state unequivocally that the above is the report that we received from Bounlert. I recognize the way the Thai operations assistants used the phrase "was strictly guarded" to mean he was confined all the time. Much has been made by DIA and CIA that a Lao Theung team would use a specific date when reporting events saying such uneducated men would not even understand the calendar we use. However, I note that the report uses the phraseology "on or about", which is the way the Thai operations assistants translated date timing received from the teams. The Thais knew we Americans wanted dates so they did their best to translate the timing used by the teams into western dating. They did the same with grid coordinates often translating what the teams told them about their movements on the ground in relation to known landmarks into grid coordinates. Again, that is what we wanted so that is what they gave us. The report was the operations assistants' version of what the team had reported.

After obtaining this information, Team Papaya/305 was never able to get any more information about Eugene DeBruin. After two years in Laos, running roadwatch and intelligence teams, I think I have an understanding how things worked with the teams. If the team were going to fabricate they would have fabricated much more to add to the above report. I gave them a very long list of questions. They would have fabricated answers to many more questions, and they would have not included negative information such as not having knowledge of whether he received packages or not. They answered only the questions their source could answer and said when they did not know an answer, which was not the pattern I saw with fabricators. They fabricated as many answers as they could and they were always able to go back and get more information by fabricating the trip and the information. Bounlert's report rings true with me, at least in that he reported what the source told him. I also believe the source was reporting reliably.

It was not until early 1991, almost twenty years later, that I was back in touch with Jerry DeBruin and we have stayed in touch ever since. I have tried to help him deal with CIA and DIA bureaucracy to get the Team Papaya/305 March 1971 report acknowledged but to no avail. It reminds me of the saying, "It only stops hurting when I stop banging my head against the wall."

Since 1991, I have met with Jerry when he visits Washington, DC to attend annual meetings of the POW/MIA group. Jerry is relentless in pushing the Lao, Vietnamese and his own government for information about the fate of his brother. I try to help him with formulating his "Action Plan" whenever he needs to understand the mindless bureaucratic monster and how best to phrase things so the monster might understand.

One thing I have never understood is the stonewalling by the CIA. Eugene DeBruin was an employee of Air America, a publicly acknowledged CIA proprietary. In this case, Air America existed only to carry out a mission for the U.S. government and it operated with funds from the U.S. government. How could any employee of Air America not be considered an employee of the CIA? Well, I can see that the CIA would be touchy about allowing the measure of employment to be whether a person carried out CIA directions and received money allocated from U.S. funds, as that would make any spy recruited to steal secrets an employee. But why didn't the CIA quietly act in a much more helpful way instead of treating Jerry DeBruin like a total outsider? Someone representing the CIA even went to Eugene DeBruin's poor parents and asked them to accept a paltry amount of money and sign a quitclaim. Eugene has now been in MIA status over 40 years. How much money in back pay would he or his family be entitled to if CIA acknowledged some form of employee status? How would the CIA have acted toward the DeBruin family if it knew it was on the hook for back pay and benefits for all the time Eugene is missing in action? I hasten to add that to my knowledge Jerry DeBruin has never brought up this issue with the CIA. He would have been satisfied with CIA assistance to determine his brother's fate before his parents died – never knowing the fate of their son.

RAVEN 42 IS DOWN

"Dignity does not consist in possessing honors, but in deserving them."

-Aristotle

C IA military operations in Laos were heavily dependent on air support. That support, provided by U.S. military aircraft, as well as Air America and Continental Air Services[39], included bombing enemy positions, bombing in defense of friendly positions, transporting men and supplies, search and rescue of downed pilots, and air dropping supplies to friendly forces. The weather played a significant role in affecting the air war. The more rain the cloudier it became, often socking in CIA sites and Royal Lao Army and CIA Lao irregular military positions.

The rainy and dry seasons in Laos both effected military operations. Rainy season made road use difficult for the North Vietnamese but allowed them to use the rivers. The rain clouds also provided extensive cover that obscured the ground from American aircraft. The dry season made it easier for the North Vietnamese to travel the roads and the smoke from dry season, rice field burning often obscured the ground, making observation from the air difficult. Nonetheless, dry season favored air strikes by American and Lao air forces.

The linchpin of the Bolovens Plateau, the city of Paksong, was located in the heart of the plateau and was the target of major North Vietnamese Army operations. The primary road from Paksong to Pakse was Route 23. Up to this time, the North Vietnamese had allowed Paksong to exist as a supply point for the communist Pathet Lao. Corrupt Lao military officers made nice profits supplying the enemy from Paksong. However, greater military considerations on the part of the North Vietnamese caused them to disregard the Pathet Lao's accommodation with the Royal Lao Army.

---

[39] Air America and Continental Air Services were airlines operated by the CIA to provide air support for its activities in Laos and Vietnam.

On 15 May 1971, the enemy captured Paksong without a fight. Paksong was only about 60 kilometers east of Pakse, on a straight line, and a bit longer overland on the Lao roads, which from the air looked like brown ribbons dissecting the surrounding green foliage.

At first, we did nothing to retake the city. The Royal Lao Army commander of the task force assembled to retake Paksong dithered and delayed. The American ambassador and CIA officials in Udorn and Vientiane put pressure on the Lao MR-IV commanding general, Phasouk Somly Rajphakdi, who finally appointed Colonel Soutchay Vongsavanh as the new commander. Colonel Soutchay, a very competent, effective and experienced combat commander, was soon promoted to General and replaced Phasouk as MR-IV commander. CIA officials from Pakse to Vientiane knew he would be the best choice if anything at all were to be accomplished. In fact, Colonel Soutchay rallied his forces, consisting of CIA Lao and Thai irregulars and Royal Lao Army regulars, and made a stand at Kilometer 28 on Route 23, which ran west – right to Pakse. If the North Vietnamese Army succeeded in dislodging Soutchay from Kilometer 28, they would be only about seventeen miles from Pakse, the headquarters for Lao forces in southern Laos. In fact, this threat caused the CIA Pakse Unit chief to evacuate all dependents to Udorn or Vientiane and send the remaining case officers to spend their nights at PS-18, a training site northwest of Pakse.

The North Vietnamese Army put heavy pressure on the Thai/Lao irregular position at Kilometer 28 on 10 June 1971. The Thai irregular commander, call sign "Right Guard", received steady support from the Pakse Ravens all during that day but as night fell the Ravens had to return to their base in Pakse. Air support was then coordinated directly between the nighttime Airborne Battlefield Command and Control Center (ABCCC), call sign "Moonbeam", and Right Guard, the Thai irregular commander. ABCCC units, like Moonbeam, flew over southern Laos in a special C-130 aircraft.

Right Guard was under heavy attack by as many as four Soviet World War II era PT-76 tanks. Moonbeam sent Spectre 17 (a USAF AC-130 gunship), Stinger 05 and Stinger 263 (USAF AC-119 gunships) and Spooky 263 and

Spooky 66 (Lao AC-47 gunships) to provide close support. Gunships like these were fearsome weapons that helped the Thai and Lao irregulars keep the enemy at bay all day on 10 June and through the night to the morning of 11 June.

All hell broke loose the morning of 11 June when the North Vietnamese Army attacked and overran the Thai/Lao irregular position at Kilometer 28. Having lost over 100 killed, an unknown number wounded and several hundred missing, the irregulars retreated west toward Pakse. However, before retreating, the irregulars had managed to destroy one of the enemy's PT-76 tanks. While there had long been intelligence reports claiming the North Vietnamese Army had tanks in southern Laos, this was the first conclusive evidence. For the Thai/Lao irregulars, the North Vietnamese were formidable enough, but tanks added a new and terrifying element to their power.[40]

Having taken Kilometer 28, the North Vietnamese Army began marching west in long columns on both sides of Route 23. This was not characteristic of the North Vietnamese but perhaps they felt emboldened because of the overcast skies and low cloud ceiling. This westward advance represented an immediate and frightening threat to Pakse. If we could not stop them, Pakse would fall. Unfortunately, for the North Vietnamese, a hole opened up in the clouds early in the morning right over Paksong and Kilometer 28. This caught the enemy in the open.

CIA case officers were putting in their own long hours on the ground, while the Ravens were fearlessly flying in support of CIA's irregular units trying to thwart the NVA advance from Kilometer 28 on to Pakse. Young CIA special operations case officers in Laos, all with some sort of military experience, easily built rapport with U.S. Air Force officer counterparts flying as forward air controllers (FAC) in the Raven program in Laos. A case officer

_____

[40] When CIA's Pakse chief of unit heard a tank had been destroyed he conspired with the Army Attaché (ARMA) assigned to Pakse, Colonel Mooradian, to fly in the ARMA's helicopter out to the tank and take a photograph of it. He enlarged the photo and sent it to the CIA chief of base at Udorn, who had long insisted there were no tanks anywhere in southern Laos. Across the photo, they wrote in bold letters, THIS IS A TANK.

could not get his job done, nor even survive alone without the aid of the Ravens and the Ravens found they could do more when they had the cooperation of a case officer on the ground. It was a symbiotic relationship and every case officer and every Raven had one or more friendships with each other. Generally, we all liked and admired each other.

The only forces available to help thwart the enemy advance were eight Royal Lao Air Force T-28s and whatever U.S. Air Force and U.S. Navy strike aircraft were available from missions in Vietnam or over the Ho Chi Minh Trail. The eight Lao T-28 pilots flew eighty-eight missions that day, an overwhelming effort by some of the bravest Lao anyone could ever hope to fight alongside.[41]

The 11th of June began for Lloyd (Dunc) Duncan when he rolled his O-1 down runway 31 at Pakse just as the sun was rising. Banking right, into the sun, Dunc pointed the nose of the aircraft eastward toward Paksong, a ten-minute flight. A pre-dawn phone call had rousted Dunc out of bed.

"Dunc, the NVA are attacking our positions near Paksong, we need you at first light."

Early morning in Laos at this time of year is cool and pleasant. As he lifted off in the early dawn light, Dunc had no way of knowing this was the beginning of more than 12 hours of grueling, horrific combat.

There were no backseaters available at dawn so Dunc took off without one.[42] He knew the Thai commander spoke good English, so he did not think he needed a Lao backseater to communicate with the ground forces. When Dunc ran low on gas or smoke rockets he had to fly back to Pakse, which he did at least three times that day. At the end of his first refuel and rearmament trip, he picked up a backseater, Nukeo, the only backseater available.[43]

---

[41] Brig. Gen. Southchay Vongsavanh, "RLG *Military Operations and Activities in the Laotian Panhandle*", U.S. Army Center of Military History, Washington, D.C., 1978.

[42] The CIA trained the men who became backseaters and made them available to the Ravens, who called them x-rays.

[43] Nukeo was a controversial backseater. Some of the Ravens did not like him at all. One of them described him as "a miserable little piece of pig shit" after he refused to

Dunc's (as well as many other Ravens') favorite backseater was Pantee. They considered him the best because he was very dependable, did not complain and was aggressive – he wanted to get after the enemy. Pantee was not available, so Nukeo was it.

Arriving on the scene, Dunc was briefed over the radio by "Right Guard", the Thai commander on the ground. Right Guard's English was quite good. Dunc was flying at tree top level to avoid the 12.7mm (equivalent to a .50 cal) guns that could chew up an O-1. The ground commander reported that the enemy had attacked using two tanks, but one was already burning alongside the road, the victim of Thai irregular anti-tank weapons. Dunc spotted the Thai irregulars in ditches and foxholes alongside Route 23.

"Raven this is Right Guard. The enemy is only fifty meters east of our position."

He was right. The North Vietnamese were all over the place. Dunc was now taking lots of AK-47 ground fire and even some from 12.7mm guns. The red trails left by the tracers were everywhere.

Meanwhile, other Raven forward air controllers (FAC) were getting into the fight. Larry "Pepsi" Ratts (Raven 41) and Jim Hix (Raven 44) soon joined Dunc in what was to be one of the epic "close air support to ground troops in contact" battles of the war in Laos. That day, cloudy weather socked in most of the rest of Laos and Vietnam. Thus, this battle on the Bolovens Plateau received almost all of the air power available in all of Indochina. For those few hours, the air war in Southeast Asia belonged to the Pakse Ravens. Hillsboro, the daytime Airborne Battlefield Command and Control Center (ABCCC) aircraft controlling all air support in southern Laos, offered the Ravens every U.S. Navy carrier based and USAF land based sortie available. The fighter jocks knew there was a set piece battle with the North Vietnamese Army going on in Laos and the skies were open. Every fighter pilot wanted in on the

---

fly during his lunch break when the Raven had a truck park target on the Bolovens Plateau with large secondary explosions on the first strike. Raven pilots were fierce warriors who could never understand a lunch break getting in the way of the mission.

action. From time to time Pepsi had to advise them there were so many stacked up he did not think he could use them all. Pepsi could detect what seemed like true disappointment from the ones highest up the stack. Many of the fighters hung around until bingo fuel (only enough to get home) just for the chance for one pass. Nonetheless, the Ravens accommodated almost every sortie they received.[44]

Route 23 runs in a generally western direction from Paksong to Pakse. That day, most of the 12.7mm guns were north of the road, with a few east of the friendly positions clustered around Route 23. Navy and Air Force air support was a mix of jets (fast movers) and propeller driven aircraft (slow movers). Close air support to troops in contact with mixed fast and slow movers, in the presence of deadly concentrations of anti-aircraft guns is tricky work that only a rare few of the most skillful and experienced forward air controllers can manage successfully.

As the day wore on, Dunc began to realize he was lucky he had not been shot down. Dunc had been careless that day.

It did not take long, however, for him to know where the 12.7 mm guns were and to stay away from them as best he could. Dunc was coordinating strikes dropping high explosive bombs, napalm, white phosphorus and CBU[45] everywhere.

After several trips back to Pakse for fuel and rockets, Dunc found another tank hidden in trees not far off Route 23. He was working all over the map all day long, but he never lost track of that tank. Nearing the end of the day, Dunc had not been able to put a strike on the tank but he had not forgotten it. Flying fearlessly in and out of ground fire Dunc was almost out of gas, tired,

---

[44] Some Ravens would say bingo fuel for them meant almost enough to get home or put it down safely somewhere and, if lucky, taxi into the chocks with the prop still turning.

[45] CBU stands for Cluster Bomb Unit. A cluster bomb is a bomb that when dropped, makes many smaller explosions covering a larger area than a typical bomb would cover. The bomb is not necessarily used for precision, but for destroying multiple targets at once or making sure something gets hit along with the outer perimeter of the target getting hit as well. (Source: the online Wikipedia)

hungry, wanted to return home to Pakse and had only one remaining smoke rocket. Nevertheless, he wanted to stay to guide an incoming flight of F–100 Super Sabres to the tank. If he did not stay, no one would be there to guide the fighters to the target.

Dunc maneuvered his O–1 and fired his last smoke rocket. By this time, previous bombing runs had blown all the trees around the tank away and Dunc's smoke marked it for the incoming F–100s. The fighter pilots radioed, "OK, we see the tank." Dunc watched the lead fighter make his run but both the lead and his wingman went by dry. The lead pilot had confused his switches and could not drop his bombs and neither did the number two. Dunc did not know what to do because he had used his last smoke.

The lead pilot called Dunc, "No problem, I see the tank, we'll come around for another pass."

Dunc thought, "I sure hope their bombs don't hit the friendlies."

The F–100s were carrying two 750-pound bombs each and Dunc watched the bombs come off the aircraft and go right into the side of the tank. When the debris from the explosions cleared, the tank was on fire. The bombs had blown off the turret. Dunc had seen many air strikes but that was the luckiest hit he had ever seen.

Dunc now had only 10-15 minutes of fuel left so he pulled away from the target area, turned south and starting climbing toward 500 feet. As he turned west towards Pakse, a 12.7 mm gun opened up on him.

Dunc thought, "I'm had", as one bullet tore through Dunc's leg and out the left side wing.

Dunc radioed Pepsi.

"41, 41 this 42, I'm hit in the leg and bleeding real bad."

It felt like someone had punched Dunc really hard. The shock of being hit made him temporarily lose understanding of what was happening. Then he remembered he was being shot at and his aircraft must have been hit.

Dunc thought, "This is what it feels like just before you die." However, Dunc was not dead and when he opened his eyes, he grabbed the stick and started flying. Then the engine quit. With the engine dead Dunc had to look for a clearing but all he saw was 30–40 foot trees. He lowered the flaps to full and when he reached the trees pulled back on the stick and stalled the O–1.

Pepsi started shouting into his radio, "He's going in, he's hitting hard, the airplane is coming apart." [46]

The O–1 smashed through the trees and kept moving as tree limbs and leaves battered the outside of the airplane. When the O–1 jolted to a halt, Dunc could see a tree about one foot in diameter halfway into the cockpit. He was pinned in because the front of the plane was crushed around his legs. Dunc struggled to get out and was able to pull his right leg free but his left leg was broken and he could not move it.

Nukeo, sitting directly behind Dunc, was not hurt in the crash. He was not pinned in and had escaped from the aircraft. He approached Dunc in the front seat and pried the fuselage metal away from Dunc's legs. It seemed to Dunc that it took about ten minutes but he was able to take hold of his left foot and pull it loose from the plane. Dunc was in a daze but it then seemed like it took another ten minutes to get clear of the crashed aircraft with Nukeo's help. Dunc could not help thinking, "If I'd had much fuel left it might have caught fire and I would have burned up with the plane."

Without Nukeo Dunc would not have been able to get out. Dunc fell out of the plane and crawled about 100 yards or so away, again with Nukeo helping him. The leg hurt a lot and when he looked back, he noticed a significant trail of blood from where he had been. Dunc decided he had to stay put or risk losing even more blood while trying to move.

Dunc's survival radio was still in the O–1, in his survival vest slung over the back of his pilot's seat. Dunc told Nukeo, "We need my radio. It's still in the plane."

Nukeo did not hesitate to immediately leave Dunc and retrieve the radio. Without that radio, neither Dunc nor Nukeo could be rescued before the North Vietnamese captured them. Dunc took the radio from Nukeo and tried

---

[46] The USAF ABCCC, Moonbeam, recorded Raven 42's shoot down at 1755 hours (5:55 PM) at 050/25/82 (on a 50 degree heading for 25 miles off Pakse TACAN 82) or about 40 kilometers northeast of Pakse.

to call Pepsi but the radio would not work. Dunc thought, "Damn radio's broken." Nukeo reached over, took the radio, and pulled the antenna all the way out. That worked and Dunc remembered learning during survival school that this was important. Good thing Nukeo knew it. Shock was beginning to set in and he was not thinking clearly at the time.

With the radio now functional Dunc was able to make contact with Pepsi. At the same time, Dunc could see Pepsi's aircraft and red tracers barely missing him. He thought, "Pepsi is going to be shot down for sure."

Jim Hix thought, "It's like the 4th of July, pretty red tracers everywhere and a little too close to my airplane to suit me."

"41, 41 this is 42. I see you. I'm about 100 feet from the airplane, west, I think."

Pepsi started circling overhead, very low. The 12.7 tracer rounds were just missing his tail. As Pepsi flew over Dunc's head, Dunc would say, "Now", meaning that Pepsi was right over him. The next thing Dunc heard were grenades going off around him. It was Pepsi shooting his 40 mm M-79 grenade launcher out the window of his aircraft at the enemy.

"41, 41 this is 42. I can hear the enemy all around. They're too close, I can't risk moving."

Pepsi could see the enemy converging on the crash site. He urgently wanted to direct them away from the crashed O-1 or perhaps convince the enemy that Dunc was somewhere else. Pepsi was desperate. He did not have any more smoke rockets or M-79 grenades or even any more ammunition for his Swedish-K, but he wanted to lure the enemy away from Dunc. What he tried next might be considered foolhardy, but in combat trying to save your comrade, sometimes you do such things without thinking them all the way through. Pepsi tried the "wounded bird" technique. He made low passes everywhere Dunc was not but which might look like a hiding place. Pepsi was frantic and he did not have any air support to bomb with, so he did the first thing that came to mind.

In fact, Dunc and Nukeo were in a tense and alarming situation. They could not see the enemy but all around there was whistling. The North

Vietnamese were keeping track of each other while they circled to surround Dunc and Nukeo to capture or kill them. The enemy whistling was alarming and eerie.

At this point, Lao T-28 sorties arrived so Pepsi had them drop bombs all around Dunc and Nukeo. In fact, Pepsi gives major credit to the fearless T-28 pilots. If there were not too many of them, Pepsi asked them to make more than one run. If a lot of them were stacking up Pepsi changed his guidance.

"Cobra Yellow, Cobra Yellow, this is Raven 41. Pickle sequentially, make your run, and beat it back home for more bombs. Don't even use your .50s."

Not using the .50 caliber machine guns minimized exposure on pull up and while coming around and let the next flight move in quickly.

"OK 41, but we gonna run our guns on roll in, too."

Using the guns was a maneuver that increased their risk as the T-28s were exposed while aiming at the target and then again as they transitioned to low altitude bomb delivery.

"Hey, Cobra Yellow, nice."

"You know it, 41."

"You're next Cobra Black. Same heading as Cobra Yellow. Lay your bombs 50 meters short of Yellow's. He took .50 cal fire on climb out, so break hard left. Cleared in hot!"

USAF and Lao bombs rained down around Dunc. Pepsi radioed him, "How was that?"

"41 this is 42, I can't stand much more of that"

Dunc was face down burrowed into the ground as low as he could go. He could hear shrapnel whizzing through the trees. He thought, "These bombs are going to kill me." The T-28 bombing stopped and Dunc could not hear the enemy anymore.

Dunc noticed Nukeo was gone and thought he might have taken off. Dunc had told Nukeo, "Save yourself if you can, don't worry about me." Dunc had released Nukeo to do what he must to survive. However, Nukeo returned and said, "We're surrounded, there's no way out on the ground, we need a chopper to get us."

"41, 41, this 42. When is a chopper gonna get here?" Neither the first nor the last time Dunc would radio Pepsi with the same question.

Up in the air over Dunc, Pepsi and Jim Hix had divided their duties. No one remembers anyone taking charge or giving orders as to what to do. Experienced pilots just know what to do, almost as linked minds thinking the same thoughts. Someone needed to suppress the 12.7 mm guns to allow air strikes to protect Dunc – Hix took that chore. Someone else needed to cover Dunc and drive away any enemy soldiers that might kill or capture him and insure the area around Dunc would be safe for whatever helicopter might come to pick him up – Pepsi took that chore.

Jim Hix was working mostly fast movers north of Route 23 against the 12.7 mm guns. Route 23 was a prominent marker that conveniently divided the area. North Vietnamese 12.7's were usually arrayed in groups of three and Hix had identified at least seven guns north of Route 23. He had also spotted at least three 12.7 mm guns two kilometers to the east where one of them was the one that probably nailed Dunc. Hix had gone after the eastern anti-aircraft guns first and took out all three using Lao T-28s. Eventually Hix wound up with all the fast movers attacking the 12.7's north of the road flying from west to east while Pepsi had only slow movers under his control flying east to west, probably because the slow movers were best for putting in strikes as close as necessary to Dunc without hitting him. Hix was directing the fast movers to dump their bombs quickly. He did not need to be concerned about hitting friendlies. There were only enemy north of the road. Hix was flying in an altitude envelope that made him a perfect target for the 12.7 mm gunners. They had marked him as their priority target. For his part, he could not mark the guns without putting himself in grave danger so he came up with the idea of Lead pulling off high and Two then seeing the tracer and coming in on the guns from behind.

"Canasta[47] this is Raven 44. Suggest Lead make a dry pass and pull off at 10 grand. Two, stay hot on Lead's ass."

---

[47] Call sign for a U.S. Navy A-7 based on an aircraft carrier off the coast of South Vietnam.

It worked. It was getting dark and the 12.7's muzzle flash was a great mark. The 12.7mm guns started shooting at the fighters and marked themselves. Once the guns were marked, the fighters went after them. The A–7's were carrying Rockeye CBU[48], which spread out in a football field shaped pattern and shut down most of the remaining guns.

How does one truly appreciate Jim Hix's nimble juggling of so many assets on up to five different radio frequencies while flying in an arcade shooting gallery where he was the slow moving duck? He had to dodge multiple first-rate anti–aircraft gunners, monitor the frequencies of ground troops (FM), T–28s (VHF), and fast movers (UHF), switch to Dunc and Pepsi on the guard frequency and check in on the ABCCC frequency. At the same time, he was directing air strikes as close to the friendlies as possible with multiple low and slow aircraft moving in and out of the area. For one hour, Jim Hix commanded the air war in Southeast Asia, not the generals, not his own chain of command – just Jim Hix, Raven 44, the unofficial but acting "one and only Air Marshal", for one hour, of all Laos.

Meanwhile, the Pakse deputy chief of operations, Ratana, was flying back to Pakse in an Air America Pilatus Porter aircraft. Ratana was on one radio frequency talking to Pakse when the Porter pilot heard, "Mayday, mayday", on the emergency guard channel. The pilot tapped Ratana on the shoulder. "There's something going on, you need to hear this."

Ratana ended his conversation and turned to listen to the emergency guard channel. Ratana and Dunc were good friends. Ratana told the pilot, "Let's fly toward Paksong and see if we can help."

The Air America porter arrived on the scene flying at a much higher altitude than the Ravens, T28s, and U.S strike aircraft. Ratana had a good overview of the area and could see red enemy tracers directed at the friendly aircraft. It helped him zero in on where Dunc was. Ratana noticed the bright color of the cloth sewn inside Dunc's hat and the difference in colors in the clothing worn

---

[48] The Mark-20 Rockeye cluster bomb unit (CBU) is a free-fall, unguided cluster weapon designed to kill tanks and armored vehicles.

by Dunc and Nukeo as compared to the surrounding foliage. He quickly calculated an eight–digit grid coordinate and passed it on over the radio.

Pepsi (Raven 41) was also monitoring the guard channel. He had probably been the first one to hear Dunc using his survival radio after the crash.

Finding Dunc on the ground happened in two separate events. First, the wreckage of the O-1 was spotted but Dunc and Nukeo had already moved away from it. Then Jim Hix saw Dunc.

Dunc was on the ground approximately an hour when two Air America helicopters, led by Hotel-88, arrived on the scene. It was dark and hard to see, except for the red tracers from the anti–aircraft guns. Hotel-88 checked in first with Raven 44 and asked for directions.

"Hotel-88 this is Raven 44. I'm busy fucking up those enemy guns and making sure I don't run into any T-28s, check in with Raven 41."

Hotel-88 came over the radio, "Guns are still firing at us, Raven 44, can you get them?"

Hix had a flight of two F-100 Super Sabre fast movers with 500-pound bombs available.

"Hotel-88 this is Raven 44. I'm putting in bombs north of the road, that'll screen you from the remaining guns so you can go in for the pick up."

It was all desperation stuff because of darkness and the need to get Dunc out.

Dunc could hear Pepsi giving them a thorough briefing on the situation. After hearing the bleak picture Pepsi described, Dunc began to doubt they would be able to get in to pick up him and Nukeo. He did not give up hope but he was bleeding badly and he did not think he had much time left.

Raven 42 had been shot down about the same time as the end of the workday for CIA up-country case officers. Most of them had already landed at the CIA irregular training site at PS-18 before Dunc's mayday went out over the radio. One of the incoming flights heard what was going on and brought the news.

The case officers had arrived at PS-18 but were in no hurry to disperse because there was still an operations meeting to attend that often lasted more than one hour. Small groups formed near each other at the edge of the runway. They stood around chatting and comparing notes on the days' events. Unexpectedly, word passed through the group that one of the Raven pilots had been shot down near Paksong.

A Raven was down. We all dreaded being shot down and wondered what we would do if that happened to one of us. Would we be on the ground in one piece? Would there be enemy all around and could we escape and evade through terrain we had only seen from thousands of feet in the air? If wounded or injured, how would we survive? There is no helpless feeling like the one that goes through your mind when your comrade, your buddy, is down and you have no idea if he will survive or not. What can you do? How can you help?

Two H-34 helicopters, each piloted by Thai pilots accompanied by a Thai flight mechanic, were on the runway preparing to fly out to rescue the Raven. As the members of the group mulled over the bad news, I bolted for the open door of one of the helicopters carrying my survival bag.

No one yelled, "Hey, Tom, where're you going?"

It was an instinctive reaction. "Get on the helicopter and see what you can do to help save the Raven." You do not have to be helpless. You can do something.

I jumped through the door just before the helicopter took off on its way to find the downed pilot. The captain of the helicopter, call sign Hotel-88, was Van U-Muang, the co-captain was Sompong Maneewan, and the flight mechanic (kicker) was Samran Kumsap[49].

I took a seat on one of the red canvas jump seats in the belly of the helicopter. I was carrying my survival bag in which I kept my maps, survival kit and a .45 cal. automatic pistol. I stowed the bag under the seat after taking out my maps. I usually carried several different maps but the one I wanted was the 1:50,000-scale map of the area near Paksong.

---

[49] The H-88 crew was identified thanks to Sarisporn Bhibalkul, former Thai Air America pilot in Laos.

I flew out over the combat zones in a Porter most days and was used to seeing the ground and knowing where the aircraft was going. Sitting blind inside the helicopter made me nervous. It was hard to sit and do nothing and not know what was happening. I decided to ask Samran, the flight mechanic, where we were going. An H-34 flying with the door open is noisy from the sounds of the engine and rotor. It is impossible to talk to anyone else without the aid of a helmet and headset tied into the pilots' and flight mechanic's communication system. The whop whopping of the rotor blades and the rush of air through the open door would drown out anything I tried to say, so I got up from my seat across from the flight mechanic and moved over to sit next to him. I showed him my tactical map, gestured out the door, and then down at the map. In response, he pointed out a position, along the side of Route 23, the highway from Pakse to Paksong. I knew this area had seen a lot of combat in the past few days.

A thought popped into my head, "Oh shit, what have I gotten myself into?"

There was nothing to do about it, however, but just return to my seat and see what would happen.

I was blissfully ignorant of all that was going on as the Ravens were fighting desperately to keep the advancing North Vietnamese soldiers from finding and capturing or killing Raven 42.

We arrived in the area and it did not take long to locate the wreckage of the Raven's O-1. The helicopter pilots bravely maneuvered the aircraft into position and hovered it in the face of intense ground fire from small arms. Hovering a helicopter in this way made it as vulnerable as it could be. But, where was Lloyd Duncan? Since I was only carrying my survival bag with a .45 caliber pistol in it, I pantomimed wanting a weapon to the flight mechanic. He pulled out a Swedish-K 9mm-submachine gun and handed it to me. I checked the magazine, chambered a round, grabbed an extra magazine and moved into a position in the open door so I could fire on anyone who tried to interfere with our rescue. I braced myself against the doorframe of the open door. The sling of the sub-machine gun was over my shoulder so I could hold the gun steady. I pointed the gun out the door and both the flight mechanic and I scanned the ground looking for the downed pilot. I could only hope I would not fall out the door, as I had nothing to secure me to the aircraft.

I was thinking, "Where are the enemy soldiers"?

Isolated from the pilots and flight mechanic communications, I could not hear any of the radio traffic among the Ravens, the strike aircraft and the rescue helicopters. I had no idea enemy ground fire was ringing our aircraft without hitting us.

I stared down into the trees and dense foliage searching for enemy soldiers trying to find and capture Raven 42. At times, all I could see was dense jungle and nothing else while sometimes the ground was more open. If anyone were on the ground, I should have seen him. With the help of the grid coordinates provided by Ratana in the Air America Porter and information from Ravens Larry Ratts and Jim Hix, our helicopter pilots located Dunc sitting with his back to a tree.

The pilots now knew where Dunc was but were standing off at a safe distance waiting for the area to be secure enough to make the pickup. They needed to hover in place to get a briefing on the situation from the Ravens and they did not want to approach Dunc until the last minute so as not to point out his position to the enemy. They also needed to stay clear of the bombing runs that were still going on. Dunc could not move anymore so the pickup would have to be a hover and sling drop operation. The trees were thick. It was rapidly getting dark, soon too dark to see into the dense trees. Shadows were making it increasingly difficult to see anything on the ground. Pepsi gave the helicopter pilot instructions to go in to make the pickup. Hotel-88 maneuvered in closer, to about 100 meters away from Dunc and Nukeo. Flying above it all, Ratana saw that it was getting dark and there was not much time left to make the pickup. Ratana now came over the radio, "It'll be night soon, don't fuck around any more. Go get him now!" Hearing this, Hotel-88 swooped in just as daylight was failing. Meanwhile, Ratana's aircraft was low on fuel and had to leave. The last thing Ratana saw was Hotel-88 flying in to begin the rescue.

Dunc had an old hat with a bright red panel sewn into the inside. He had already been displaying it, turned inside out. Now, Nukeo waved it.

In the meantime, Raven 44, using the T-28s and the Navy A-7s with Rockeye CBU, had silenced the anti-aircraft guns. Raven 44 had also directed a screen, using bombs from the F-100s and his own smoke rockets, between the gun positions and Dunc's position - just in case.

The pilot of Hotel-88 began to maneuver to get into position to lower a cable with a sling to lift Dunc out. The helicopter hovered while I stood on one side of the open doorway and Samran, on the other side of the door, lowered the sling toward the backseater and the Raven. I kept up my surveillance of the ground and made sure I stayed out of the flight mechanic's way. I had never operated a sling like that so I did not want to muck anything up. Samran, the flight mechanic, was prepared to ride the sling down to help Dunc, an incredibly brave thing to do because there were enemy tracers flying all around our aircraft. That became unnecessary, however, because the backseater helped Dunc into the sling, since Dunc could not do it himself. We hovered, exposed and defenseless. The rotor blades were whipping the trees and other foliage all about. The sling extending down to the ground seemed to tether us to the ground. We wanted Dunc and Nukeo to move as fast as they could as we still had to remain out in the open while the sling, now encumbered with the weight of both airmen, came back up slower than it had descended.

On the ground, as soon as the backseater had gotten Dunc into the sling he immediately placed one foot in the harness and, holding on to the cable leading up to the helicopter, rode the sling up to the relative safety of our aircraft. I thought to myself, "That backseater is not taking any chance that we won't lower the sling a second time." He may have even been thinking the ground fire and enemy presence were so intense we might not be able to make two sling extractions.

Dunc and his backseater came up to the level of the door and the backseater had to slip around the flight mechanic as we jostled Dunc into the aircraft. The backseater jumped into the helicopter and sat exhausted on the floor of the airplane in the tail area.

The flight mechanic and I grasped Dunc as best we could and pulled him into the helicopter. We carefully sat Dunc down on the floor with his back to the sidewall of the helicopter. The flight mechanic went back to his seat and used the internal communications to tell the pilots they could get out of there.

I thought, "I better look him over for wounds."

Dunc wondered, "What the hell is Tom doing here."

It was late in the afternoon and the sunlight was rapidly waning. Inside the helicopter bay, it was hard to see because of the dim light. Dunc had a gray pallor and his movements were sluggish. I noticed a rip in his jump suit and a lot of blood on the lower half of his pants leg. He had a nasty leg wound and must have lost a lot of blood.

They used to tell us in first aid training that you should not use a tourniquet unless it is very urgent. I decided I could control his bleeding at an arterial pressure point next to the wound and above it nearer to his heart, with my fingers. I became a human tourniquet. The blood was not spurting, the sign of a cut artery, but rather bleeding slowly the way cut veins bleed.

I maintained the pressure. I began to worry that I might be missing something. I did not want to sit there mindlessly being a human tourniquet while something else went wrong. I reviewed the situation in my mind. Dunc had a lot of blood on his flight suit. If he lost too much he could die. I knew we were flying to our training site at PS-18 where we had a first class field hospital with surgeons who could save Dunc but they had to know how much blood he had lost. What if he arrived there and they did not have enough blood to replace what he had lost?

I had to briefly leave Dunc and get close to Samran, the flight mechanic. I moved quickly from Dunc to the jump seat next to Samran and leaned over so I could speak to him as close to his helmet as possible.

"Ask the pilot to radio PS-18. Tell them the Raven has lost of lot of blood. He'll need transfusions when we arrive."

I quickly returned to Dunc's side and resumed pressure on the arterial pressure point above the wound. Dunc did not seem to be conscious and never spoke to me during the entire flight. I don't know how long it took but it was arduous and stressful, bouncing around kneeling on the deck of the aircraft while trying to maintain a steady hold on Dunc's pressure point so he would not bleed anymore.

As we flew steadily from the combat zone toward the hospital, the pilot relayed my message back to PS-18. A call went out for volunteers to give blood. CIA case officers already at PS-18 began to line up. Arriving Raven pilots and USAF ground personnel assigned to Pakse to support the Ravens joined them. All had flown to PS-18 from Pakse, gone to the hospital and given blood. By the time Hotel-88 arrived, there was a good supply to use on the wounded Raven.

Hotel-88 swept into PS-18, headed straight to the hospital and landed as close as possible. Hospital personnel, shuffling along bent over at the waist, rushed up to the helicopter with a stretcher. Even though the rotors would never be able to hit anyone, most people did this when approaching a helicopter with the rotors turning. They brought the stretcher up to the side door. Hands reached out, moved Dunc to the stretcher and took him into the hospital. I stood in the bay of the helicopter watching Dunc disappear into the hospital. We used this hospital to treat our Lao and Thai irregulars brought in wounded from combat. The hospital had two excellent Filipino surgeons led by Dr. Val who operated on Dunc, gave him transfusions and prepared him for evacuation to a rear area hospital. The skill of the surgeons, plus stanching the flow of blood during the flight and having enough blood for transfusions, saved Dunc's life. The Air Force medically evacuated Lloyd Duncan back to the United States and I never saw him again in Laos.

———

Postscript

I had not thought about this event in a long time when one day in April 1999, twenty eight years later, my good friend Eli Chavez, called me out of the blue, from Caracas, Venezuela. Eli called me to tell me that he had long considered it a grave oversight that I had never been recognized for what I had done to save Lloyd Duncan. Eli was then a DEA Special Agent in Caracas and had regular dealings with the CIA deputy chief of station (DCOS) there. Eli had convinced the DCOS to submit a recommendation about me to CIA head-quarters and Eli wanted me to write up a description of what had happened. I eventually sent Eli an excerpt from Christopher Robbins' description of Raven 42's rescue from his book[50]. I also sent Eli a description of the rescue as best I remembered it.

Having dredged up this old history, I decided to visit the Ravens web site on the internet. I wound up getting in touch with Larry "Pepsi" Ratts, Raven 41. Larry and I exchanged emails about the rescue and Larry eventually put me into contact with Dunc. Dunc and I also exchanged emails.

We eventually had a reunion in Crystal City, Virginia. I learned that Dunc had met his wife in the hospital where he recovered from his wounds from being shot down in Laos. They had two fine children and a happy life until she tragically died at a young age. Ratana, who had been a close friend of Dunc's in Pakse, joined us. We drank a few beers and told war stories. It was great to see Dunc and to hear about his life after the day he was shot down. Dunc was then living in Texas and was a commercial airline pilot.

More recently, Dunc (Raven 42), Pepsi (Raven 41, Jim Hix (Raven 44), Ratana and I had a reunion in Cocoa Beach, Florida. Dunc is now retired in Montana, Jim is a retired commercial airline pilot living in Florida and Pepsi is working in medicine in Washington. More than once, when thinking about the events of that day, Dunc has said, "An amazing number of things all had to go just right in order for me to survive that crash."

The details of Dunc's rescue and the dialogue described in this chapter were reconstructed, to the best of our memories, from extensive email correspondence among Dunc, Pepsi, Jim, Ratana and me.

---

[50]Christopher Robbins, *The Ravens: The Men Who Flew in America's Secret War in Laos*, Crown Publishers, Inc, New York, 1987.

Nothing much has come from Eli's recommendation, but I have come to a much more important realization. I told Eli it means much more to me that he knows what happened and he believes what I did was worthy of recognition. Eli received an Intelligence Star, the CIA's highest award for bravery, for his actions while with his GM at Long Tieng, and if he believes in me, that is all I need. I also have the satisfaction of meeting Lloyd Duncan all those years later and learning that he continued his career in the Air Force, had a happy marriage and fine children of whom he is proud. I know that what I did made it possible for those people to have the lives they did and that, too, is reward enough.

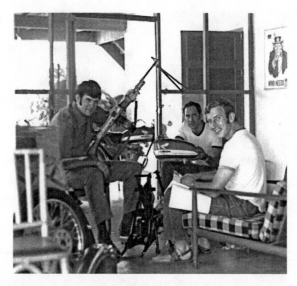

[L–R] Lloyd Duncan (Raven 42), Frank Kricker (Raven 40) and Jim Hix (Raven 44).
Photo courtesy of Lloyd Duncan

Larry "Pepsi" Ratts (Raven 41)
Photo courtesy of Lloyd Duncan

**Lloyd Duncan (Raven 42) with Royal Lao Air Force T–28 pilots
Photo courtesy of Lloyd Duncan**

**The tank destroyed by Lloyd Duncan just before he was shot down on 11 June 1971
Photo courtesy of Lloyd Duncan**

Lloyd Duncan's crashed O–1
Photo courtesy of Lloyd Duncan

Tail Number H–88 – the helicopter that picked up Raven 42
Photo courtesy of the Air America Association

FRAGGING THE NAI KOU

———◆———

And I looked, and behold a pale horse:
and his name that sat on him was Death.

-Revelation, 6:8.

I started my two-year tour in Laos supervising one of the three Pakse based roadwatch operations from PS–38, Guerrilla Zone II headquarters, on the southern end of the Bolovens Plateau. In 1970, the Pakse chief of unit moved the SGU operations, as well as my roadwatch operations from PS–38 to PS–22, Guerrilla Zone I headquarters. While on PS–22, I was given supervision of the other two roadwatch projects (the one based on PS–22 and the one originally based at LS–171, Guerrilla Zone III headquarters). As the Bolovens Plateau came under more pressure by the westward advance of the North Vietnamese Army, Pakse management decided to transfer my roadwatch operations from PS–22 to PS–47. Pakse Unit management felt there was too much danger of PS–22 being over run. It would be better to move the road-watch operations while it was still safe and easy to do. PS–47, not far off Highway 13 the road from Vientiane to Pakse and then on to Phnom Penh, was not quite fully operational as an irregular battalion base. The chief of unit and chief of operations decided I should share PS–47 with the Guerrilla Zone III irregular units that had moved there from LS–171.

From time to time, I held formations for all my men in camp. I usually did this when several teams had returned from missions and were due to receive their pay. I liked to pay teams in front of all the troops so the team members would know how much the team was receiving. That way the team leader could not cheat them. I had learned early in my time running roadwatch teams that there were team leaders who would tell the team I had paid a lesser amount than I had. Then the team leader could keep the difference from what I had paid and what he actually paid them. Sergeant Vouk commanded the formations. First, he said a few words to the men, thus confirming his position as their leader. I had inherited Sergeant Vouk from the LS–171 roadwatch program. The PS–

38/PS-7 and PS-22 roadwatch programs did not have a camp commander. Sergeant Vouk was a Lao Theung (tribal Lao) and had a good reputation with the LS-171 case officers, so on the recommendation of Viroj and Hom I retained him as the camp commander of the overall roadwatch program, which we named Team 300. Then the teams due to be paid were called to a nearby hut where I was ready to pay each team. The Thai operations assistants usually set up a table where I sat with the money and a roster. I used the roster as a checklist for paying the teams and would file the original copy with my finance accounting and keep the second copy as a record of who had been paid. Sometimes a team leader would not be able to sign his name in Lao so we let him make an "X". Hom used to get a kick out of pointing out to the team leaders who could not sign their names that I could write Lao. He then asked me to show the team leader how I could write my name, "Tan Chanh", in Lao script, which he had taught me once when I asked him to show me how to do it. Hom then told the team leader he should at least learn to write his own name, since the American Nai Kou had been able to learn to write Lao. While the team leader was at the table receiving and signing for the money, the men in his team stood outside the hut but could see what was going on. The idea was that the team leader had to go back out of the hut and face the men with the money I had paid him. This made it harder for the team leader to lie to the men about how much he had been paid. A team member would never go behind the team leader's back and ask me how much had been paid. It would cause loss of face both for the team member and for me. However, the team leader would lose face if it turned out that he had lied to them.

We were sitting in the team headquarters building waiting for the men to form up in formation. I was with Hom and a couple of the other Thai operations assistants because Hom had told me he wanted to go out and check the formation before I went out there. We heard an explosion; the kind of thing that makes your heart beat faster and wonder if we were taking incoming fire or if we were under ground attack. The fact that it was only one explosion was actually reassuring since any kind of enemy attack would entail more explosions and small arms fire.

Hom had not been acting normally and seemed tense. I started to jump up to go out and investigate. Hom said, "Wait, Tan Chanh, let me go first."

I sensed that something was definitely wrong, as I had not seen Hom act this way before. I decided to let Hom go and stayed behind waiting. Hom went out with one of the other Thai operations assistants.

After a few minutes, the other Thai came back. "Tan Chanh, one team leader is dead. There are several wounded. We need a helicopter right away to take wounded to the PS-18 hospital.

I went to the single side band radio and called the Pakse air operations officer.

"Grey Fox, this is PS-47. We have an emergency. We need immediate medevac from here to PS-18 hospital."

I then radioed the chief of operations and told him we had casualties from an accident. He told me to file a report as soon as I knew all the details. I went out to where the soldiers had been forming up and found Hom giving directions to get the wounded to the runway. I went to the runway as I heard over the radio that the Air America H-34 pilot wanted assurance that it was safe to land. He was worried that the soldiers on the ground might be in revolt and he was not going to land if he thought they would fire on him. I presented myself out in the open on the dirt runway and talked to him on an HT-2 VHF radio to assure him that the site was still under the supervision of the site customer, me. When he saw me, he came in and landed. Some of my men, carrying one man with blood all over his uniform placed him sitting up in the aircraft. His arm was heavily bandaged. Flying shrapnel had hit my supply officer. There was a lot of blood and he looked dazed but he was walking to the aircraft. As soon as all the wounded were loaded, the aircraft took off for the hospital.

I went back to Hom and asked him to fill me in on what had happened. Hom told me that one of the team leaders had had a live grenade in his hand with the pin pulled and it had exploded blowing off his arm at the elbow. It had also killed the soldier next to him and wounded our Lao supply officer. In the past, I had called for formations when I was going to pay teams for their completed missions. If I believed a team had fabricated their mission, I sometimes reduced their mission pay and sometimes I refused to pay them at all. This team leader had decided the night before that I was going to refuse to pay his team for their mission and had decided to use the hand grenade on me if I did. He had consumed a large amount of alcohol before the formation and had lost control of the hand grenade allowing it to explode in his hand. Hom had gotten wind that something was up and was worried that violence was planned against me. That was why he had not wanted me to go out to the front of the formation until he had a chance to go out there and see if he could tell if it was safe or not.

One can only guess what caused the team leader to think he would not be paid and why killing me would be a solution. He was under the influence of a large amount of alcohol, but I am not sure that explains it. One might infer that the team had probably fabricated some or all of their mission and my reputation for uncovering fraud and my inclination not to pay mission pay for fraudulent reporting had led the team leader to become desperate. Ironically, whether he had committed fraud or not, in this case I was unaware of it and was prepared to pay the team for a full mission.

THE TRAGIC CRASH OF XW–PCL

To live in hearts we leave behind is not to die.

-Thomas Campbell, (1777–1844) Scottish poet. "Hallowed Ground", (1825), Repr. in Complete Poetical Works, ed. J.L. Robertson (1907).

When I arrived in Laos and began working with the roadwatch teams, I could not speak Lao. Special operations case officers were not given language training. Traditional case officers assigned to Vientiane were usually trained in French or Lao and some special operations case officers, who had been in Laos for several tours, could speak a certain amount of Lao, but most special operations case officers had young Thai, or young Lao men, assigned to them to work as operations assistants. The young Thai men could speak enough English to communicate with the case officers. Some of them spoke better English than the others. They did not always speak good Lao but the lowland Lao and the hill tribesman usually understood their Thai or "Thai accented" Lao. To be sure, there were problems. A Lao hill tribesman was speaking Lao as a second language and often could not read or write Lao. A Thai operations assistant who spoke Thai or "Thai accented" Lao would be difficult for a hill tribesman to understand unless the hill tribesman had become very fluent in Lao. As far as I knew, all of my Thai operations assistants were college graduates except one. They were generally hard working young men and I came to like them all. While their full names were on record, we called them only by their first names or by nicknames. The best of my group were Hom, Viroj and Niphon. After Viroj and Niphon's tragic deaths, Somneuk and Thong developed into very competent operations assistants and I came to value them very highly.

Hom had been involved in Lao operations for many years. I once had a long talk with him about his past career and he mentioned that he had started out with what he knew as "White Star." As far as I know, White Star was a code name for U.S. Army Special Forces (Green Berets) who operated in Laos in the early 1960s. I first worked with Hom in mid–1970 after my arrival at

PS-22, so he had probably worked in Lao operations for almost ten years by that time. Hom was Thai, but he was married to a Lao woman and had children. His Lao was native and he could pass for a Lao. While Thai and Lao often seemed to be indistinguishable to many Americans, they could tell each other apart. Hom and I got along very well and I respected him very much. He had a charisma that beguiled Thai, Lao, hill tribesmen and Americans alike. Hom was always sober on the job but when he drank, he often got very drunk. He maintained a refined demeanor even when drunk but he would drink to a point of passing out. I worried that he might be an alcoholic or terribly vulnerable to becoming one. I owe my life, or at least that I was not severely wounded, to Hom. His long experience in Laos and his attention to what was going on among the team soldiers made it possible for him to avert a tragedy. I was very fortunate to have such a professional, experienced and loyal assistant.

Pete, also known as Boonsong, was Hom's assistant. Peter was his Christian name as he had converted to Christianity. He was quiet but competent. While Hom was willing to accept responsibility and liked to exercise authority, Pete just wanted to do his job and was not interested in taking on any authority or additional responsibility. He seemed introverted and shy, not socially outgoing. He was absolutely competent and always got his assigned tasks completed.

Thong was my senior operations assistant at PS-38. Initially, his English was not good and I had a hard time communicating with him. He was, however, a very earnest young man and worked hard to do his job the best he could. Over many months, his English improved and by the end of my tour in Laos, I would have rated him one of the best of my operations assistants. He was another dedicated, loyal young man and the more experience and confidence he gained the better he became. By the end of my tour, I could depend on him to work all day long without my direct supervision and I would be completely happy with what he had accomplished.

Somsit was Thong's assistant at PS-38 and arrived in Pakse about the same time I did. Somsit marched to the beat of different drummer. He spoke very heavily Thai-accented Lao and made no effort to try to improve. I first noticed his attitude when he was assigned to be the interpreter for Bob, the senior polygraph operator in Laos at the time. Bob liked to tell the roadwatch team members who were being polygraphed that there was a spirit in the polygraph machine that could tell if the team member was telling the truth or not. Somsit thought that was stupid and was not translating what the polygrapher told him. Bob knew enough Lao/Thai to recognize that he was not being translated accurately. He came to me to complain and Hom and I had to talk to Somsit and convince him to just translate what was being said and not to interject his personal beliefs into the job. He was a very intelligent young man, seeming quite bookish. In another day and age, he might be seen as a geek, a translator of documents, not someone who would climb aboard an aircraft and fly out over the Ho Chi Minh Trail to coordinate military activities on the ground below. Somsit would have become an excellent operations assistant if he had not met a sudden death.

Viroj was one of the finest young men I have ever known. He was married and had a child. His family lived in Thailand and was not with him. He was the only other operations assistant, besides Hom, who was married. He was quiet but effective. He and Niphon were a very effective team. They were the LS-171 operations assistants and I inherited them when I took over those roadwatch operations. Viroj had a charisma about him that made him difficult not to like. The team soldiers he supervised looked up to him and the case officers who worked with him liked and respected him. If I wanted to sit with him and ask questions about Thai or Lao food, culture or traditions he was more than happy to describe them to me. When I wanted to learn Lao, he enjoyed trying to teach me. He saw the value of the procedures I wanted to establish and readily adopted them and tried to make them better if he could. His loss was a great tragedy for all of us.

Niphon was quite big for a Thai. He had a lot of natural charisma and was well liked by everyone I knew. His complexion was much darker than the other Thais and he had a good sense of humor. He exuded an aura of power and bravery. He was confident and would do anything he was asked and would try to do it the best he could. He liked to pilot the Porters and whenever a Thai Porter pilot was working in Pakse, he would let Niphon fly the airplane. It eventually cost him his life. The loss of Viroj and Niphon were very hard for me.

Somneuk was one of my favorites. He never failed to try to do his very best. He worried about the team soldiers and always wanted to make sure they were well supplied. I felt very close to him. After I left Laos, I received a Christmas card from him. He had become the director of security at one of Bangkok's big tourist hotels. At my departure, I felt my successor would be well taken care of by Hom, Thong and Somneuk. They were less than half the number I had but they were so experienced and professional I felt they would be able to support him in any manner he required.

By the middle of my assignment to Laos, I had the jobs formerly held by four or five different case officers and one job that the chief of unit had established just for me. Carl, the Pakse chief of unit (COU) during my second year in country, was a believer in making sure the collectors had proper requirements and he wanted good intelligence production. Prior to Carl's arrival as chief of unit, the unit reports officer was totally responsible for receiving the intelligence information collected by the case officers, analyzing it, and preparing intelligence disseminations for transmission to Vientiane and Washington. In addition to the reports officer there was a part time reports assistant. The reports officer was also supposed to provide requirements to the case officers but this was a random process. Generally, the chief of operations, DCOU and COU directed the case officers in accordance with what they thought were Pakse's intelligence requirements. Carl did not think that process was good enough and he wanted someone besides Pakse's managers to focus on requirements. Carl asked me if I wanted to take on the responsibility for the unit's intelligence requirements and reporting, he called it "IRR", and wanted me to supervise the reports officer and the reports assistant.

While the idea had some attraction, I did not want to convert into a desk jockey, sitting back in Pakse reading intelligence reports all day long. I countered with a proposal that I would take on the IRR responsibilities in addition to all my other tasks. The reports officer was doing a good job on the essential task of writing and disseminating intelligence reports and I did not see any need to spend much time looking over his shoulder. Indeed, he would have resented that. After agreeing to become responsible for Pakse IRR, I sat down with the reports officer and explained that I did not plan to spend much time interfering with his work, but rather that I wanted to concentrate on requirements and validation. Having observed the reports process for about one year I felt that not much was being done to insure that the information we were reporting was valid. The reports officer felt he had enough to do and as long as I did not interfere with what he was doing, he had no problem having me as his supervisor, or that is what he told me and he never said anything different as long as we worked together.

We had one case officer assigned to traditional intelligence collection, that is, he was supposed to spot, investigate, assess, develop and recruit sources that could report information that provided answers to our requirements. I always thought this was a wasted effort. It did not seem to me that he could recruit sources in Pakse who would have access to what the North Vietnamese Army were doing out in the denied areas. He might be able to find sources with access to Lao communist activities but that did not seem to be worth the effort, as it seemed to me that the Lao communists were total lackeys of the North Vietnamese Army. In my opinion if you wanted intelligence on the North Vietnamese Army you had to find a way to recruit North Vietnamese Army soldiers and traditional methods were not going to help anyone do that. The one other target for a traditional case officer would be recruiting sources in the Royal Lao Government so we could keep current on what they were doing and try to determine if anyone there was working with the communists.

Our one traditional case officer had a less than sterling reputation with the unit's special operations case officers. He had a large stable of sources but they never seemed to report information that was worthwhile in any way or that was verifiable. Among the special operations case officers we used to snicker about some of the stories he told. One of the favorites was the story of his principal agent running a network collecting intelligence on the Lao communists. A case officer with a network of agents usually only dealt with one agent who was known as the principal agent. Sometimes the case officer insisted that he would only deal with the principal agent for security reasons. This type of network is often used in denied area operations where the principal agent infiltrates the denied area and recruits the sub-agents. The principal agent has to have a way to cross back and forth from the denied area to the friendly area. If the security forces in the denied area are efficient and competent, the principal agent does not travel back and forth much while still being the primary communicator. In a place like the denied areas of Laos, it would be difficult to have very many valuable reporting sources. They would not rise to the level that would justify giving them real time technical communications equipment nor would it be worthwhile to set up traditional tradecraft reporting via dead drops or secret writing. The most reasonable method to communicate with low-level agents is to have the principal agent travel into the denied area to contact the sub-agents and get their reports. The principal agent would then return to the safe area and report to his case officer.

I will call this case officer, Terry Malone. His nickname by the time he left Laos was "House of Cards." Terry paid the network's sub-agents by giving the principal agent all the money and sending him into the denied area to pay them. One day the principal agent returned to tell Terry that on his way to pay the sub-agents he was crossing the river and the boat rocked back and forth and the satchel holding all the money went over the side into the river. Terry wrote this up as factual and asked to write off the money so he could give the principal agent a second bag of money. All of us who had been in country a while, and had to be constantly on guard not to be ripped off, laughed and snickered when we heard this. We were all sure that the principal agent was ripping Terry off. In light of this and other stories and events surrounding Terry, I paid close attention, in my new IRR job, to the information he turned in to the reports officer. One day I came across a report that Terry had submitted from one of the agents in his best network. The report described how the agent had learned that a North Vietnamese Army unit of about 100 men had moved an amount of rice and ammunition to a storage location and stored them. I decided to analyze the information. The agent had reported the amounts of ammunition and rice that the North Vietnamese Army soldiers had carried. It was easy enough to calculate how much the rice and ammunition weighed and then divide it among the 100 men. If every man, including officers, carried equal weight, each man would have had to carry 100 pounds of rice and ammunition, in addition to his personal weapon, ammunition and equipment, making the total load at least 120 pounds. In addition, I calculated the distance the agent said was covered and calculated that to cover the reported distance the unit would have had to travel 12 hours a day at 10 kilometers an hour. A well-conditioned American soldier would be lucky to be able to carry 40-50 pounds total at two to three kilometers an hour. North Vietnamese Army soldiers had a reputation for being indomitable soldiers but there really was no way to believe they could carry almost triple the weight, five times faster for 12 hours at a time, with no rests.

I then turned to the part of the report that concerned the rice storage depot. I got in touch with a United States Agency for International Development officer I knew well and asked if he could tell me how much storage space 100 kilograms of rice would take up. Terry's report did not describe what the rice storage depot looked like. However, it did state the size of the space and the amount of rice being stored. Using the USAID officer's information, I calculated that the reported amount of rice would have to have been stacked 300 feet in the air in the reported 12 by 12 foot space.

I told the reports officer that he should not bother with this report because we could not disseminate it. When Terry heard from the reports officer that his agent's information was not going to be sent out as an intelligence report because I had rejected it, he went to the chief of operations. This officer had replaced Ray as the Pakse Unit chief of operations. He listened to Terry's complaints and then went to the reports officer and ordered him to disseminate the report. When the reports officer mentioned to me that the chief of operations had ordered that the report be put out I went to see him and asked him if he was aware why I had decided not to disseminate the report. After describing my analysis to him, the chief of operations changed his mind and agreed the information could not be disseminated.

Terry was not happy with what happened and tried to go around me after that. One day I came across a report that Terry had submitted from one of his agents that reported that his agent had walked through an area and not seen any enemy activity. I checked the date and location and realized that I had been flying in a Porter over the same area on the same day. The Porter pilot had flown down to tree top level and we had seen North Vietnamese Army soldiers in combat with some local guerrilla force soldiers. I had not previously had much opportunity to observe the enemy and it was fascinating to see them as they ran hiding and shooting. A Raven FAC was beginning to put in air strikes on them. They needed to hide and we needed to clear the area so that we would not be in the way of the strike aircraft. How could Terry's agent have gone through the same area and not reported a thing? On that day and in that area there had been combat and air strikes and the agent reported nothing. I decided it would be better if I talked to the chief of operations first, so I went to him and explained the problem. He still did not want to do anything about it. I suggested that I could draw up a series of questions to ask Terry's agent. I framed the questions in the form of requirements for a more in depth debriefing of the agent. I sent them to Terry with a request that he talk to the agent again. Terry came back and actually had the balls to report that the agent had now remembered that he did in fact see enemy activity on the day in question. It was obvious from the new report, however, that the agent was giving just vague responses without any real detail. Terry's position was that the agent had redeemed himself and should now be trusted to have given a good report. Most of the special operations case officers I knew would have been pissed off that an agent had tried to take them to the cleaners and would not have rested until learning the truth. You had to wonder if maybe Terry had some other reason to want to validate the agent. Terry later served in another Asian country. I met a woman who had served there with him. We began trading Terry war stories and I mentioned that we called him "House of Cards" because when he left none of his agents could be turned over to anyone else. The whole structure he had been running just collapsed like a house of cards. She was amazed because they used the same phrase for the same reason when he left that country, too.

No one likes to think that a colleague may not have been honest. It is called a "red flag" when a case officer's cases collapse like a house of cards and none of his agents can be turned over. It is almost a 100 percent certainty that something is wrong with the case officer when none of his agents turn over and when it happens in two consecutive assignments there really can be no doubt. Terry went on to become a chief of station and then suddenly and mysteriously resigned during that assignment. There were many rumors about why but I never heard any details. If he had been committing fraud, it took long time to catch up to him. If he was not committing fraud, I am one who would like to know why he resigned. He was a likeable guy and got along well with most of us in Pakse.

As it turned out, my assignment to this desk job probably saved my life. Before the assignment, I got up every morning (except Sundays) and flew in a Porter to my up-country site, whether it was PS-38, PS-22, PS-47 or lastly PS-18. I spent the day on the site, sometimes flying out of the site on missions, and then flew back to Pakse in the evenings. Of course, there were days when I might make more than one trip back and forth but usually we spent the whole day on site.

Most of the Continental Air Services Porter pilots were Americans, but there were times when the pilot was Thai. There were many days when I sat in the back while Niphon sat up front with the Thai pilot. The Thai pilots were very friendly and let any of us take the controls if we were interested in flying. I had a vague idea that Niphon liked to fly and was doing some of the flying but I had no idea how much he was flying or that he was taking off and landing as well as controlling the aircraft once it was at altitude and making its way up-country.

I had taken my own turn at flying the Porter at the urging of one of the American pilots. He let me take over the stick and pedals once the Porter was level. He continued to handle the flaps and the throttle while I had the stick and foot pedals. On one flight, he insisted I handle the stick and foot pedals on take off and landing but I was very nervous the whole time even though he was ready to take the stick if necessary. It was a nervous but thrilling thing to do, but I only tried taking off and landing that once. After I took on the desk job, I either spent a half-day in Pakse or sometimes the whole day. The up-country assignment and the desk assignment were not compatible and I was getting to the point where I wanted to give up the desk job and just concentrate on my teams up-country. The tragedy that happened one day when I stayed behind in Pakse might have happened to me if I were not still working on the desk assignment.

On this tragic day, instead of flying up-country, I was sitting in the office near the single side band radio we kept for maintaining communications with all the up country sites and with other locations in Laos. A horrifying message came over the radio that the Porter taking my operations assistants to PS-47 had crashed while on approach to the runway. It was not clear how bad the crash was but I raced out of the office and down to the airfield to find an aircraft and fly to PS-47 to find out what had happened. From what I could piece together from witnesses who were on the site that morning, the Porter had flown the approach leg and the base leg and then after turning into the final leg almost immediately went down short of the runway in an area overgrown with trees. There were a lot of trees but it was not thick, dense foliage. I never found out just what had caused the Porter to crash, other than that Niphon was at the controls and he must have made a mistake that the Continental Air Services pilot could not correct.

When I arrived at the site, we walked out to the crash scene. The aircraft was sitting there on its bottom with no wheels holding it up. The engine and wings were largely intact but broken, as it seemed to have pancaked. The wings, which usually carry most of the highly flammable fuel and that were across the top of the fuselage over the pilot's compartment, were broken on either side of the fuselage. When the wings broke across the fuselage the fuel, highly flammable JP-4, spilled continuing forward and splashing across the extremely hot engine, igniting in an intense gush of fire and flames that engulfed the pilot and passenger compartments. A massive intensely hot wave of burning fuel hit all the occupants. They died in place. I could see each of them, what was left of their blackened bodies, sitting just where they were when the fire hit them. They looked like blackened sculptures. To this day, my memory is permanently seared with the image of Pete (Boonsong), with his hands frozen in front of his face as if to ward off the fire and his mouth wide open, grimacing in horror. It was an overwhelming scene. I was severely overcome by the loss of my friends. In two years of working steadily with the same young men, I had come to like them personally. They did a good job and worked hard, but more than just good employees, camaraderie had developed between them and me. They taught me about Thai and Lao customs and I learned the Lao language from them. They asked me questions about Americans and what it was like in the USA. We flew over the Ho Chi Minh Trail and other combat zones in Laos together, risking death in many different ways, accidental crash, shoot down, being over run while on forward sites, etcetera. It was such a sad thing to see their young lives snuffed out so quickly and cruelly. We knew we worked in a dangerous environment but we did not dwell on it. When death did come, it was surprising. I thought, "How could death have found us? Why in this way?"

I stayed at the crash site while the necessary work to remove the bodies from the wreckage was accomplished. Once I determined that everything was being done to properly take care of the bodies, I flew back to Pakse to go to the office of the Thai military intelligence officers who were responsible for my operations assistants. I had to tell them that four of their men had died. I was in a highly emotional state and I could only get out a few words of my first sentence before breaking down crying. I was sobbing so hard I could not talk and I seem to remember the Thai officer hugging me and trying to comfort me and calm me down, asking me what had happened. I was finally able to tell him.

Niphon, Somsit and Pete (Boonsong) were bachelors and I am sure their families were devastated by their loss, but I felt really bad for Viroj who was married and had a small baby. What a terrible loss for his young wife and child. All of these young men had their charming characteristics, but Viroj was a particularly charismatic young man. We were a pretty well meshed team, in my eyes, and I really felt their loss for a long time. I really think I never actually got over it. Funeral services were held in Pakse and it was a very sad time for me.

DEPARTURE

———————•◆•———————

"*War is an ugly thing, but not the ugliest of things: the decayed and
degraded state of moral and patriotic feeling which thinks nothing worth a war, is
worse. When a people are used as mere human instruments for
firing cannon or thrusting bayonets, in the service and for the selfish purposes of a
master, such war degrades a people. A war to protect other human
beings against tyrannical injustice; a war to give victory to their own ideas
of right and good, and which is their own war, carried on for an honest purpose by their
own free choice––is often the means of their regeneration.
A man who has nothing which he cares about more than he does about his personal
safety is a miserable creature who has no chance of being free,
unless made and kept so by the existing of better men than himself. As long
as justice and injustice have not terminated their ever renewing fight for ascendancy in
the affairs of mankind, human beings must be willing,
when need is, to do battle for the one against the other.*"

–John Stuart Mill, "The Contest in America", pp. 208-09,
in John Stuart Mill, Dissertations and Discussions
(Boston: William V. Spencer, 1867).

During the second half of 1971, Pakse management became more and more apprehensive. Every time there seemed to be any possibility that Pakse would be threatened with being overrun by the North Vietnamese Army the chief of unit would react. First, he would order that everyone had to abandon their houses on the airfield side of the Sedone River and sleep in various accommodations on the Pakse city side of the one lane bridge over the river. That ended when he cried "the sky is falling" and we spent five nights on the other side of the bridge until nothing happened at all and he allowed us to return to our houses. Finally, he began ordering evacuation of the families. Such an evacuation would leave only case officers behind. During one evacuation my wife and the chief's wife were designated "Pakse Rear", the source of no end of friendly jokes, most typically referring to them as "Pakse's Rear." One evacuation had all the case officers living on PS-18 instead of in our own houses in Pakse. There were a number of two man cabins on PS-18, built for some reason I don't think I ever knew, and parceled out among the case officers. Now as I write this so many years later I cannot remember that management lived on PS-18, too. For a while, it was like going to football camp before school starts in the fall; after a while though it became tiresome. All the spouses and children were cooped up in the Vientiane Embassy Guest House where a good deal of time was spent at the swimming pool with the children.

Now, from a perspective many years after the fact, I might be able to see that the chief of unit really had our welfare at heart, but unfortunately, he had no real leadership skills. He seemed to arrive in Pakse with the idea that he knew exactly how to run the program better than it had been run in the past. I would have to agree that things needed to be run better but he had his own ideas and never tried to test those ideas with us or even solicit our opinions. He made many changes, in many different things and then, as often as not, he would change them back. One source of great amusement to many of us was the constant movement of our mailboxes. Of course, in the beginning it was not amusing at all. In the army, they used to say, never mess with a soldier's pay or tamper with the timely delivery of a soldier's mail. Put civilian men and women in a dangerous, hostile situation and they view mail the same way. Our mail arrived twice a week and we eagerly awaited it. Someone in the Pakse Unit, in the distant past, had built a mail receptacle with a "pigeon hole" for each person or family to have one. The mailbox stood in its time-honored place in the office. One day the chief of unit decided to move it. There was turmoil and uproar, not for any good reason other than you just do not mess with someone's mail and the chief of unit never provided any particularly good reason for the move. Then a few weeks later the mailbox moved again. This repeated several times until it finally ended up right back where it had started. For many of us, we could only roll our eyes and shake our heads in wonder. It just did not make any sense. Just as often, the chief of unit made other decisions reflecting on our standard of living while not making many changes in the way we conducted operations. We needed to have a settled home front so that we could confront the dangers and hostilities of running special operations and unconventional warfare (by this time actually conventional war conducted by irregular units) without worrying about our home life. He probably believed he was making the home front safer but he was creating upset and turmoil doing it and that was counterproductive and undercut his ability to lead us.

The final few months then were chaotic. We suffered through two family evacuations and when it came time for our departure, we were enduring the second evacuation. My wife was in Vientiane while I was in Pakse in charge of our final pack out. Pack out was not a big deal because we only had what we carried in suitcases on the flight out to Laos and air freight. We were subject to the same rules as those in the State Department Foreign Service. Normally, a person is allowed to take air freight and sea freight, including furniture, to an unfurnished overseas post. However, if the housing in an overseas post is furnished, you are allowed a smaller amount of sea freight than when the housing is unfurnished. You can not take your own furniture. Going to Laos, they told us not to send any sea freight at all, that we would only need a few personal things and should send only air freight. Thus, I did not have a lot to deal with but it was in a chaotic context, created by the chief of unit, of imminent enemy attack. You had the feeling that any day you would look up and a North Vietnamese Army soldier would be at your door to take you away to Hanoi. That may be a bit of hyperbole on my part but the constant pressure of evacuate, sleep across the river, evacuate, sleep at PS–18, etcetera, created chaos and havoc over top of just dealing with the military situation and what was going on at the up-country sites.

Despite all that was happening on the home front, my Thai operations assistants did not want to let me go home without holding a big party for me. We had been together for all of my two years and we had been through a lot. I like to think I know how to take care of those whom I supervise. I found out, in a round about way, that none of them had had a raise in their basic salaries in more than five years. I say "round about" because they would never have brought the subject up themselves. They did not come to me and ask me for a raise. I was not directly responsible for paying them so I was not aware of how much they were paid. At one point a cable had come from CIA headquarters asking for information about one of them. In the process of getting the information I asked CIA headquarters how much they were paid and how. The cable reply mentioned that information and included the date the most recent salary amount had commenced. That was how I learned they had not received a raise in quite a long time. Without mentioning anything to them, I wrote a cable to CIA headquarters requesting raises for all of them and providing laudatory comments about them to justify the raises. The money to pay them was funneled through the Thai government for payment to them. When they began to receive more money, they asked why and their Thai management told them their American counterpart had recommended it. They let me know they knew I had made the arrangements and that they were very pleased to receive recognition after such a long time. I also think they appreciated my time with them because I was not a micro-manager or a control freak. I gave them specific responsibilities and let them do their jobs. To be sure, I knew everything that was going on and I only included myself in the details of operations that were of particular importance and only then in a way that treated them as colleagues whom I happened to supervise. I think they appreciated that.

This was going to be one hell of a party, with roast pigs, plenty of lao-lao[51] and all the men from the roadwatch teams (Team 300) at PS-18 in attendance who were not on mission or on leave. The Thai operations assistants told me that the only way you could have a powerful Buddha was if someone gave it to you as a gift. They gave me two Buddhas that I still have. Each Buddha engraved with an image of the King of Thailand. One had been a gift from the King to the Thai Border Patrol Police (BPP) and they re-gifted it to me. The boys from Thailand felt these were the most powerful Buddhas they could give me. I sometimes wonder if they thought that in going back to the United States, I might need all the protection I could get.

Some of the Lao believed a strong Buddha could keep them safe from harm even in combat. Khamsing had a commando/raider team leader who was absolutely fearless in combat. He was known to stand up in a hail of bullets to fire back at the enemy, believing his Buddha would deflect the bullets. One day Khamsing got into a discussion with the team leader about whose Buddha was more powerful. Seeing he could not shake his team leader's belief in his Buddha, Khamsing decided to have a test of which Buddha was more powerful. Khamsing set up a 60mm mortar with tube and base plate and stood on one side of the tube. He told the team leader to stand on the other side of the tube. He then dropped a mortar round into the tube. The idea was that if the Buddhas were strong they would protect Khamsing and the team leader from any harm. Khamsing, however, knew the mortar

---

[51] Lao-lao, meaning Lao alcohol, was a locally made alcoholic drink, which we would probably term moonshine if it were made in the United States.

round would not come directly back down on them and was counting on the round landing far enough away to not hurt them (a very dangerous thing to do on any account). The poor team leader did not realize the round could not come straight back down on top of them and dove for cover before the round hit. The shrapnel did not hit either of them, but the team leader lost face and his confidence in his Buddha was destroyed. He was never again the same fearless warrior and I often wondered just what Khamsing had gained from his little exercise in playing "chicken."

My going away party at PS-18 was a rousing success. Two whole pigs were roasted over an open pit and large quantities of beer and lao-lao were drunk. Songs were sung and there was a lot of dancing by the firelight. It was a good thing that we could stay over night and sleep at PS-18 because most of us were in no shape to do anything but try to sleep it off. Besides, the party did not begin until after nightfall and project aircraft did not normally fly at night and certainly not to come pick me up to take me back to Pakse after midnight. All the same, it was a bittersweet ending to my stay in Laos. I am still good friends with a few of the case officers I worked with in Laos, but of all the Lao and Thai I worked with I was the closest to my Thai operations assistants. I respected them very much. Obviously, I could not have done my job without them because they were my interpreters and translators. However, more than that, they tried to do everything I asked, they risked their lives every time they flew out on infiltrations, exfiltrations, re-supply drops and air to ground radio contacts. Of the seven original interpreters, only three were still alive and working for me. The three, Hom, Somneuk and Thong, were experienced, diligent, competent and brave. Young men who made me proud to have worked with them. There were many things to miss in leaving Laos, but one of the most important to me was leaving behind these good friends.

I arrived in Laos, a 28-year old Vietnam veteran and left a 30-year old CIA veteran. We lived in a small community of CIA, U.S. Air Force, U.S. Army, United States Agency for International Development, and State Department volunteers, mostly young singles or young married couples (some with children) who depended on each other in good times for our social contacts and in bad times for mutual support in survival or even escape to safety. The work was extremely rewarding in many ways and now many years later, I view it as one of the best experiences of my life. I made friends I still have today and I have memories that I will never forget. If Thailand were not so far away, I would want to look up the surviving operations assistants and find out how they are doing these days. What happened to them over all these intervening years? The Lao members of Team 300 intelligence collection and action teams fought on the side of keeping Laos independent and neutral. They now live under Lao, really Vietnamese dominated, communism. How did things work out for them? After the end of the war, were they imprisoned or executed? What did they do with their lives? Did any of them decide to leave Laos and live in Thailand or elsewhere? How are they living now?

When you work with people like that, you think the greatest betrayal is to walk away and leave them to their fate. I am not alone, among CIA veterans of special operations around the world and over many years, to develop a special feeling for the people we train and often guide in special operations. The war in the north, at Long Tieng in support of Vang Pao and the Hmong people, received the most publicity and is the best known. Some Hmong were able to leave Laos and settle outside the country, including the United States. The world does not know much about the people of southern Laos, who also worked with us. My good feelings about the positive things we did in Laos are tempered by the fact we abandoned them. Now with communist regimes having failed almost everywhere we can only hope that if the Lao people continue to live under communism it is their choice to do so. Failing that, I can only hope that some day, if they so choose, they will be able to rid themselves of the yoke of communism imposed on them by the North Vietnamese communists.

SPEAKING TRUTH
TO POWER –
LESSONS LEARNED

———◆———

"Wish to advise that this will be final message from Saigon Station...It has been a long fight and we have lost...Those who fail to learn from history are forced to repeat it. Let us hope that we will not have another Vietnam experience and that we have learned our lesson. Saigon signing off."

–Declassified final cable from CIA's Saigon station, April 1975.

Wayne, a branch chief in Special Operations Division (SOD), now deceased, was a believer in after action reports. He also believed that a good after action report was the basis for lessons learned and it was important to learn from experience. Of course, it is also important that after action reports and lessons learned are available to those who come later and that they read and digest that experience. Those who follow us have to have the mindset that there are lessons learned. They need to look for them, find them and read them. Unfortunately, my experience in 32 years of government service, in the military, law enforcement and intelligence, is that after action reports and lessons learned end up, more often than not, locked away in safes or destroyed unread. My favorite saying about this is, "Yeah, he has twenty years of experience, one year repeated twenty times." Nonetheless, here is my attempt to say something about lessons learned.

The CIA's covert action program in Laos consisted of two parts, special operations and unconventional warfare. I am defining special operations as clandestine, irregular, small teams intelligence collection and action operations, where action operations means operations that are primarily intended to kill the enemy rather than covertly collect intelligence. I am also defining unconventional warfare as the use of indigenous irregular soldiers, formed into teams, squads, platoons, companies, battalions and even regiments for the purpose of carrying out guerrilla type combat operations. My definition would not allow these unconventional units to be used for conventional combat, that is, to attack the enemy to seize and hold territory. I would argue that if you want a country to have conventional forces you should bring in U.S. military personnel capable of training and advising conventional units and you should provide arms and equipment for those conventional forces. If political considerations prevent the use of uniformed U.S. advisors and you cannot sponsor conventional forces, then your goals and objectives in the country may never be more than unconventional forces can achieve, that is, you probably will not be able to seize and hold territory.

It has long been military theory that conventional ground forces have the mission of closing with and killing the enemy and seizing and holding ground. Unconventional ground forces are to be used to fight guerrilla style, that is, fight only when having numerical superiority and/or the element of surprise, and melt away and hide among the civilian population or in unreachable redoubts in order to fight only on their own terms. It is a basic fact of bureaucratic life, both military and civilian, that one does oneself no good reacting to requests from higher authority by declaring that you can not really do what has been requested. Thus, for example, when asked to employ unconventional guerrilla units as conventional units for political reasons, the military or civilian bureaucrat does not explain why not, but says, "Yes, sir, can do." That then, is what leads to failures. How many times in the history of this country have operationally benighted civilian leaders asked the professionals to do something that was not reasonable or feasible or both? How many times have those professionals told their leaders, no? An interesting project for research, but the most recent example comes from the decision to invade Saddam Hussein's Iraq. The fate of General Eric Shinseki is a shining (or tarnished, depending on your point of view) example of what happens when you do not just stand to attention and say, "Yes, sir."

Another factor is that unconventional guerrilla operations, including special operations, only work against open societies. It is impossible to conduct such operations against closed, totalitarian societies. Thus, when asked to operate against a totalitarian society, the correct reply is that it cannot be done. The most that can be hoped for is to be able to conduct intelligence collection operations by recruiting agents while they are located out of the closed, totalitarian country and then clandestinely communicate with them once they return to their home country.

When the primary activity of the North Vietnamese Army in Laos was to use the country as a corridor for its supply line into the Republic of Vietnam, the CIA's objectives were to organize and run irregular units that would reconnoiter the Ho Chi Minh Trail area to find targets for American fighter/bomber aircraft and to conduct hit and run guerrilla style attacks against North Vietnamese Army targets. CIA in Laos initially used the larger 50-man Special Guerrilla Unit (SGU) patrols for ambushing smaller North Vietnamese Army units and for collecting intelligence. Small roadwatch and action teams were intended more for reporting enemy locations for bombing than to try ambushes, but if the North Vietnamese Army unit were small enough, the teams might also ambush them. SGU and roadwatch case officers were operating like their OSS predecessors who operated with resistance movements to harass the enemy and tried to collect intelligence about enemy activity behind the lines.

When the North Vietnamese Army began to expand its control westward from the Ho Chi Minh Trail toward the Lao cities on the Mekong River, the CIA tried to turn the larger irregular guerrilla units into regimental units (Groupement Mobile or GM) for use in confronting the North Vietnamese Army and taking them on in main force combat. The CIA's GM case officers were then more like MACV advisors assigned to the Army of the Republic of Vietnam (ARVN). However, the ARVN was an actual main force army, equipped, trained, supplied and advised by U.S. military personnel, while the CIA organized and trained irregular guerrilla forces were far from being anywhere near that level, as low as some American military officers might have believed the ARVN were. Nevertheless, roadwatch case officers were still in the business of collecting intelligence behind enemy lines and taking on the North Vietnamese Army only in typical hit and run guerrilla style operations. A good special operations case officer in roadwatch operations was not going to collect intelligence that would end up on the President's desk, but he could still collect valuable intelligence for use in conducting unconventional special operations against the enemy.

During the 1990s, because of the increasing threat of terrorism, narcotics trafficking and the proliferation of weapons of mass destruction in the hands of people who might use them against us, the issue was raised that American Intelligence does not have enough people who can pass for foreigners and infiltrate the cultures of the terrorists, narcotics traffickers and weapons proliferators. In my opinion, and I believe the history of intelligence would support me, if it could be fully known, many more people betray trust and provide secrets voluntarily than are ever convinced to do so when first they had not thought to betray. It is much better for a potential volunteer to believe the person to whom he is volunteering is an American than for him to worry that the person who claims to be American is a double agent actually working for the host country's intelligence service. The ability to speak a language fluently while obviously appearing to be an American is more important than being ethnically identical to the people of the target country. A subtle point but quite valid.

Moreover, in the milieu of law enforcement intelligence there are two types of cooperating individual, also known as a snitch or informer: the "involved" and the "non-involved" cooperating individual. Generally, the most useful and sought after cooperating individual is the one who is involved in the criminal activity. How much could a person who is not actually involved in crime really know? Criminally involved people do not go looking for law enforcement officers to volunteer their services. Rather, criminally involved cooperating individuals begin to cooperate when a law enforcement officer finds a way to coerce that cooperation, known sometimes as "twisting" or "flipping" a criminal. One obvious example is to convince the criminal that you have enough evidence to convict him but you are willing to put in a good word with the judge if the criminal will provide information about criminals higher up in the criminal enterprise. Another example, often seen in television dramas, is to tell each of two criminals that one is about to make a deal and implicate the other, indicating that the first one to cooperate will get the favorable deal. Usually, law enforcement cooperating individuals do so because they have no choice, but sometimes they cooperate in order to eliminate their competition or for revenge. In any case, the goal of law enforcement intelligence operations is to gather enough evidence to arrest criminals, put them on trial in a court of law, and get convictions. To do that, law enforcement usually wants the cooperating individuals to testify in the court proceedings, thereby making the cooperation public.

The collection of intelligence about the acquisition and use of weapons of mass destruction by the governments of other nations would be a proper objective of national security intelligence collection operations. Our government could negotiate with such nations and seek to establish foreign policy in relation to those nations based on the understanding gained from such intelligence reporting. The collection of intelligence on terrorism, narcotics trafficking, or the acquisition and use of weapons of mass destruction by non-governmental entities is the collection of intelligence on criminal activity. It is law enforcement in nature, that is, it has short–term goals. Law enforcement intelligence collection seeks to arrest, to try and to convict. In military or special operations environments the goal of intelligence collection, also relatively short term, is to locate and capture or destroy the persons involved in the enemy activity in order to win battles and end the war. When it comes to traditional intelligence collection in support of national security the goal is, more often than not, to recruit a person with access to secrets and leave that person in place for as long as possible. Secret activity changes once the opposition knows it is no longer secret. False secrets, known as disinformation, are passed via the uncovered spy. Denied area special operations intelligence collection, sabotage, or other such activities are short term, military oriented in their goals. If war has been declared, it would be more appropriate that special operations are conducted by uniformed military personnel, but when war has not been declared and there is reason to want to be able to deny that the U.S. government is involved then special operations might best be conducted by CIA special operations officers. That is not to say that the CIA officers just take the place of the military personnel in the denied areas, but that CIA officers clandestinely run the operations from safe havens. A government cannot plausibly deny that it is involved in special operations if its CIA officers are killed or captured in the denied area.

In the case of denied area operations, we either have to send our own in-telligence officers (here I mean employees of CIA) behind enemy lines or send agents (citizens of foreign countries) we have recruited who are inhabitants or former inhabitants of the denied area. Of course, we can send combinations of the two. When sending our own intelligence officers behind enemy lines we intend for them to avoid all contact with the enemy. Their function would be to contact rebels or partisans and become their liaison with our forces and to remain hidden from the enemy. When we send our own intelligence officers behind enemy lines to mix in with the enemy population, we need officers who can blend in with the local population. During World War II, we sent Italian–American OSS operatives behind enemy lines to try to blend in with the local population and we also sent native Italians, who had joined us in the fight against fascism, behind enemy lines.[52]

There is a variety of missions that might be carried out in denied areas: intelligence collection, sabotage, liaison with local partisans, commando raids, political action, propaganda, psychological warfare, kidnapping important enemy officers or officials and more. The World War II era American OSS and the British Special Operations Executive (SOE) established methods of operation that remain the same in principle and change merely to accommodate new and different local conditions. For example, infiltration methods change because the nature of the enemy's border protection methods, its sophistication of detection methods and its economic status affect our choice of overland, aerial or maritime operations. By economic status, I mean, for example, that maritime infiltration into a tropical country that only has dugout canoes is different from infiltration into a country with modern shipping and ports.

No matter the adjustments for local conditions, there are fundamental basic methods of conducting special operations in denied areas: requirements, planning, recruitment, training, infiltration, communications, re-supply, exfiltration, debriefing and intelligence or operational reporting.

---

[52] Max Corvo, *The O.S.S in Italy 1942-1945, A Personal Memoir*, Praeger, New York, 1990.

It is difficult to plan and run any clandestine operation until we know the intelligence collection requirements or the targets for covert action operations. As a special operations case officer, you want to know the requirements so you can decide how many men you will need and what skills and experiences they should have. What languages should they be able to speak? Do they need to pass for natives or just be able to communicate with the people they meet? Will they carry their supplies with them and return without needing re-supply or will they attempt to remain in the denied area for a long time and therefore require re-supply?

There is another side of requirements that is not obvious but is important. What are the political considerations? If our government can accept American casualties then it might be possible to send Americans behind enemy lines. If American casualties are not acceptable, or we do not have any or enough of our own personnel who can pass as native then we are required to send agents recruited from the local population.

The intelligence requirements drive all elements of planning, which should take into account: equipment, weapons, explosives, codes, maps, radios, clothing, documentation and transportation. The end result of planning is the production of the military five-paragraph field order or its equivalent. This field order provides the team with the situation, both enemy and friendly, in the target area; describes the mission to be accomplished; describes how the mission will be executed; gives the team administrative details; and describes command and control for the mission.

The key to recruitment is first to build a program that is attractive to the potential recruit. In a special operations context that means developing a good reputation for taking care of the men who serve as soldiers, exercising good leadership and military judgment, providing good combat support, and taking care of dependents while the soldiers are out on missions or if they do not return. Once a program has a good reputation, the second key is recruiting men whose characters suit the missions and objectives of the program. The most important are the team leaders, deputy team leaders and communicators.

The trainer needs to tailor the training to the men receiving it. It needs to be obvious how the training applies to the particular mission. The trainer needs to teach at the educational and experience level of the men receiving it. It needs to take into account the cultural realities for the men receiving it. One example of this is to recall the problems the British Army in India was supposed to have had from supplying their Indian troops with Enfield rifles. The rifle's cartridges were supplied in greased paper. The soldier was supposed to bite through the paper before using the cartridge. Rumors spread that the grease was from cow or pig fat. Both Muslim and Hindu soldiers were offended.[53] A specific example of understanding the culture of the men being trained is described in the previous chapter, "Remote Sensors and Beacons."

There are many ways to approach the problem of infiltration; one is to decide on the method of transportation. In World War II in Italy[54], OSS used submarines to transport teams to the Italian coast, while in the Far East OSS used small fast cutters as mother ships to deliver small paddled boats close to the coast. In World War II France, OSS infiltrated by jumping from aircraft with parachutes. Infiltration will fail if in moving from the base of operations to the target area of operations the enemy discovers the team and captures or kills its members. How can the team move successfully into the area of operations and remain there without being discovered? Past methods of special operations infiltration have been helicopter, boat, parachute, glider, walking, train or combinations of two or more depending on the operational environment. Planning for infiltration requires as much knowledge of the target area as can be acquired. The goal is to get the team into the target area with its equipment or with a plan to receive the equipment separately. During World War II, OSS and SOE infiltrated teams or individual agents into Japanese held Thailand by using a mother ship to carry motorboats into the general area. The case officers then went on the motorboat with the team and its small boat.

---

[53] Alex von Tunzelmann, *Indian Summer: The Secret History of the End of an Empire*, Macmillan, 2007.

[54] Corvo, *The O.S.S in Italy 1942-1945, A Personal Memoir.*

The motorboat then approached the coast to a point where the small boat could reach land with the team paddling it. The case officer put the team off the motorboat in the small boat and they paddled for shore while the motorboat returned to the mother ship. OSS dropped operatives into France by parachute during World War II where they expected to be met by resistance forces. During the Vietnam War MACVSOG carried teams into Vietnam and Cambodia by helicopter and dropped them off on helicopter landing zones from which they made their way further into the area of operations. During the "Secret War in Laos", I sent my teams from PS–18 down the river by water taxi then overland in wheeled taxis through friendly territory. Upon reaching the limits of friendly territory, the teams walked by foot the rest of the way to their areas of operations.

Communications between the team and the case officer need to satisfy various objectives. An intelligence collection team needs to report the intelligence it collects reliably and securely. The team also needs to be able to report administrative matters and ask for guidance. At other times, for example, when being resupplied or exfiltrated, a team needs quick and easy communications. In that instance, security is less of an issue. When security is important, a team needs a method of transmitting encoded messages. When teams are infiltrated long distances into denied areas, that is, behind enemy lines, radio becomes the means of communications and batteries and battery life become important. Certain types of radios require antennae – the ability to string an antenna so it functions properly and at the same time concealing the antenna are both important. If CW (continuous wave used for Morse-code) radios are to be used, training Morse-code key operators and having enough of them on hand is important. Of course, Morse-code radiomen are needed both in the field and at the operations center to receive the field radio reports.

If a team is operating behind enemy lines but will be able to contact indigenous inhabitants of the operational area, some items such as food, will be available for purchase or barter. Other unique items, such as codebooks or batteries, will need to be delivered to the team. If a team is operating behind enemy lines but will have to remain hidden from both the enemy and indigenous inhabitants, or there are no indigenous inhabitants, then all re-supply will have to be delivered. The preferred method of re-supply behind enemy lines is dropping by parachute. The parachute drop must be covert so that the enemy is not alerted to the team's presence or its specific location. Often parachute drops are made at dusk when there is enough light for both the aircraft to locate the drop zone and at the same time failing light so once the drop bundle is received the team can use the oncoming darkness to conceal its movement away from the drop zone. A drop bundle should have enough supplies to be worth the risk but not so much that the team is over-burdened and cannot carry the weight away with them. Parachute drops must be accurate. The best drop is right on the team's location, which is not always easy given wind conditions and terrain. A bad drop forces the team to move from the drop zone and search for the drop bundle. When the drop bundle is actually lost that forces the team to leave the area empty handed and dispirited by the prospect of having to do it again too soon and enduring more time without supplies. A lost bundle means finding a new drop zone not in the same area. Time is lost, even when the team has an alternate drop zone, by having to move carefully away from the old drop zone to the new one.

The best exfiltration is when the team covertly walks out of enemy con-trolled territory and returns to the operations base on its own. The riskiest exfiltrations are when plucking the team from enemy territory by helicopter. A helicopter exfiltration requires two aircraft, one for the team pickup and one to pickup the first crew if their aircraft is downed by enemy fire or fails mechanical-ly on the helicopter-landing zone. It also requires a command and control aircraft carrying an interpreter-translator to talk to the team and the case officer to coordinate the exfiltration, and strike aircraft flying cover to provide suppress-ing fire if the enemy has found the helicopter-landing zone and is trying to attack the team or the helicopters. Strike aircraft cover requires a forward air controller (FAC) to mark targets, to converse with the case officer coordinator, and to orchestrate the bombing and strafing runs of the strike aircraft. In Laos, Continental Air Services, Incorporated (CASI) pilots flew Pilatus Porter PC-6 aircraft, Air America pilots flew the Sikorsky H-34 helicopters, U.S. Air Force officers (Ravens) flew the FAC O-1 aircraft, and U.S. Navy, U.S. Marine Corps, U.S. Air Force, and Royal Lao Air Force (RLAF) pilots flew the strike aircraft. All air operations, and thus all ground operations, in Laos were dependent on these skilled, courageous military and civilian airmen, some Lao, some Thai, and some American, all brave and resourceful.

At the end of every operation, a debriefing is necessary and required. Each and every mission needs to be documented, not just for the historical record or the intelligence product, but also to evaluate what the team did and how well it did it. If a team's mission did not result in something tangible, such as a North Vietnamese Army prisoner or secondary explosions or fires observed by a Raven pilot, a debriefing was necessary to gather enough details from the team to enable a judgment as to whether the team was fabricating any or all of the events it described during the mission. When any source of intelligence provides information, there usually isn't any way to tell immediately if the information is valid or fabricated. The information has been a secret. The recipient of reports describing secret information is at a disadvantage unless some means to validate the information or the reporter is possible.

The CIA effort in Laos was primarily special operations in nature. True, there were case officers in the capital, Vientiane, who worked in the tradition-al way, targeting Soviet, Chinese and other hard targets and working against other foreign intelligence targets, but throughout the rest of the country, Nam Yu, Luang Prabang, Long Tieng, Savannakhet and Pakse – the effort was special operations. The emphasis was on irregular guerrilla style operations and later on irregular main force combat operations. The collection of intelligence behind enemy lines, in the manner pioneered by the OSS in World War II was also an objective, but it was an adjunct to the combat operations. Some of the irregular combat operations were not done well and some were quite excellent. Some day, perhaps, the general public will learn more about them.

From an American point of view, the CIA covert action program in Laos was nothing less than a success. SGU and GM combat capability, amply assisted by U.S. air support, required the North Vietnamese Army to keep significant forces in Laos to protect the Ho Chi Minh Trail, forces that could not go to the Republic of Vietnam and fight against U.S. and ARVN forces. The Hmong units of northern Laos and the lowland Lao and Lao Theung mountain tribe units of southern Laos, later augmented by Thai and Cambodian irregular units had only to tie up North Vietnamese Army forces and keep them in Laos, and they did that. Lao irregular roadwatch and commando/raider teams collected intelligence on North Vietnamese Army activity in Laos and harassed the North Vietnamese Army by conducting ambushes and guiding American air support to attack and bomb the North Vietnamese Army. There never could have been any expectation that CIA led irregular forces would defeat and drive the North Vietnamese Army out of Laos. The CIA irregular forces would merely harass the North Vietnamese Army in conjunction with U.S. efforts in Vietnam and when the President of the United States decided to withdraw from Vietnam the fate of Laos was tied to the fate of the Republic of Vietnam.

For a Lao point of view, one would have to analyze both the reaction of the ruling class and the peasants (there was not much of a middle class, if any) to the U.S. government use of their country and people in support of the war in the Republic of Viet Nam. The ruling class was generally conservative and royalist and wanted to maintain an independent, non–Communist Laos. CIA led activities were the only thing between that and a very early collapse and fall to the North Vietnamese communists. For the peasants, the CIA led activity provided well-paid employment, brought money into the country, and bolstered the economy. I do not recall any peasant uprisings against the Royal Lao Government or calls by the peasants for a communist government. In my opinion, the CIA was helping the majority of Lao citizens try to maintain an independent country. In the final analysis, the American government's effort to help the Lao remain free of communism and Vietnamese domination failed, but that was tied directly to decisions related to the Republic of Vietnam rather than anything the CIA did or did not do. The one significant disservice that was done to the Lao was to encourage them to use the CIA trained unconventional, irregular, guerrilla units as conventional units asking them to seize and hold territory. When CIA led irregular units, using superior aerial movement and American bombing support, attacked the North Vietnamese Army they often defeated the North Vietnamese Army units. However, when then asked to hold the ground they had seized they were then routed by the North Vietnamese Army despite aerial bombing support. Had CIA's unconventional units been immediately withdrawn after inflicting surprise losses on the North Vietnamese Army, those units would have suffered far fewer casualties and been able to make life in Laos very miserable for the North Vietnamese Army. There was never any possibility that Lao irregulars would have been able to seize territory from the North Vietnamese Army and then hold it but they might have been able to bleed the North Vietnamese Army in a way that would have caused them to commit more troops.[55] In the end, however, the result of war in Laos was always tied to the results in the Republic of Vietnam. Moreover, without using American forces to physically cut the North Vietnamese Army supply lines into the south, the goal of bleeding the North Vietnamese Army turned out to be useless as the North Vietnamese Army was willing to take many more casualties than anyone in the U.S. government could possibly conceive. If we failed the Lao, it was in not using the irregular units properly and causing them to take excessive casualties while acting as conventional units.

In the aftermath of 11 September 2001 and the commencement of the Global War on Terrorism, special operations and unconventional warfare have been much more in the limelight. The high point for special operations has been the war in Afghanistan where the modern version of special operations was used to the most dramatic effect ever. In the future, military historians may look back on these special operations as one more in a long line of significant developments in the history of warfare. In my opinion, the deadly and efficient combination of having small teams locate the enemy, advanced location-finding technology to pinpoint the small team's positions and precision guidance of bombs to the targets identified by the small teams are

---

[55] Vongsavanh, *RLG Military Operations and Activities in the Laotian Panhandle.*

developments that rival the introduction of the long bow, gunpowder, the machine gun, the tank or aircraft into warfare.

As a retired former special operations professional, I was fascinated to read, in news accounts of the action in Afghanistan, about these developments and how they were being used. However, I was aghast to read about the presence of CIA teams in Afghanistan and how they were contributing to special operations. In some cases, it seemed from the news media reporting that the CIA and U.S. military special operations units were in competition with each other. CIA activities should never be publicized until some time in the future when such activities might be declassified. CIA case officers must operate in total secrecy. There is no justification for allowing any publicity at all to ongoing CIA operations. In Laos, even though there were U.S. Army and U.S. Air Force personnel in the country, the CIA was the lead agency. In Vietnam, the U.S. military was the lead agency and the CIA was there in a supporting role. The news media reporting from Afghanistan indicated that CIA teams were operating, with help from Afghanis, on their own in competition with U.S. military special operations forces. This should never happen. If the U.S. government can politically sanction the use of U.S. military personnel in combat then they should be the ones out in the field conducting special operations. If there is a need for CIA special operations personnel, they should be operating special CIA equipment or providing intelligence they have collected. The function of CIA special operations officers must always be the collection of intelligence to provide it to those who will take action. The exception being, of course, when the CIA is the lead agency in a country and then the action element should be indigenous military units. CIA should not be hiring special operations case officers to go out and operate in the field as U.S. military special operations forces do. In all cases, CIA special operations officers should be program managers, managing activities designed to produce intelligence for U.S. military special operations forces or managing the production of intelligence and the actions by indigenous forces to take advantage of the intelligence. CIA special operations officers need to be accomplished intelligence collectors and clandestine operators as well as experienced in U.S. military special operations forces methods and techniques. Hiring CIA special operations officers who only go out into the field and act exactly like U.S. military personnel is a mistake, a redundancy and just bad practice.

It is also important for CIA special operations officers to immerse themselves in the history of special operations, both military and CIA, and the lessons learned from them. Since many CIA officers who are committed to general intelligence collection operations also served tours of duty in the military, they tend to think they have all the military experience they need. They don't know what they don't know. It is necessary to recruit CIA special operations officers who have military experience and then give them rotational assignments in traditional intelligence collection assignments, as well as giving them special operations assignments. They also need to receive special operations training that emphasizes the history of special operations, the successful as well as the failed special operations, and they need to be able to recognize the lessons learned from both. When it comes time to place a CIA officer in charge of special operations, that officer should be this type of traditional plus special operations officer.

The best way to view CIA special operations officers is to see them as program managers. Where U.S. government policy prefers not to use uniformed U.S. military men for special operations in a country, then CIA special operations program managers would function as training officers and operations officers. As training officers they would have the experience and skills to train the trainers or to give the training themselves, in a foreign language or through interpreters. Where possible, trainees could be taken to a neutral location and trained by the U.S. military, or by the military of another country, especially where the military of that other country speaks the same language as the trainees. Sometimes, the other country's military might visit the trainees' country to give the training. In the case of operations officers in a country where the U.S. military is not allowed, they should perform all the necessary functions to prepare, launch, monitor, support and exfiltrate indigenous special operations units. They also would be responsible for any intelligence collection activities apart from field intelligence collection and combat action operations, such as, low power radio intercept, aerial photographic reconnaissance, document exploitation, interrogation and debriefing, and other such intelligence collection activities. Sometimes, they supervise indigenous personnel and sometimes third country personnel, capable due to language and cultural affinity, of operating in the country. It just does not make sense for the CIA to employ personnel who have only the same military experience and skills as the U.S. military and compete with U.S. military special operations forces in the same missions. If the CIA's special operations officers are the traditional intelligence collectors as well as special operations officers I have described, then it is a misuse of them to use them in the same manner as U.S. military special operations forces. Moreover, the CIA should have an investment in training and experience that it should not want to squander duplicating what U.S. military special operations forces do. Misusing CIA special operations officers by duplicating what U.S. military special operations forces do also misses the opportunity to develop intelligence collection in a special operations environment, something that is difficult to do and not often done well.

CIA special operations officers need to be able to work in military as well as law enforcement environments. The "Global War on Terrorism" will confront terrorists in both field combat type operations as well as in urban criminal type operations. Some times terrorists must be fought using military methods and techniques and some times terrorists must be fought using law enforcement methods and techniques. CIA operational management must be able to distinguish the difference to be able to make plans and commit the appropriate resources. CIA special operations officers must be able to plan and conduct intelligence collection operations as well as plan and conduct action operations, whether working with military or law enforcement personnel.

The U.S. government needs a strong, professional, non-political centralized intelligence agency.

CIA leadership that fears doing its job because it fears political backlash is a leadership that becomes risk-averse. When the executive or legislative branches of the government use the CIA to advance or defend their own agendas, they are doing the nation a great disservice. The one thing that stands at the forward edge of the battle area in any war on terrorism is intelligence collection. Decisions cannot be taken and plans cannot be made without accurate intelligence information to inform the policy makers. There must be a strong, vibrant, well-led intelligence community, especially a centralized intelligence agency. Rather than pander to a political agenda, the executive and legislative branches need to work to insure that the foremost quality of its intelligence agencies is good leadership; a leadership that knows when to tell the policy makers when it can and when it cannot get any particular job done. A leadership that is not afraid to make mistakes will be a leadership that will not make many mistakes.

There is no such thing as a peace dividend. When one threat is contained, another threat soon emerges. The proliferation of weapons of mass destruction, terrorism, narcotics trafficking, and any number of future threats will always be out there to endanger the Free World. There will never be any time when free, democratic nations will be at peace. There will always be danger in this world but the time of most peril will be when it appears there is none. At minimum, an intelligence agency must work just as hard in apparent peacetime to learn where the next threat will come from. Moreover, there is no such thing as "surging" intelligence operations. A surge merely leaves one or more other areas understaffed. Clandestine sources of information and technical methods of intelligence collection must be constantly and consistently developed and nurtured so that intelligence on how peace is continuing or new threats are developing will always be available to our nation's policy makers. The U.S. government cannot just turn intelligence sources and methods on and off. They take time to develop or build and employ. Every time we declare peace and begin to downsize our intelligence capability we are only giving our enemies a window of opportunity during which they can attack without fearing our ability to know what they are doing and when they will do it. The USSR may have changed into Russia but we still need intelligence on the plans and intentions of the Russian government, as well as the plans and intentions of China, India, Pakistan, Japan, Germany and many others too numerous to list here.

The United States of America needs a centralized intelligence capability. If you have read this book to this point, you should not close it with the idea that I would espouse any less. In my 32 years of government service in military, law enforcement and intelligence, I have become convinced that our leaders will always need to know what is going on in the world, in the secret deliberations of our friends as well as in those of such nations or groups that would do harm to our citizens or our country. What I would wish for the reader to take away from reading this book is that there is not now or ever a point when our leaders will not need an efficient, professional intelligence service. The CIA was not formed to fight the Cold War, in my opinion it was formed to prevent future Pearl Harbors. That it did not prevent the 9/11 terrorist attacks on the World Trade Center and the Pentagon does not mean anything more than the CIA needs to be examined to see how it can do better. It does not need to be reorganized by politicians. What the politicians need to demand is that the CIA is led by the best officers that can be found and led in the best way possible. The best professional intelligence leaders will determine how to organize it or they are not the best.

Morale problems beset the CIA. Its leaders, especially in field stations, are afraid to be bold. It is better to do the safe thing rather than that which needs to be done. Middle management has been decimated. There are not enough experienced, competent mid-level officers to provide mentoring for the new, young officers being recruited. The new, young officers are not staying in sufficient numbers to provide an experienced, competent mid-level. The mystique and the cover of national security classification prevent an understanding of what is really going on. If you understand what is happening you have to gag when you read books written by former high-level CIA officers who were so afraid of having trouble in their foreign postings that they eliminated every operation that had any chance of backfiring on them. One reduced the intelligence report output from over 200 a month to less than 20 a month and relied almost exclusively on the relationship with the host country's intelligence and counterintelligence services (called our liaison partners). Having done better than any opposition intelligence service to reduce the CIA's intelligence collection in that particular country we now have to gag on what this stalwart "yes" man has to say about what's right and what's wrong with the CIA. The CIA can do better; the question is, will it?

The CIA's special operations cadre was decimated at the end of the Vietnam War. Special operations officers who had special operations field experience were either encouraged to leave or to transfer into traditional foreign or counter intelligence. The next time there was a need for special operations experience the CIA recruited former military officers who had no CIA experience. Their leaders were then mid-level officers who had no special operations experience. Following that, CIA began to recruit pure military types with no intention of ever encouraging them to become traditional intelligence officers. The best special operations officer for the CIA is someone who has military experience, an understanding of intelligence and a desire to be both special operations and an intelligence collector. Pure "ammo-humpers" need not apply.

In my opinion, the Vietnam War began for the right reasons, to provide the people of Vietnam and Laos the opportunity to choose freedom and democracy and not to have communism forced down their throats by terror and violence. That our nation's leaders chose not to fight the war to win, nor recognized that the war should have been ended immediately if it could not be fought to win for whatever political reasons they had, is a moral outrage. It is a crime to sacrifice the lives of so many soldiers and innocent civilians, American, Vietnamese both northern and southern, Lao, Thai, Korean and Australian by pursuing a war determined by political considerations rather than military principles. North Vietnamese communist leaders who sacrificed the lives of millions of their own so that today they can come whining to the West asking our help in building their country back up also committed that crime. Why didn't they pursue peaceful, diplomatic means to get to where they are now? Why did they have to fight a war and lose millions of lives against the same people from whom they now seek aid and assistance? Americans would not have been fighting in Vietnam and Laos if the Vietnamese communists had not been trying to impose their will by violent means, murdering tens of thousands of innocent Vietnamese civilians.

The CIA's war in Laos was a success even though the war in Indochina was lost. The CIA was not asked to win a war in Laos. It was asked to do what it could to impede the North Vietnamese use of Laos for the infiltration of men and materiel into South Vietnam. It was asked to bolster the government of Laos, keep its capital from being overrun and keep it from toppling into the communist camp. It was asked to cause the North Vietnamese Army enough problems it would have to keep a large number of its troops in Laos defending its supply line. CIA did all of that at the cost of dollars, not the lives of any American soldiers, but at the cost of the lives of patriotic CIA officers who wanted to be there in that fight. The Lao who lost their lives while fighting in CIA sponsored units did so voluntarily, no one forced them to join. The communists murdered many more Lao civilians than were killed because of the fighting.

CIA special operations in Laos received publicity, but it was unwanted. There is no place in such operations for CIA provoked publicity about what its special operations officers are doing. I despair when I read in the newspapers today, information that could only have been officially leaked, about the activities of CIA special operators in Afghanistan and Iraq. If I am wrong and information was not leaked; shame on them for not being able to provide the proper security for their operations.

I despair for CIA's young officers who are sent into special operations situations with little or no military background just because they are willing and volunteer to go. I despair for CIA's young officers who are supervised by mid-level and higher officers who do not know what they are doing or are too beleaguered to give them proper supervision. My military police training and experience with prisoner of war (PW) operations[56] tells me that the CIA in Afghanistan had no idea how to handle prisoners of war. True, the prisoners

---

[56] In 1967, the 504th Military Police Battalion operated a prisoner of war facility at its headquarters location in Qui Nhon. I supervised the facility as part of my duties as a platoon leader in C Company.

of war were being handled by Afghans, but had the supervisors known what was to be expected they might not have risked their officers in dangerous situations. All prisoners of war, when taken into custody by friendly combatants, must be searched and rendered harmless before they are passed on to the next stage of imprisonment. At each stage, the receiving unit must not take control of prisoners of war until it has insured that those prisoners of war have been searched again and rendered harmless. In the U.S. military, military policemen will take charge of prisoners of war at the earliest point possible and control them. When CIA officers go to a place where prisoners of war are located and those prisoners of war turn out to be armed, they were not under control. They were at a rallying point where control had not yet been established. In Afghanistan, the friendly combatants who corralled numbers of enemy combatants inside a fortress and had not searched them for weapons and taken control of them did not have a PW camp, they merely were trying to control a rallying point. The CIA officers who went to that rally point thinking they were interviewing prisoners of war were going in to a very dangerous situation without knowing it. Their supervisors failed them miserably. Those supervisors did not have the requisite experience or the understanding of what they did not know. A CIA officer died because of it.

Do not get the idea that any organization will understand what it does not know and want to identify and bring back experienced officers who do know what they are doing. It seems to be a conceit of movie producers and fiction writers that when things get really bad someone will suggest bringing back some "old war horse" who is the only one who can get the job done or the only one who has the experience or skills for the problem at hand. In reality, this almost never happens and I actually would love to hear about just once when it did happen. It has been written[57] that extensive planning for war in Iraq and its aftermath, drafted under the command of Gen. Anthony Zinni, had been discarded when planning was underway for the invasion of Iraq in

---

[57] Thomas E. Ricks, *Fiasco: The American Military Adventure in Iraq*, The Penguin Press, New York, 2006.

2003. Former Director of Central Intelligence (DCI), the late Richard Helms, has written[58] that he knew the security of the American embassy in Tehran better than most people but was never contacted when plans were being made to go in and rescue the hostages being held there in 1979. In my own experience, I was assigned to Germany from 1994-1997 and sent to Munich to help out with a visit of the DCI, who was going to visit our offices in Munich and then a relative who was working at the George C. Marshall European Center for Security Studies in Garmisch-Partenkirchen, Germany. Now, in this case, it so happened that the former chief of the DCI security team was assigned to Bonn as chief of support and his former executive officer was assigned to Munich as the support officer. In addition, there was another security officer, assigned to Bonn, also available to help out with the planning and execution of the DCI's security during his visit to the Munich area. These men, quite experienced in VIP security, as well as specifically, security for the DCI, needed additional help and I was one of those sent to Munich to join others assigned there who would be helping out with the escort work.

Arrangements were made for armored cars to be used to transport the DCI and his entourage and drivers were assigned to all the vehicles. A member of the office in Munich and I were assigned to drive a truck carrying the group's luggage. The person assigned to drive the DCI's car was a part-time spouse who had never been a staff employee of the CIA. His part-time work in Munich was the first time he was working for the CIA. His military experience was far from anything to do with this type of security work. What the trio from security with all the experience did not know or had ignored was that I had spent three years in the U.S. Army Military Police, one year in Vietnam, and was qualified with the .45 cal pistol, shotgun, M-14 and M-16 rifles, had spent two years in Laos as a special operations case officer, had been through the CIA's defensive driving course where you are taught to break through roadblocks and make 180 degree turns, and had been a DEA Special

---

[58] Richard Helms, *A Look Over My Shoulder: A Life in the Central Intelligence Agency*, Random House, New York, 2003.

Agent, qualified with the Smith & Wesson Model 10 .38 caliber pistol and Smith & Wesson Model 59 9mm pistol and had the highest qualifying score on the combat shooting course during DEA special agent training in a group made up almost entirely of former uniformed police and detectives.

The DEA combat pistol training in 1974 was a uniquely designed course. DEA headquarters was located at 14th and K Streets in Washington, D.C. and Special Agent training was conducted right there. Adjacent to the headquarters building was an old time very narrow building like the ones that used to house banks. The basement was a locker room, showers and athletic trainer's rooms, the ground floor was a narrow gym set up as a basketball court, the first floor was a workout area setup with free weights, weight machines, and a variety of stationary bicycles and other such machines, and the top floor was a small pistol firing range. All the special agent trainees were gathered in the basement having been told to bring their issue .38 caliber Smith & Wesson Model 10 revolvers and 12 rounds of ammunition. Each trainee was told to put the bullets in his pocket and to put on a vest holding twenty pounds of weights. The trainee was then required to do ten pushups and then run up the stairs four floors to the top floor. In the beginning, the instructors were gathered in the stair well and shouted and screamed at them as they ran. Later, each trainee completing the exercise joined others on the stairs to harass the next trainees. I remember that for some reason one of the trainees was lying on a stair when I ran up and I stepped on him as I went up. Upon reaching the top floor, a trainee found himself in the anteroom outside the actual pistol range, where breathing strenuously from the push-ups and run carrying the weighted vest, the trainee received instructions.

"Take out your weapon and load 6 rounds."

"OK, now, inside that room is an unknown number of criminals holding hostages. One of the people in the room is an undercover agent."

"Now, go into the room."

Entering the darkened room instructors were yelling and throwing garbage can covers at the trainee. You were supposed to use available cover and figure out what to do next. Suddenly a light came on and a target came toward you.

If the target represented the figure of a criminal (a menacing figure holding a gun) you were to shoot at it but if it represented a hostage (in the form of a woman holding a baby or the undercover officer holding a badge) you were not supposed to shoot. The instructors had taught that you should fire in sequences of two shots per target. I remember being in the basement when a former big city policeman, the highest scoring trainee on the pistol range when firing at targets with bull's eyes, went up the stairs. After the delay for the time it took to run up, get instructions and load the pistol, we heard six rapid-fire shots followed by six more. He could not possibly have been identifying what he was shooting. Evidently, there was more stress involved in this type of pistol firing than in standing sideways to a bull's eye, with one hand on your hip, while slowly lowering the pistol with the other hand and squeezing off one round at a time.

If I had been in charge of security for the DCI, the one person I would have wanted to drive the DCI's car was a person with my background. They did not have a clue. Moreover, that's the way it goes not the way it is in the movies or the thriller novels. When the planning is done, they usually do not bother to make sure they have the best people or they do not want someone coming in who might show them up. If you have to call in the old warhorse, doesn't that mean you can't handle it? You do not get the awards and recognition by bringing in the savior; you make sure you are the savior. It is a myth that needs to be put to rest.

The American preferred model is that the only way to get a job done is to send an American to do it. The next best thing is sending Americans along with the indigenous assets. Indigenous assets cannot be trusted to get the job done by themselves without American supervision and Americans witnessing what is done. Many a mission in Laos, carried out by indigenous soldiers, was not carried out as reported or not at all. However, many missions were successful and, given the case officer's desire to drive his men to conduct the missions honestly and his efforts to validate the missions, it was possible to conduct successful missions using only indigenous personnel. If it ever needs to be done again - it can be done.

A successful CIA special operations officer needs to be more than a weapons specialist or just one form of "ammo–humper" or another. He needs to be an intelligence officer and an intelligence analyst. As an intelligence officer, he needs to assess the character, personality, experience and cultural background of his assets so he can best determine what they can and cannot do. Such analysis will help him to formulate the best missions for his men and the best way to train them to perform those missions. Special operations must be planned and executed with all the knowledge of the target personalities and the target area that can be obtained. The case officer must study the available intelligence himself in order to become more knowledgeable than anyone and to be able to make the best plans, supervise them and validate them.

I have been writing this book, off and on, for several years. I would have made the last paragraph above the last sentences of the book, but as fate would have it, I ran into Khamsing, who is also retired now. Khamsing has been working as an independent contractor, volunteering for Afghanistan and Iraq and other such places, just as he did before he retired. When it comes to running snatch operations, I like to think of myself as the champion of the war in Laos. I did it first, I did it longer and I captured more than anyone else did. However, Khamsing was runner up in Laos. While I chose to move on to traditional operations, other than three years in special operations in the early 1980s in Central America, Khamsing stayed in special operations, rising to the Senior Intelligence Service and the top special operations job in the Directorate of Operations. Along the way he managed to serve in the field, I believe, everywhere there were special operations in the past thirty years and his story, if he ever chose to tell it, would be one of the most amazing books in the history of CIA special operations.

So we chit chat a bit, and then Khamsing says something like this, and I have to paraphrase as I don't remember word for word what he said. "You know, I've been out in the field where they have a real need to run snatch operations, and I bring up your name and the operations you ran in Laos as examples of how it has been done successfully, but they don't want to hear it. They say, 'Now, now, Khamsing, that's not what you're here for, just do the job you're here for and let us worry about that.' I've been around and I've seen how it needs to be done, but do they want to listen to me? No. You know why they don't want to listen?"

I nod my head imperceptibly as I do not want to interrupt. I know what he is going to say but it is best to let him say it.

"These people are younger than we are and they don't have our experience. But they don't want to let us tell them how to do it because they'd have to share the credit, or maybe just give it to you or me. I wasn't the first one to say this, but, do you know how much could be gotten done if no one had to get credit for what gets done?"

It is an amazing, unfathomable thing. Wouldn't you think that in defense of our country and in defense of innocent men, women and children who might die in future attacks on the United States, those of us who serve in foreign lands would want to do anything that had to be done to find Islamic terrorists and insurgents, no matter who gets the credit? If they could have the advice and consultation, perhaps even the operational services, of men who have successfully run special operations around the world - wouldn't you think they would make use of them?

That only happens in books of fiction and the movies.

And finally, this book was still being drafted as the report of "The Commission on the Intelligence Capabilities of the United States Regarding Weapons of Mass Destruction" was published. As I read the Washington Post, I was struck by the irony of reading only quotes from one disgruntled person who left CIA after a few years, or another who as one of the most senior managers has the most to protect in reply to the report's criticisms. So now, I present the comments of someone who spent thirty-two years in government service, who did not leave disgruntled, who did not rise to a high position and now have anything to protect, who speaks the truth as he sees it with no hidden agenda, and who believes this country needs a strong, well-led, well-funded, centralized intelligence agency.

The Washington Post did a reasonable job of casting doubt on this report because the report put all the blame for what it perceives as failure on the intelligence community and did not address how the policy makers used the intelligence. Intelligence collectors and analysts do not make policy. They merely collect, analyze and disseminate intelligence to the policy makers. This report should never have any validity until it addresses the issue of how the intelligence was used.

I am not, however, a total apologist for the CIA. There are many problems, many of which are the result of intense public scrutiny and blame laying, plus the proliferation of lawyers at every level of the Directorate of Operations. How could anyone be anything but risk averse if every move that is made is subject to public scrutiny and the endless hand wringing of an army of lawyers? How did this come about? Right or wrong the profusion of congressional oversight mechanisms, with members who are dishonest about what they have been told and when, and the need to have one's backside totally covered by legal advice does nothing but create risk aversion. Having created a risk averse environment why is anyone surprised that CIA leaders are risk averse?

Having declared a "peace dividend" and reduced CIA funding and required the CIA to reduce personnel numbers why would anyone be surprised when large numbers of mid-level officers take the early out and leave the CIA with insufficient numbers of mentors to help young officers reach mid-level with the appropriate competence to become competent case officers or leaders? You cannot find experienced case officers at mid-level pay grades elsewhere and just transfer them in to the CIA to replace those who have left or those you would fire. Young officers need two to three operational assignments in field offices to learn their trade well enough to reach journeyman status. Young officers need mentors to help them directly or they need to have competent journeymen colleagues they can observe and copy. Where are those journeymen? There are not enough of them. It makes no difference how many young officers you bring in each year if they do not have mentors or good examples to emulate and if they do not stay to become journeymen.

Having declared that the CIA must adopt "business" methods and then changed the retirement system so that it is portable via the 401k, why would anyone be surprised when larger numbers than ever up and leave? When I joined CIA in 1969, I learned the term "velvet trap." If you reached age 50 and had 20 years of federal service, of which 10 years was with CIA and five of that was in overseas assignments, you could retire with a decent annuity. I was 27 years old and would have 20 years service by the time I was 44 years old because my three years of Army service would count as federal service. I then would only need six more years to qualify for an annuity. The "velvet trap" was that if you lasted at least 10-12 years you were about halfway to the annuity. Why not stay on and finish it off? This was especially worth considering because if you left either you could take a payout of only what you had paid in or you could leave it there and collect a small annuity when you reached 65 years old. Some CIA employees ignored this "velvet trap" and left anyway, but a very significant number remained, becoming the journeymen backbone of the CIA's Directorate of Operations. Today, you just take your entire 401k with you if you want to leave after one year or two or five years. It does not make any difference whether you put federal money or any other money in your 401k - it is all the same. Given the special way that an intelligence case officer population has to be grown, this new retirement system only works against developing and keeping young officers so they can become journeymen and, perhaps, later the competent senior leadership that is so necessary.

That said there is a crisis of leadership. That crisis is the result of a vicious cycle. Talented young officers are recruited but do not remain because they recognize the lack of quality leadership. The CIA has always attracted new recruits from the middle of average to the very best. The problem has always been that only a small percentage of the very best stay on for careers of twenty or more years. Only a small percentage of the very best remain long enough to move up to the senior levels of management. Of those that remain, the ones who rise to the top are the ones who have mastered the bureaucratic skills for rising in such an environment. Those skills do not include taking risks, telling higher management and the policy makers when something cannot or should not be undertaken, being totally honest all the time about all subjects. To be very blunt, you learn whose ass to kiss and how or you do not make it very high. There must be many reasons why larger numbers of the very best do not stay on but you can imagine that if the average and only slightly above average are populating a high percentage of the upper management positions, they do not encourage the very best to stay on and challenge them. You can also understand that if the very best, with a variety of opportunities available to them in other career fields, see the type of manager that makes it to the top they can more easily make the decision to move on. Some one else said this more succinctly than I have, "Higher rank means longer organizational experience, greater commitment to the organization, and more selecting out of deviant perspectives."[59]

Back in the late 1970s I used to stop by to chat with a colleague of mine, a fellow Special Operations Division case officer, who occupied a small office for two. The other occupant was a young African-American man who had graduated from an ivy-league university and an ivy-league law school. He also had an aunt who was well connected in Detroit politics. My friend and I would sometimes exchange war stories about Vietnam and Laos and the young officer would often turn his chair around to join us by listening to our stories. As I came to know his background after one or two visits, I finally asked him what a young man, with such credentials and connections, was doing working in a bureaucracy like the CIA.

As part of our conversations, we would often tell stories of this or that mid level or upper level manager who had done something we thought was well below what we expected of the managers we thought we should have in the CIA. Having been overseas in combat zones, we thought it was incredible that we had encountered such incompetence at the leadership levels. The young man took it all in but really did not comment much on our stories. One day I visited and his desk was bare. I asked where he was and was told he had resigned. I do not think anything we had said was the direct cause of his resignation; I believe he just added what we were saying about life in the field

---

[59] Morris Janowitz, *The Professional Soldier: A Social and Political Portrait* (New York: The Free Press, 1971), p. 239. As noted in *Learning to Eat Soup with a Knife: Counterinsurgency Lessons from Malaya and Vietnam* by John A. Nagl, p.202.

to what he had seen in the headquarters environment. He realized it was not going to get any better.

It probably is wonderful that so many politicians, wide variety of pundits and family members of victims of terrorist attacks have taken such an interest in the organization of the CIA and other intelligence community agencies. I see no reason why they should not criticize what they see and understand about what the CIA has or has not done. However, they do not know the full story and they ought to know they do not know it. Yet, they proceed to suggest just how the CIA should be re-organized, without any experience in the collection, analysis and dissemination of intelligence and without all the details of how any particular intelligence, and certainly not how all of it, was collected, analyzed and disseminated. Most often, the solution they suggest boils down to rearranging the lines and boxes on organization charts. People populate the boxes on organization charts. How can it be that the perceived failures they are correcting were merely the result of the boxes not being connected properly among the lines? If the failures were the fault of the people, why don't they ask that all those people be fired or demoted? Would that do any good? You cannot just go out and hire experienced intelligence professionals from a vast pool that just happens not to be working for the CIA at the time. Intelligence professionals must be grown from seed; they cannot be transplanted from mature plants. Yet, reorganizations are always proposed as changes of the alignment of lines and boxes or the creation of more lines and boxes added to the top of the whole structure, e.g. the National Counterterrorism Center or the Director of National Intelligence. Just how does adding more people to boxes and placing them on top of a bureaucratic structure make it better? Where do the people come from? If they are experienced intelligence professionals, how did anyone figure out how to identify the ones who were not part of the problem? If they are not experienced intelligence professionals why does anyone believe they will have what it takes to lead such a complex undertaking that has no valid lateral experience other than to mature within the intelligence structure?

I challenge anyone to describe a successful reorganization of one or more bureaucracies. How about the "War on Drugs"? The original drug enforcement bureaucracy was the Federal Bureau of Narcotics (FBN). I am not completely familiar with everything that was done in the history of drug enforcement but I do know that eventually the FBN disappeared during the 1968 reorganization that led to the formation of the Bureau of Narcotics and Dangerous Drugs (BNDD) from the *"Bureau of Narcotics, in the Treasury Department, which was responsible for the control of marijuana and narcotics such as heroin, (and) the Bureau of Drug Abuse Control (BDAC), in the Department of Health, Education, and Welfare, which was responsible for the control of dangerous drugs, including depressants, stimulants, and hallucinogens, such as LSD. The BNDD became the primary drug law enforcement agency and concentrated its efforts on both international and interstate activities."*

"In 1973, President Richard Nixon declared 'an all-out global war on the drug menace' and sent Reorganization Plan No. 2 to Congress. In the spring and summer of 1973, the U.S. House of Representatives and the U.S. Senate heard months of testimony on President Nixon's Reorganization Plan Number 2, which proposed the creation of a single federal agency to consolidate and coordinate the government's drug control activities. At that time, the BNDD, within the Department of Justice, was responsible for enforcing the federal drug laws. However, the U.S. Customs Service and several other Justice entities (ODALE and the Office of National Narcotics Intelligence) were also responsible for various aspects of federal drug law enforcement. Of great concern to the Administration and the Congress were the growing availability of drugs in most areas of the United States, the lack of coordination and the perceived lack of cooperation between the U.S. Customs Service and the BNDD, and the need for better intelligence collection on drug trafficking organizations."[60]

And so, where are we now? The "All-Out Global War on the Drug Menace" began in 1973 and it is now 2009, thirty-six years and counting and can anyone say the war has been won? I think not. What were the 1968 and 1973 reorganizations all about – bottom line? They moved boxes and lines, created new boxes and lines, and they never really changed the people. Now don't get me wrong, I do not think the real answer was changing the people, I just mean

---

[60] The text in italics comes from the DEA Museum, DEA History Book.

no one ever looked at what was really wrong with the people. In my opinion, nothing was wrong with most of the working level people. What was lacking was competent, effective leadership. What all the politicians, pundits and victims' families do not know how to do is identify leadership problems and then fix them.

Before piling more bureaucracy on top of what is already there in the CIA and other intelligence community agencies, the glaring need is to correct the vast deficiency in leadership. Force the best of what is there to become competent, effective leaders and develop a program to identify and nurture future competent and effective leaders. Then work to reduce the forces that create yes men and the risk averse. If competent and effective leaders manage a bureaucracy, there will be no need for outsiders to force organizational change. Competent and effective leaders will find and implement the best and most effective changes.

One of the recent criticisms of the CIA and the intelligence community is that it is incapable of communicating effectively among all its members. When was that criticism first brought forth? At the end of the First Gulf War, General Norman Schwarzkopf declared that too many of the messaging systems in use in the defense and intelligence communities were incompatible. From that "lesson learned" came the Defense Department (DoD) requirement to build the Defense Messaging System (DMS). Supposedly, the entire intelligence community was to adopt the DMS or build new messaging systems compatible with the DMS. The DoD took the lead and built the DMS but allowed other agencies to keep their own messaging systems. The DMS established protocols for other agencies to use to convert their proprietary messages into and out of DMS compatible messages so another agency's outgoing messages could be received by the DMS and incoming DMS compatible messages could be received at other agencies. Once an agency could write its messages in its own messaging system and then the message could be converted into something compatible with the DMS and then receive DMS compatible messages – the entire military and intelligence community would have interoperability, a post Desert Storm buzzword. The DoD awarded a contract to build the DMS in May 1995 and implementation began at ninety-eight sites in October 1997. Contrast that with the CIA that, as of March 2005, was not yet DMS compatible. That means that the CIA was incapable, during the Second Gulf War, of sending DMS compatible messages to the warfighters in Iraq or Afghanistan - more than 10 years since DoD awarded the DMS contract and more years than that since General Schwarzkopf made his plea for interoperability.

Why not find out why this deplorable situation exists so many years down the road - instead of piling more bureaucracy on top of what is there. No matter what else you think you are fixing by piling on more bureaucracy and rearranging lines and boxes, if the intelligence community can not send information electronically among its members there is a glaring deficiency that needs fixing.

On 9 October 2002, John Helgerson spoke to the members of the Central Intelligence Retirees' Association (CIRA) at a luncheon meeting. Mr. Helgerson was the CIA's Inspector General at the time. At the end of his talk, he asked for questions from the audience. His speech and the subsequent question and answer session were published in the CIRA Newsletter, Winter 2002. I stood up and asked, "The CIA does a lot of contracting, including with independent contractors. Inevitably, there are occasionally things done that ought not to be either ethically or legally involving both Agency officers and contractors. What does the OIG do about this?"

Mr. Helgerson's reply was, "Yes, this is a problem (*section deleted*). So far as we can tell, the problem of contract fraud or abuse in our Agency is less a problem than one finds in many other departments of our government." He goes on to describe two cases of identifying and correcting contract fraud. Unfortunately, he did not really grasp the essence of what I was saying. I was especially interested in what the Office of the Inspector General knew about the participation of Agency officers in contract fraud and abuse. Many Agency officers who deal with contracts are not really skilled in such matters or are skilled enough to know how to "use and abuse" the system.

In the CIA's effort to achieve interoperability with the DMS it was pursuing what it called the Enterprise Messaging System (EMS), an effort to keep it own proprietary messaging system but make outgoing messages compatible with the DMS and be able to receive and convert incoming DMS messages into its own EMS. By the first half of 2001, CIA was ready to install a system in all its field offices that would be the first step toward DMS compatibility. The CIA manager responsible for budgeting for the large number of installs had grievously underestimated the amount of money needed to complete the installs. The first thing he did was sabotage the first install so that the first field office would not find the new system acceptable. Company "A", a large contracting company, was developing this system. He contrived to illegally give a sole source contract to Company "B" that would be developing their work with software belonging to Company "A." Without going into all the arcane details of federal contracting it is more than bizarre that Company "B" could be awarded a sole source contract, meaning they were the only ones who could do the new work, when they would be using Company "A's" software. Moreover, one of his subordinates, who was directly supervising contracts for Company "A" and "B", had a relative employed by Company "B", unethical if not actually illegal. The messaging system being used overseas, which was not DMS compatible, and would have been replaced by a system that was the first step toward compatibility, was installed about 1992. As of early 2005, it was still in place, still not DMS compatible. In their defense, these CIA officers might claim that the system to be installed in 2001 might not or would not have resulted in DMS compatibility, but they do not really know that. Moreover, they did not successfully install anything that was DMS compatible - and the same people managed these programs from 2001 to 2005.

In another scandal of major proportions, CIA spent millions on another system for installation in overseas offices and has yet to deliver that system and make it work. All the time that money was budgeted on this failed system, money was taken away from the enterprise messaging system that might have led to DMS compatibility. If nothing else, enough money might have been found in the failed system to give it to the enterprise messaging system for initial installation in all overseas offices. More discussion of that would take us into the vast murky world of budgeting and the internecine wars fought among the various CIA directorates. I watched but I would not be able to give a cogent description of it.

When CIA decided to reorganize its Directorate of Administration (DA) into an array of big business styled support functions it moved the Directorate of Operations' own information technology development component over to the Corporate Information Officer (CIO), thus placing it under non-DO officers. The Directorate of Administration was transformed into a business like entity. Eventually, the DA was re-established as the Directorate of Support. Once more, we see the failure of merely reorganizing the lines and renaming boxes.

The real cause for any failures in providing proper information technology support to the DO falls on its managers who do not understand information technology and have no interest in managing it directly. When information technology was housed within the DO, non-DO information technology officers were brought in to manage it. They did not fully understand the DO's needs and requirements, but at least they worked for the Deputy Director of Operations. Once you take all management of DO information technology out of the DO, you lose any leverage over it.

The lifeblood of an intelligence agency is the creation or receipt, storage and retrieval of information. From the beginning the DO had a records management component. Operations officers generally regarded its members as second-class citizens within the DO, seeing them as merely the clerks, file room monitors, archivists, etcetera. However, as part of the DO they did yeoman's work for many years insuring that when documents were created or received they were stored properly and the documents or the information in them could be efficiently retrieved. Most recently, the records management function has been severely downgraded to where it is not even on a par with the divisions, centers and staffs that make up the DO. The result is that document and information storage and retrieval have never been in more disarray. The DO is incapable of conducting a search for all the information on an issue and then declaring that it has found every scrap that pertains to the question. This issue in itself is much more important than whether some lines and boxes are rearranged. What is going to be done to correct this glaring fault?

A lot has been said about changing the government system of pay and promotion and once more, it is nothing more than just rearranging all the same blocks without affecting the most important aspect of pay and promotion - the performance appraisal system. However, I am not here to prescribe some new system. The real problem with all performance appraisal systems is that the performance evaluators do not write honest evaluations. It is well known that if you were to write an honest evaluation you would be in more trouble than you could handle, unless you worked 25-hour days to document to an infinite degree each subordinate's performance. Today's managers are not about to put in the effort it would take, so they write dishonest performance appraisals usually giving the subordinate higher ratings than deserved. The average manager does not have the intestinal fortitude to write honest, uninflated appraisals. To be sure, there are managers who are bullies and know which subordinates can be bullied resulting in some appraisals being rather tough, but that is the exception rather than the rule. Moreover, in an effort to achieve a high level of equal employment opportunity, the CIA has hired a significant number of minority employees. Given the extreme sensitivity of equal employment opportunity, a manager has to be very brave to give a harsh, but perhaps well-deserved, performance appraisal to a minority employee. Many an employee, of all types, has learned that if you get a poor performance appraisal and you raise a big stink over it, more often than not you can get the performance appraisal rewritten. Finally, a significant number of performance appraisals are written by the employee. The managers have found it much easier to lightly edit the employee's draft of the performance appraisal. That way, the manager knows what the employee wants included and what left out. If the manager can live with that, the performance appraisal is submitted and the manager does not have to worry about the employee complaining. So, what difference does it make to install a new pay for performance system when the majority of performance evaluators are too cowardly to give honest evaluations and usually give ratings that are too high?

In the long history of the CIA, its case officers have been judged by the number of recruitments of new spies, often called assets, each case officer makes. In the Directorate of Operations case officers, field stations and spies are not judged by the quality of the intelligence they produce. Files are kept on all spies but the intelligence reports that are written from what they give the case officer are not kept in those files. It has always been difficult to evaluate a spy by reviewing all the intelligence reports he has provided. A special effort has to be made to try to accumulate all a spy's reports in one place. Case officers are also not evaluated on the intelligence reports provided by the spies they recruit. Thus, a case officer can recruit several assets near the end of a tour and then depart. His last performance evaluation reports the high number of new recruitments and he is promoted – never mind if the recruits turn out to be duds that never produce quality intelligence. The production of intelligence is evaluated, for gauging the performance of a chief's field station, by the number of intelligence reports produced and the grades received. One might think, well all right, they do evaluate intelligence by giving it grades. However, you would be hard pressed to really evaluate the intelligence because all reports are basically equal. A report on the activities of opposition political parties in Peru can receive a "10" as well as a report on the intentions of a terrorist group to attack the embassy in Rome with biological weapons. There is no attempt to apply a degree of difficulty similar to that used in calculating a college cumulative grade index. Getting an A in a four credit course is worth more to your cumulative grade index then getting an A in a one credit course. As mentioned above, there is also no attempt to have each spy recruited by a case officer tagged to that case officer so that all future reporting is attached to the recruiter as well as to the spy's subsequent handlers.

The chief of a field station is not evaluated by the quality of the intelligence his entire office produces. Why not develop an overall cumulative grade index for the intelligence reporting of an entire field station and then give that grade to everyone in the field station? That way, all the members of the team in the field station would have to pull together to support the case officers in their pursuit of high quality intelligence? Why not publish internally in the DO a list of all the field chiefs and their overall cumulative intelligence reporting grade index, in descending order? Would DO management want to take a close look at why the bottom ten or twenty percent do not have higher intelligence reporting indexes? Why not then also assign the overall intelligence reporting grade index to all the people in CIA headquarters who support the field station? Why not make the intelligence grade index an important part of the performance evaluations of all these people? It seems to me that making fundamental changes that encourage the collection and dissemination of high quality intelligence is more important than rewiring the hierarchical lines and boxes. If the most important thing that human intelligence collectors can do is collect and disseminate the highest quality intelligence why isn't the evaluation of that the most important criteria for evaluating the performance of everyone working overseas and in CIA headquarters? Why are we even talking about rewiring lines and boxes and adding more bureaucracy on top of what we have when we do not even do everything we can to encourage and evaluate the collection of high quality intelligence? If anyone thinks the CIA has not done its best to collect high quality intelligence that is because there is more emphasis on how many new spies are recruited than on how much high quality intelligence is produced.

Finally, why is it that so much attention is paid only to retired high-ranking officials? When someone who has not reached the upper levels deigns to speak out he or she is often dismissed as not having had access to the inner sanctums of the high and mighty. When that happens you need to think about who has the most to protect. Not everyone who reaches the highest levels did so by compromising their integrity but a hell of a lot of them did. When it comes to commenting on something specific, some particular event or operation, perhaps it is partially valid to point out that a lower ranking official did not have access to all the data. However, it is not conclusive. Lower ranking officials may still be able to comment with enough validity to, at least, be heard. Beyond that, an entire working career confers enough validity on any employee that he or she ought to be heard.

Frankly, I chose "speaking truth to power" as part of the title of this chapter because it is a current buzz phrase. In reality, only those subordinate to power may be called on to speak to power. Anyone speaking truth to power that is not in the chain of command is, honestly, pissing in the wind. Power often blows a strong wind of obfuscation back on anyone speaking out against it. You do not have to look any farther than Ambassador Joseph Wilson for an example. Moreover, if you speak truth to power from a position subordinate to power you merely have to be removed from your position and ignored. General Eric Shinseki comes to mind as an example. However, it is an American tradition to speak out with the truth, as we know it. One can only hope that somewhere, someone is listening and thinking. I firmly believe in the need for intelligence collection, analysis and dissemination. The government of the United States of America cannot determine its foreign policy without accurate and timely intelligence. I also believe that this country needs a strong, effective centralized intelligence collection capability, best accomplished by an organization such as a competent, vital, independent Central Intelligence Agency. Finally, I believe it is possible to achieve success in small unit special operations, or even in battalion sized unconventional operations, using surrogate indigenous irregular soldiers. It is not necessary to send Americans into combat zones. When properly led and managed by Americans or surrogate program managers success can be achieved. I am not suggesting that surrogate combat units can completely replace American units, but they could be used much more than they are being used.

"If I tell you the truth, why do you not believe me?"

–John 8:46

Vero Nihil Verius

INDEX

LaVergne, TN USA
29 November 2009

165475LV00002B/18/P